AMISH ALLIANCE

THE COVERT POLICE DETECTIVES UNIT: BOOK 9

ASHLEY EMMA

Copyright © 2024 by Ashley Emma

All rights reserved.

No portion of this book may be reproduced in any form without written permission from the publisher or author, except as permitted by U.S. copyright law.

Contents

The Real Amish Church of Unity, Maine:	1
Author's note	2
Chapter One	3
Chapter Two	12
Chapter Three	25
Chapter Four	34
Chapter Five	44
Chapter Six	50
Chapter Seven	56
Chapter Eight	59
Chapter Nine	64
Chapter Ten	70
Chapter Eleven	76
Chapter Twelve	85
Chapter Thirteen	94
Chapter Fourteen	107

Chapter Fifteen	112
Chapter Sixteen	124
Chapter Seventeen	133
Chapter Eighteen	141
Chapter Nineteen	150
Chapter Twenty	158
Chapter Twenty-one	172
Chapter Twenty-two	185
Chapter Twenty-three	201
Chapter Twenty-four	205
Chapter Twenty-five	217
Chapter Twenty-six	225
Chapter Twenty-seven	238
Chapter Twenty-eight	246
Chapter Twenty-nine	254
Chapter Thirty	259
Chapter Thirty-one	265
Chapter Thirty-two	274
Chapter Thirty-three	284
Epilogue	303
All of Ashley Emma's Books on Amazon	307

Other Books by Ashley Emma (ebooks)	319
Excerpt of Undercover Amish	328
About the Author (Ashley Emma)	335

GET 4 OF ASHLEY EMMA'S AMISH EBOOKS FOR FREE

www.AshleyEmmaAuthor.com

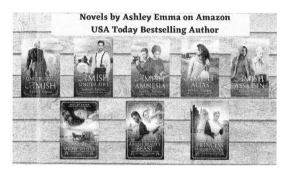

The Real Amish Church of Unity, Maine:

The Real Amish Church of Unity, Maine:

Unity, Maine, is a real Amish community about two hours north of where I live, and they are one of the few communities with their own church building. Theirs also doubles as their school. I've been there several times, and they welcome visitors. You can read about the church/school here:

ARTICLE ABOUT THE AMISH CHURCH/SCHOOL BUILT BY THE COMMUNITY IN UNITY, MAINE:

https://www.amish365.com/can-outsiders-attend-amish-church/

Author's Note

There are characters in this book that are featured as main characters in other books in this series.

For example, there is an entire storyline that leads up to Detective Olivia Mast finding Ava in the basement. To read about Olivia's story, read *Undercover Amish,* book 1 in this series, which is about how Olivia left the Amish, became a police officer, and rescued Ava.

To read about Maria's story, read *Amish Under Fire,* book 2 in this series, which is about how Maria fell in love with her bodyguard, Derek.

To read about Freya's story, read *Amish Accident,* book 6 in this series, which is about how she met and fell in love with Adam.

To read about Liz's story, read *Amish Espionage,* book 8 in this series, which is about how she and her sister Anneliese were kidnapped.

Chapter One

Six-year-old Ava Sullivan bounced on the balls of her feet, her small hands fidgeting with the straps of her prayer *kapp*. She could hardly contain her excitement about her trip to the pond with her brothers, a marvelous treat on a scorching hot summer day.

Before they could step out of the house, their father's stern voice cut through the air, calling her brothers aside. Ava watched, trying to catch her father's gaze, but he was focused entirely on speaking with Ian.

"You're the oldest," Bill Sullivan said in a low, commanding tone, "it's your responsibility to keep an eye on Ava. She's only six and can't swim well. Don't let her out of your sight."

Ian nodded, his expression firm. "*Ja, Daed.* I understand."

Jake and Samuel, her other two brothers, also nodded.

With a curt nod, Bill said, "Go on then. Be back in time for dinner."

Ava scampered out of the house with her three older brothers. The path to the pond was a familiar one, etched into their memories through repeated visits. When they arrived, Ava's eyes danced as she took in the cool, inviting water.

Samuel, Jake, and Ian were quickly swept into the raucous play of their friends, their laughter mingling with splashes. The game was a simple one: catch and toss the ball without losing your footing in the slippery mud of the pond's edge.

In the warmth of the summer sun and the joy of her surroundings, she splashed in the shallow parts of the water, but Ava's attention easily drifted. A butterfly, its wings a brilliant orange, flitted by, and she followed it with wide-eyed wonder, moving away from the water's edge toward the woods. Her small feet padded across the grass, pursuit-driven and carefree, leaving the laughter and splashes at the pond far behind.

Her three best friends, Maria, Liz, and Anna, ran by, playing tag. Ava joined in the fun, forgetting all about how her brothers were supposed to be watching her.

As they drew closer to Ava's house, their innocent laughter echoed across the yard, harmonizing with the sound of horse-drawn buggies and the clucking of hens nearby. The sun illuminated the white prayer *kapps* of the four girls as they played beneath the expansive blue sky, surrounded by the simple yet sturdy homesteads of their Amish community.

Since the girls all lived close together, their game brought them running into Maria's yard, then into Ava's yard.

Without warning, the air split with yells piercing the calm from within Ava's home—it was her father and mother arguing. Somewhere in the kitchen, something was knocked over and shattered. Probably a plate or a glass. The sounds sent a shiver down Ava's spine, causing her to halt mid-step. Maria, Anna, and Liz, with worry shadowing their youthful features, looked to Ava for an explanation.

Ava's eyes widened in fear.

"What happened?" Maria asked.

"Oh, my mother broke a dish, I think. She must be upset. I'll go see if she's okay," she blurted to her friends. "Bye!" Ava turned and ran into the house. She turned to see if they'd left, but they were still standing there, looking concerned. "Go on home, now. Go!" she barked.

Without another word, they scurried away, throwing worried glances over their shoulders as they rounded the corner of the white-washed fence.

Ava sprinted to the house, her small hands fumbling to push open the heavy wooden door. The chaotic sounds escalated, guiding her trembling legs toward the kitchen, where her mother and father were.

She pushed the door open to a horrifying sight. Her father, Bill Sullivan, his face red with fury, had his large hands wrapped around her mother's slender neck. Diana Sullivan's face was drained of color, slipping in and out of unconsciousness as she slumped. Bill let her drop to the floor.

"*Daed*, stop!" Ava cried out, her voice slicing through the thick air of violence. "I'm going to tell the bishop!" She ran to her mother. "*Mamm? Mamm!*" Ava grabbed her mother's shoulders.

Her mother opened her eyes just slightly. Amidst desperate gasps for air, she managed to wheeze, "Ava, my *liebling*, darling, don't tell anyone."

But the desperation in Diana's eyes told Ava the truth that her words tried to conceal.

Her father's reaction was immediate and thunderous. He turned his seething gaze upon Ava. His voice was a growling whisper, thick with menace. "You'll tell no one," he spat, veins in his neck bulging. "I'll make sure of that. Don't tell anyone, you hear?"

She hesitated. "On Sunday, the bishop taught us that the husband is supposed to love his wife as Jesus loves the church, remember?"

"Ava, if you tell anyone, I will hurt your mother again, do you understand?" Bill threatened.

Diana, her breaths shallow and uneven, pulled Ava close. Her voice trembled as she whispered, "Ava, my sweet girl, I'm fine."

"I thought you were dead, *Mamm*," Ava cried.

"Really, I'm fine. You must promise me you won't speak of this to anyone."

Ava's eyes, wide and brimming with tears that threatened to spill over, met her mother's. "But it's not right," she protested, her small hands balling into fists at her sides. "The bishop says we should love one another and be kind to one another."

Diana's eyes darted toward her husband. "We must obey *Daed*. He's our head, and the good Lord asks us to follow him."

Ava's chest tightened at her mother's words. The very fibers of her being screamed in rebellion. She knew deep down that what her father had done was wrong.

Ava froze in fear as he walked toward her, but instead of striking her, as she expected, he opened the door to the basement and grabbed her arm.

"Come with me, Ava." Bill guided Ava into the basement.

"Why are you bringing me down here? You told us never to come down here," Ava protested.

Her father's grip on her was firm as he now guided her to the basement. Ava's heart pounded in her chest as she stumbled down the wooden stairs.

"I'm changing the rules, but only for you. Now you are not allowed to go upstairs anymore. That way you won't tell anyone about what you saw," he explained.

"You mean I can't go outside anymore?" she asked, panic rising in her throat. "How will I play with my friends?"

Ava felt her world crashing down around her. It was finally summer, and now she wouldn't be able to play tag or hide and seek with her friends outside anymore. She wouldn't be able to go to the pond with her brothers anymore or go to the store with her mother. And she would not be able to go to school in the fall. Would she really be down here for that long?

"Your life outside this basement is over," her father explained in a hollow voice. "I'm going to tell everyone you drowned in the pond. Everyone will think you're dead. You can't let anyone see you, even your brothers, so you can't go upstairs, understand? You have to be quiet, and you have to stay down here."

"For how long?" she asked, her heart sinking.

"Well...forever," he said flatly, his brow furrowed in thought.

"Forever?" she cried. At six years old, she couldn't even comprehend what could happen in the next decade of her life, let alone the next twenty to thirty years. And what about her mother and brothers? What would her father do to them while she was down here?

She made one last desperate plea. "But *Daed*... I won't tell anyone. I promise."

"It's too late for that. You are too outspoken. You're not like your mother. You don't follow orders. The only way I can make sure you don't tell anyone is if I keep you down here." He picked up some boards and turned around, starting to hammer.

Ava stood there, stunned and confused. He couldn't be serious. Surely, he would let her out in a few hours or maybe a few days...wouldn't he? And if he wouldn't, maybe her mother would. Her mother always protected her.

***

Samuel felt a strange unease settle in his stomach. He squinted against the sunlight, his gaze sweeping across the water, searching for Ava. The game of catch and toss continued around him, but he found himself unable to focus. He realized Ava was missing.

"Ian," he called out to his brother, who was knee-deep in the water. "Have you seen Ava?"

Ian shook his head, his brows furrowing in confusion. "She was just here..."

Their laughter faded into an uncomfortable silence as they scanned the pond and shore, their young friends joining them in their search. "Ava!" they called out, their voices echoing through the still afternoon air.

Minutes passed with no sign of her. A knot of panic tightened in Samuel's chest. He looked to Ian for reassurance but found none.

"She's probably just playing somewhere else," Ian said, but his voice wavered with uncertainty. "Maybe she wandered into the woods."

After looking in the woods and not finding her, the brothers decided to go home, thinking maybe she was there. Realizing their game was over, their friends went home.

Jake, Samuel, and Ian walked up to their house hesitantly, reluctant to face what came next.

"Is Ava here?" Ian asked his father. Diana was hanging laundry on the clothesline while Bill was outside, building a new section on their chicken coop to expand it.

"No," Bill said. "You weren't watching her?"

"We were playing a game, then a few minutes later we realized she wasn't there anymore..." Ian explained. "It was only for a few minutes."

"I told you to watch her!" Bill boomed, then stormed past them. He whirled around, staring at Ian. "I'll go look for her and you three stay inside the house with *Mamm*. If something happened to her, it will be all your fault."

Diana tried to comfort her sons, but she knew she would never be able to tell them the truth—that their sister was actually downstairs and their father was lying to them. Why did he have to make his sons feel so guilty? He was always playing mind games, gaslighting them, trying to control them in any way possible—especially manipulating their emotions.

Finally, Bill returned. By then, the boys had gone inside the house with Diana as instructed.

"Boys," he called out to them as he walked through the door. His voice was grave. "While you were playing, Ava drowned. I found her body in the pond and locked it in the shed."

"What?" Samuel cried.

"No!" Jake bellowed.

Ian shook his head vehemently, denial etched across his face. "No... she can't be..."

Bill cut him off abruptly, "*Ja,* she is dead." His gaze hardened on Ian. "You didn't even notice. You were supposed to be watching her."

Samuel felt tears prick at his eyes, panic gripping him like a vice as he looked at his brothers.

As the boys began to cry, Diana rushed to them, trying in vain to comfort them. "This is not your fault, boys." Her heart broke in two from seeing her sons in so much pain.

"But it is," Bill argued.

"I'm sorry," Ian said. Samuel and Jake could only nod. "It's all my fault. I'm the oldest."

"How could you let her die, Ian?" Bill demanded.

Diana felt the world spin around her. She sank to her knees, her cries echoing through the house. Bill took her arm, pulling her into their bedroom down the hall.

She stared at him in confusion. "Why are you doing this? Why are you letting them think this is their fault?"

He ignored her question. "I am going to build a secret room downstairs," he said quietly. "In the basement."

Diana pulled back, staring at him in disbelief. "You are going to do what?"

"She's safe," he continued, ignoring her question. "But she needs to stay hidden and quiet."

Her mind reeled at his words. "Hidden? Bill, she's our daughter! You can't just..."

"I'm doing this for us," he interrupted her sharply. "If the bishop finds out what happened or how I choose to run this house, I could go to prison."

Diana felt her neck where she knew bruises had already formed. She kept it hidden with a shawl despite the sweltering heat.

"You know how he is not as traditional as our former bishop. He would call the police. You don't want to tear our family apart, do you? I am doing this to protect us," Bill said.

Diana stared at him, tears streaming down her face. "No," she whispered. "Look what you're doing to your children. You're already tearing our family apart. You're doing this for yourself."

Bill took a step toward her as she recoiled. "The boys can never know the truth. And don't you dare tell anyone about this or try to get her out. If you do, you will regret it. And if you ever let her out, I will kill her. I'm going to tell everyone that she drowned today. No one will know the difference if I kill her after today because they will already believe she is dead."

His words hung heavy in the room as Diana's sobs filled the silence and she sank to the floor. Her heart shattered, and she knew it would never be whole again.

Chapter Two

Bill took the next two weeks off from work to build a secret room in the basement with a small access door that blended into the wall and a pile of stacked firewood. He added some sound dampening materials just in case, even though he had told Ava to stay quiet, threatening to hurt Diana if Ava did not comply with his demands to remain unheard upstairs.

He never usually let his wife or children go into the basement, saying it was his workspace, so they didn't dare go down to disturb him while he was working. He told them he was building a casket for Ava and didn't want any interruptions. He worked day and night. No one questioned him on why it took two full weeks, as they were processing their own grief.

Ava stayed in the basement the entire time, watching him construct her prison, but she didn't understand what he was building. She thought maybe it was a closet.

Meanwhile, word of Ava's death spread through the community like wildfire. The community rallied around the Sullivans to comfort them, all the while having no idea that Ava was downstairs when they brought the family casseroles and prayers.

Bill finished constructing a small casket, secretly filled it with some rocks, and the family had a small funeral in the field behind their house. He had invited some of their neighbors and friends to have them witness the casket being buried, only making his ruse more believable.

Diana watched, her heart weighed down with sorrow as the small, makeshift casket was lowered into the earth. The field near the woods behind the Sullivan home, usually a place of life and growth, had become the stage for a harrowing charade.

Distraught, her sons—Ian, Jake, and Samuel—stood by the grave, their young faces overcome with grief. They seemed to shrink under the weight of a guilt that was never theirs to carry, believing they had in some way contributed to Ava's death, unaware their sister was alive in their own basement.

With a mother's instinct, Diana gathered her sons in her arms, trying to comfort them. The entire time, Diana wanted to tell her boys the truth, to tell them this was not their fault and their sister was actually alive, but the words died in her throat. The truth clawed at her from within, begging to be released. She wanted nothing more than to reassure her sons, to lift the burden of guilt from their young shoulders and tell their neighbors the truth, but she feared her husband would take her daughter's life if she told them. He always followed through on his threats.

***

For two weeks, Bill kept Ava downstairs while he worked on his secret project. He moved a small mattress downstairs for her to sleep on with some things from her bedroom to keep her busy, but she only grew more confused as she watched her father. She asked questions, but he wouldn't answer her. Each day, she hoped this would be the day he would change his mind and let her out, but she also had a deepening sense of dread that this would be her new bedroom.

She didn't realize he was building her a prison.

Finally, the secret room was finished. It was narrow and long, the length of the basement, and the outside of it looked like that wall had always been there. In a corner, a pile of firewood was stacked high up to the ceiling. With a swift movement, Bill reached into the stack and pulled a hidden lever. Ava watched as a portion of the wall slid open, revealing a secret room that she had watched him build.

"What is it?" she asked.

"This is your fault, Ava," Bill said, his voice harsh in the silence of the basement. "You've forced me to do this. You saw too much, and you're too much of a chatterbox. I know you won't keep our secret."

He shoved her towards the secret room, his words bouncing around in her mind. She turned back to face him, but his gaze was like steel. "I'm doing this for your own good," he insisted. "To protect you. To protect all of us."

"*Daed*, what do you mean?" she asked, confused.

But he ignored her question. He nudged her into the room. It was narrow yet long with a small amount of sunlight coming from a small window high on one wall. There was a single bed with a battery-operated lantern that sat on a table beside it. Bill picked up the mattress from the other end of the basement and put it on the bed he had built, then added her faceless doll and her other toys and books from her bedroom upstairs that he'd brought down earlier.

"Why are my toys and bed in here? Do you mean I will be sleeping in here?" she asked in confusion.

"*Ja*," he said. "This is your room now."

"For how long? I know you said forever before, but will it just be a few days?" her voice cracked. "You don't really mean forever, do you?"

Bill sighed. "*Ja*, Ava, I mean forever."

"But why? Can I please have my room back? I won't tell anyone anything, *Daed,* I promise," she pleaded.

"No, Ava. I'm not going to let you out. You have to stay down here. Forever." He paused, and she searched for any flicker of sympathy or love in his eyes, but all she saw was a cold emptiness.

He closed the secret door.

"No!" she screamed, plunging into panic, rushing forward to bang on the solid door. Her small fists pounded against it. "Let me out! *Daed,* let me out!"

"Ava, listen to me," Bill said in a muffled voice from the other side of the door. "You must stay quiet. I don't want anyone to know you're here, or bad things will happen to them. Do you understand?"

"*Ja, Daed,*" she said, her heart sinking. Would she truly be down here forever? What did he mean by forever, anyway? How long was forever? A few weeks? She couldn't even imagine a year from now.

Maybe *Mamm* would convince *Daed* to let her out, or maybe she would sneak down and let her out soon. Yes, maybe she would, then everything would be fine.

"Good girl," he muttered.

All she could hear were his retreating footsteps on the wooden stairs above and the basement door shutting.

Then silence.

Ava's fingers traced over the cold metal of the door handle, and she tried to open it, but it was locked from the outside. She was trapped in this hidden room. The small window was her only link to the outside world, a world that felt far removed from the chilling confines of her new prison.

Ava sank to the floor, her small body shaking with sobs. Her heart pounded in her chest, each beat echoing the grim reality of her situation. She was alone and locked away, hidden from the world by a man she had once trusted. It had already seemed like forever that she had been down in the basement, bored, lonely, and fearing the future. She would now have to depend on her parents, the only two people who knew she was still alive, to bring her food and care for her.

She sunk into the bed and stared at the walls which confined her in now a smaller space. Curling up into a ball, she grabbed her faceless doll and hugged it to her chest.

"Please, God, be with me," Ava whispered. "God, why is my *daed* doing this?"

She wiped away a tear and hugged her doll tighter.

"It'll be okay," she said to the doll, but mostly she was saying it to herself.

***

The dust danced in the single beam of light that snuck into the basement through the high, narrow window into Ava's tiny world. The rest of the community, her friends, and life itself became nothing but fragmented memories, echoes of laughter and warmth long gone. She escaped through the power of words, both read and written.

Mamm became Ava's only lifeline, softening the harshness of her existence. *Mamm* risked *Daed's* wrath each time she crept down those creaking wooden stairs with her hands full of treasures—books, paper, pencils, and art supplies to color the dreary grey of Ava's captive life. Yes, Bill had told Diana that she could bring her these things, but Bill also was known to change his mind and lose his temper without warning.

A few times, Ava even heard her friends playing outside without her. She could hear their playful shouts from a distance, probably from Maria's house. They had no idea that she was still alive, trapped here.

Ava watched the years slip by in her dark little basement hideaway, counting the seasons by the supplies Diana would sneak down to her. If not for the books, which *Mamm* taught her to read, paper, pencils, and the colors from the paint sets, every day would've blended into the next, dull and never-ending.

Ava found joy in the stories that leapt from her imagination onto the worn pages of her notebooks. Ava began writing her own stories and was just twelve years old when she finished writing her first full-length novel, which had taken her a year, and that was just the start. More stories followed as she grew into a teenager, the notebooks her mother brought her filling and piling up beside her and even under her bed.

Sometimes when her *daed* was out and her brothers at school, Diana would let Ava sneak upstairs. It felt like a dangerous game of hide-and-seek, especially if someone came to the front door and she had to scramble back to her hiding spot.

Then one day, her mom came down with some surprising news. "Ian's left the church and moved away," she said, and Ava felt a twinge of jealousy. Her brother Ian had gotten away from their father's strict rules. Now that she was a teenager, she couldn't help but dream about escaping and leaving to join the outside world. She even imagined becoming an *Englisher*, or a non-Amish person, and also a successful author.

She had often imagined the life of her family and often played out scenarios of what life was like for them. Now she wondered what life was like for Ian in the outside world.

Later on, Diana told Ava that her brother Jake had married a young Amish woman named Olivia. Jake had turned out to be just as violent as his father and Olivia had killed him in self-defense, then she left the community to become a police officer.

"He tried to strangle her," Diana explained. "She acted in self-defense."

Diana and Ava mourned Jake's death together, but in Ava's mind, still in shock from the latest news, all she could picture was the little boy she hadn't seen in years. She wished he had broken the cycle of violence, but instead he'd become like *Daed* and paid for it with his life. Ava couldn't blame Jake's wife for defending herself. It surely wasn't her fault.

Years later, everything changed one day when Diana came downstairs, looking conflicted. "Your father...he's been murdered, right out in our barn," she said, her voice shaky. Ava's heart stopped for a second. She couldn't believe it. Her father was dead. She knew she should be sad, but she wasn't, not at all. She only felt relief that the tyrant was gone.

Then, the question burst out of her, "Does this mean I can be free now? You will let me out, won't you?"

But Diana shook her head, her eyes sad and fearful. "No, I can't. I could end up in prison for what we did to you. I'm sorry, *liebling*. But this whole time, I knew you were here, and I didn't let you out. Everyone will blame me. You understand, don't you?"

"What? You're not going to let me out?"

Ava sat in the shadows, the news of her father's passing wrapped around her like a fog. Her mind spun with questions and a touch of hope—freedom felt so close she could almost taste it.

Diana's voice was solemn. "Ava, I'm so sorry, but I can't. I've told Samuel about you. He knows the truth now that your father is gone. I told him about how you've been hidden away all these years. He wants to come see you now."

The basement door creaked open, and the silhouette of a man she barely recognized descended the stairs. Samuel, her older brother, stood before her, a stranger bonded only by blood and distant memories. "Hello, Ava," he said, his voice strange and unfamiliar.

A rush of emotions flooded Ava, and she stepped forward, but Diana pushed the metal door to the secret room closed. "*Mamm*, open the door. Please let me hug my brother!" Her voice cracked with a mixture of longing and desperation.

But Diana's face was stone, her body a barrier as immovable as the walls that caged Ava in.

Samuel—no longer the boy she'd played with but a man with the weight of reality on his shoulders—shook his head. "We can't let you out. If you try to run, to escape, they'll lock up *Mamm*. And since I am involved now and I can't claim ignorance, and *Daed* isn't here to threaten us, so we can't claim we acted under duress as we were afraid of him. I'm not a minor anymore. I'd go to prison. And *Mamm* would get an even longer sentence. I am sorry, but I have to be the man of the family and protect *Mamm* now."

"I won't try to run away!" Ava's promise spilled out, pledging words she felt deep in her heart. "I don't want either of you to go to prison."

"We can't risk it, Ava. You've been down here too long. I would go to prison for years," Diana said. "This family has been through too much already. I can't let that happen. However, we will not lock you in the secret room anymore when we are home. We will give you full access to the entire basement, but you can't come upstairs anymore. I am sorry, Ava, but I feel I must do this to protect what's left of our family."

Diana's gaze was shadowed with a fear that spoke louder than her assurances.

"You don't trust me?" Ava asked, eyes filled with tears.

"I'm sorry," Diana whispered.

The door to the basement closed once more as her mother and brother left, leaving her alone with the door to her secret room now open to a slightly larger prison, standing there in shock once again amidst her books, her art, and the ache of a longing unfulfilled.

"God, why are they doing this to me? Please change their minds," she prayed. "I thought this was finally my chance at freedom."

It felt like a punch in the gut. How could her mother still keep her locked away like this, with even less freedom than before? Ava felt more trapped than ever, all the stories in the world couldn't write her out of this one.

***

The heavy sound of Ava's door opening was a bitter reminder of freedom just beyond reach. Diana stepped into the secret room. With a gesture that passed for kindness in their twisted normalcy, Diana was allowing Ava to walk around in the basement at will, to use the toilet there, and clean herself up in the large sink, leaving her with a clean towel to dry off.

"I need to go clean up," Diana said. "I'll be back later."

As Diana ascended the stairs, the light from above seemed to offer an illusion of hope before the door closed, plunging the basement back into shadows cast by the single battery-operated lantern she was allowed and a window to the outside in her secret area and one in the main space. Ava's heart beat with a sense of urgency. This was the small window of opportunity she had learned to seize—her family's temporary absences.

She hurried to the basement window, a high and narrow piece of glass that offered a sliver of the world outside. The sun was out, so dust danced in the shafts of light from the window as Ava's fingers, smeared with paint from her art supplies, moved with desperate intention. "HELP," she wrote backwards, the letters a silent scream for someone to do something. She had been doing this for years, but maybe today someone would finally see it and call the police and get her out of here.

But then that would mean her mother and brother would go to prison. Was that really what she wanted?

If a neighbor came down here and found her but no one called the police, then no one would go to prison. That was also a possibility.

Ava's chest tightened with a blend of fear and anticipation. Every moment that her message stood on the window increased the chances that her neighbor might glance over and see her silent call for help.

This was not her first time doing this—she had done it countless times. But her neighbor, Jonas Miller, never seemed to notice or perhaps he chose to look the other way, not wanting to get involved.

Or maybe he just didn't care.

Loud footsteps above signaled Samuel's return. Ava surged into action, erasing the evidence of her silent cry for help just as quickly as she had written it. She couldn't afford to be caught or risk losing her art and writing supplies that helped her bear the isolation and confinement. The paint had barely disappeared when Samuel made his descent.

Ava's brief glimmer of hope was extinguished, leaving her once again to wait and endure.

***

A few weeks later, Diana's footsteps echoed down the basement stairs, each one foreboding a sense of dread that Ava sensed even before her mother appeared at the entrance of the secret room. There was something different about Diana this time; her usual fear-laden caution had given way to a tremor of urgency.

"Ava," Diana's voice broke as she pushed open the door. Her face, pale and drawn, bore the imprint of news that has yet to be spoken. "It's your brother, Ian. He's been arrested."

Ava felt a chill that had nothing to do with the coolness of the basement. Her brother Ian, the sibling who had managed to escape their father's tyrannical grip by leaving the Amish community, had become little more than a memory, a silhouette of freedom on their family's horizon. Because the Amish did not allow or have photographs in her community, she did not even know what he looked like now, and his younger image in her mind had faded quite a bit.

"For what?" Ava's question emerged as a whisper, a thin thread of hope that perhaps the reason was anything but what her heart had already concluded.

Diana's eyes pooled with grief, the words seeming to stick in her throat before tumbling out. "For murder, Ava. They're saying he killed your father."

The room spun as Ava struggled to comprehend the gravity of Diana's words. They hadn't heard from him since he'd left the community.

"Why did he come back after all this time?" she murmured more to herself than to Diana. "To kill *Daed*?"

Ava was going to ask why, but she knew why. Ian was the one their father had blamed for her falsified death. He had probably carried around the guilt for years, and the guilt could have been taken away if only Bill hadn't kept the truth from him. That, combined with their father's abuse toward his family—both mental and physical—must have turned Ian's mind into a war zone. Ava knew it was always wrong to murder, but she was not surprised her brother had sought revenge on Bill Sullivan, if the police were right.

Diana nodded, her body wracked with a sob. "I know Ian did this, Ava. Who else would want to kill your father? He blamed Ian for your death. Ian must hate him."

They had not even known Ian was nearby, let alone possibly harboring intentions of murder. And Ian had never been told Ava was really alive.

"There's something else. They're also saying he kidnapped Jill Johnson, the little girl who lives down the lane, because she looks like you when you were about six. I think she reminded him of you, and it was like he was pretending she was you, maybe to ease his guilt. I'm not sure what he was thinking. She's home safe now. That poor little girl."

"He kidnapped a child and pretended she was...me?" Ava asked in shock.

He must have missed me more than I realized all these years, she thought. Yes, she had been close with all her brothers, but to her, it seemed as though they had continued living their lives without her. She had often wondered if they'd missed her because she hadn't witnessed her brothers grieve her death.

Ian had always looked out for her when they were young. He'd often take the blame for something that was not his fault just to protect his siblings.

Now she realized he was not who she remembered at all. What had happened to him? What had her father done to them after locking her away?

The truth was as confining as the walls that held Ava, a new prison made not of stone and mortar, but of betrayal and blood.

Chapter Three

Note from the author: This scene is also in Undercover Amish, book 1 in this series. In that book, it is told from Olivia's point of view. This scene is a pivotal moment in Ava's life, so I also included it in this book. If you want to read more about how Detective Olivia Mast found Ava, I recommend reading Undercover Amish.

The stagnant air of the basement was all too familiar to Ava, the silence a constant companion within her hidden chamber. But today, a foreign sound provided an unwelcome duet—a murmur of unfamiliar voices, slicing through the stillness. Her heart lurched with panic; were they police? What had she been thinking, writing on the window for help? Perhaps she was only being selfish.

As fear constricted her throat, she stayed silent, praying they would leave as mysteriously as they had arrived.

Then she heard it—the sound of her room's well-concealed door creaking open. Ava quickly turned off her battery-operated lantern, casting herself into darkness once more. Who could've found the hidden lever her father had made?

A shadow of a woman stepped into the threshold, a glint of metal in her hand—a gun. In the woman's other hand, she held a flashlight, illuminating the basement. Ava's pulse hammered in her chest, a silent scream lodged behind her clasped hand.

"Police! Who is in there?" The woman's voice was firm, authoritative.

Ava shivered, unable to move.

The woman spotted her, shining the light on her. "What is your name?" the woman pressed.

Ava shielded her eyes from the light, too curious not to answer. "You saw what I wrote on the window?"

"Yes. That's why we're here. To get you out."

The words tangled in Ava's mind. Escape had been a daydream, and now the opportunity clawed at her with sharp, frightening talons. "I thought I wanted to escape, but I'm too afraid. You should go," Ava pressed herself against the wall, her figure shadowed by the side of the bed. "Please. Just go. And don't tell anyone I'm here."

"No. I can't do that." The woman's resolve was unyielding. "My name is Olivia Mast, and I'm an undercover police detective. This is Isaac Troyer. He lives here, in this community. Now, I need to know your name." She gestured to the Amish man standing next to her. He wasn't police, so why was he here with her?

Ava studied this Olivia Mast, her heart a confused knot. "My name... My name is Ava Sullivan."

"Ava?" It was almost a reverent echo from both Isaac and Olivia.

The woman, Olivia, continued, ripples of disbelief in her tone. "Everyone thinks you're dead," she murmured. "Why are you down here?"

"Really, you can't be here. If Samuel or my mother find out, it will be very bad," she stammered, the motion of pushing her blonde hair from her brown eyes an unconscious bid for comfort. "My mother and brother went out to run errands, but they could be back any minute."

Olivia's determination was clear as she stood in the grim shadows of Ava's prison. "Look, I won't let Samuel or your mother hurt you ever again. Please, just tell us why you are down here. So, you wrote help on the window today and the other day?"

Ava clung to the little hope she had as she responded to the questions. "Yes. Sometimes they let me out into that room for a little while. Sometimes I write help on the window in there because it faces the neighbor's property, but no one has ever seen it or done anything about it... until now. I did it the other day too, but then I got afraid Samuel or my mother would see it or that they would be arrested, so I wiped it off after a little bit. I don't want them to go to prison."

Acknowledging the seriousness, Olivia continued, "I saw it. That's the reason why we came. Who kept you down here? Was it your parents and Samuel?"

With a nod that felt heavier with each motion, Ava confirmed the truth. "My father put me down here when I was little. My mother always knew, and Samuel has known since my father died."

Olivia retreated to the adjacent room, where she hastily called her sergeant. Backup was on the way to safely arrest Diana and Samuel.

Returning to Ava, Olivia affirmed, "Look, I know we have so much more to talk about. But it's not safe for us to stay here. We need to get you out now, okay?" She extended a hand to Ava.

As she moved closer, Olivia's eyes were drawn to the neatly organized stacks of Ava's writing. Titles like Freedom and The Secret City adorned the top pages, each stack a testament to the time Ava spent entombed yet breaking free in her own mind. There were also dozens of sketches and paintings on the wall, mostly of farm landscapes but also some cityscapes—visual escapes.

Ava recoiled to a tight corner, the old fear surging as she objected. "No! Samuel will find out! He'll be so angry! If he is like my father, he'll hurt me, and probably you too."

Olivia was insistent. "I told you, we won't let him hurt you. Do you know if there are any weapons in the house?"

"No. And I can't go with you!" Ava refused.

A sudden sound from above—Samuel's footsteps thundered, signaling their return. "They are home!" Ava whispered urgently.

Isaac, quick on his feet, urged her, "Come on. We have to go right now. You'll be safe with us." But clumsiness followed as he knocked over a metal bin, the sound echoing loudly in the basement.

Liv reacted with frustration. "What, are you trying to wake up the dead? Let's go. Now."

As Samuel's presence loomed closer, Liv called out to Ava, "He heard us. Come on, Ava."

Ava was rooted to the spot, her reply filled with fear. "I can't!"

Liv prepared for the worst, positioning herself near the stairs to take out Samuel if necessary.

"Get her out of here!" she directed at Isaac.

He appealed to Ava once more, but she wouldn't budge. "She won't come!" he exclaimed in frustration.

"Throw her over your shoulder, drag her, carry her, I don't care. Just get her out!" Liv's voice was tense with urgency.

Samuel's voice boomed from the stairway. "Who is down there?"

Olivia's voice boomed, "Police! Approach slowly with your hands up where we can see them. You are under arrest."

"No!" Samuel barked, his heavy footsteps pounding as he descended the stairs with dangerous speed. Just out of his direct line of sight, Liv readied herself. As Samuel passed, she lunged with the urgency of a panther, aiming to incapacitate him with her .45 pistol—but he saw her at the last second in his peripheral vision and twisted out of reach, her blow missing its mark. His fist cut through the air toward her, but Liv dodged with grace, spinning into a brisk roundhouse kick that connected with a thud to Samuel's ribs.

Samuel staggered, then locked eyes with Isaac. Charging like a provoked bull, Samuel lunged, shoving Isaac to the ground with a thud.

"I told you to stay away from here!" Samuel roared, his fist connecting brutally with Isaac's face.

"No!" Olivia yelled.

An opening came when Olivia was able to push Samuel from behind as he focused on Isaac, throwing Samuel off balance. She then brought the butt of her gun down onto his head, and Samuel folded, collapsing into unconsciousness, but was breathing steadily. As he lay still, Olivia secured him with handcuffs from her holster with practiced efficiency.

"The police officers providing backup should be here any second," she confirmed, glancing up to see Ava hovering apprehensively in the doorway of her secret room.

Ava's mind whirled with questions. Were her mother and brother really going to prison? Did this mean she was finally free now? But what would happen to her mother and brothers in prison? She feared for them, not wanting them to be confined like she had...

She wouldn't wish it on anyone.

"What about *Mamm*?" Ava's voice was a fragile whisper, laden with complex emotions.

Then Diana thundered down the steps. "Samuel? Samuel!"

Her eyes flitted over the scene—Samuel slumped against the floor, face down and hands cuffed behind his back, slipping in and out of consciousness; Ava in the doorway, a ghost finally given form; Isaac's bruised face and Olivia holding her gun.

"What did you do?" Diana shrieked as she surged towards Olivia. Yet her strike was futile against the trained reflexes of the undercover officer; Liv blocked and skillfully maneuvered Diana's arms behind her, securing the cuffs with a cold click.

Ava's eyes filled with tears, her heart twisting at the sight of her mother, who was also a victim, being handcuffed. Ava's arm reached out instinctively for her mother.

"You can't do this. I was protecting her!" Diana shouted, trying to wriggle free, but Isaac came and helped Liv hold her still.

After reading her Miranda rights, Olivia stated her position firmly, "Diana, I am Detective Mast from Covert Police Detectives Unit. And yes, I can do this. What you didn't have the right to do was hold your daughter captive here for almost her entire life."

Standing aside, Ava watched her mother's eyes darting frantically, taking in the grim sight of her son handcuffed on the floor and her daughter, now at the threshold of freedom.

In a desperate plea, Diana turned to face Liv. "You took all my children away from me!" Her wail was a blend of anger and despair. "You killed Jake, my son! You arrested Ian, and now you're arresting Samuel. Who knows what will happen to Ava now?"

Ava's eyes went wide with realization. This was Olivia, the same Olivia who had grown up here and had married Jake, then killed him in self-defense. She had become a police officer.

"I had to arrest Ian for murdering your husband. That is not my fault. And Jake almost killed me multiple times. The day I killed him in self-defense, he almost strangled me." Olivia told Diana, rich with empathy yet edged with sternness. "I know you were a victim of the abuse from your husband because I was a victim of abuse. You went through the same thing I did. You and I have a lot in common. But I would never, ever hurt someone else on purpose like you hurt Ava. You stole over a decade from Ava and wouldn't let her out even after your husband died, when you could have set her free. There is no excuse for that."

"But my husband would have killed Ava if I had released her when he was alive. He made that very clear to me. Then after he died, I feared that I still would have gone to prison!" Diana's protest was like a cry from a cornered animal, one last attempt to justify the unforgivable.

"And now you are," Olivia replied, standing up, looking out the window at the red and blue lights signaling the beginning of justice for this family.

Ava stood frozen as police officers entered the basement. The sight of her mother and brother, restrained by the law, sent a shock through her. She couldn't decide if she was relieved to be free or devastated at seeing the only two people she had left in her life be arrested.

She watched, torn between the chaos and the fear of what lay ahead for her family. There was so much confusion, so many unsaid things between them, but this wasn't the time or place. Her throat tightened as her eyes met her mother's, who looked back with fear and confusion of her own.

"Ava!" Diana screamed. "Ava, I'm sorry."

Ava noticed the pain in Samuel's expression when their eyes met. She knew he had endured so much more of their father's abuse than she had because she had been protected in her prison, shielded from their father's anger.

The officers didn't hesitate, quickly escorting Diana and Samuel up the stairs. Ava's eyes followed them until they reached the top of the stairs, cutting off her view. When would she see them again? How long would they be in prison? Would she be able to visit them? So many questions flooded her mind.

Suddenly, she began to weep with a physical pain in her chest, her heart aching to see her mother and brother arrested. Yes, what they had done to her was wrong, but she understood why they had done it, and she knew they had been victims, too.

But now I'm...free, she thought. Yet she couldn't bring herself to step through the doorway of her prison.

For the first time, Ava's life was her own to shape. What would she do with her freedom? There were so many possibilities that her mind swam, but she couldn't think about that now. All she could think about was how she hated seeing her mother and brother in handcuffs, being taken away by police.

"Ready to go?" Olivia's voice touched Ava's ears, a murmur of hope amid the remnants of her life. Her hand, an offer of freedom, reached out.

Ava caught sight of Olivia's hand, a gesture that seemed to bridge her years of captivity and dreams of liberty, but was Ava ready to step into the unknown?

As a smile broke across Olivia's face, Ava's fingers tentatively found their way into the detective's grasp. Olivia gently pulled, and together, with Isaac close behind, they stepped towards the expanse of the outside world.

Thank you, God, for getting me out of there, finally, she prayed. *But now what?*

The brightness of the setting sun greeted Ava, urging her to shield her eyes—such an ordinary part of everyday life, but it was something she hadn't experienced since childhood. It felt warmer and more comforting than she ever remembered.

"You're very brave, Ava," Olivia assured her.

But she didn't feel brave. She felt overwhelmed. She had managed to calm herself so her weeping was reduced to crying, but tears still flowed down her cheeks. Ava's gaze flickered from the rolling fields to towering trees, absorbing the beauty of the world she'd been denied.

Neighbors, drawn by the sirens, clustered outside, their curiosity piqued by the scene unfolding. As Liv accompanied Ava out of the house, the crowd's shock rippled through the air with their collective gasp. Ava Sullivan now stood before them, the veil of her captivity finally lifted.

Chapter Four

"That's Ava Sullivan!" a woman shouted, recognizing her. "She's alive!"

More people gathered around, all asking questions and talking amongst themselves. Olivia, Isaac, and Ava watched as Samuel and Diana were taken away in police cars. As the police vehicles drove away, she felt a hollowness in her heart that she hadn't expected. She had always imagined being overjoyed if she ever got out, but now all she felt was uncertainty.

But one thing was for sure—she was free now, and she would never go back. She would rebuild her life and live the life she had dreamed of for so long.

"I can't believe this is finally all over," Ava said quietly.

"Ava, you may have to testify in court about this," Olivia said.

Ava gave her a timid look. "Testify? Oh, no, I couldn't possibly."

"You're a lot stronger than you think. I can tell," Olivia told her. "So, why did they keep you down there all those years? What happened?"

"Well, it all started the day my father tried to kill my mother…" Ava continued to explain the story.

Afterward, Isaac and Olivia looked at each other, not knowing what to say.

After they took a moment to let her story sink in, Olivia said, "Ava, I don't know what else to say except I'm so sorry you had to go through all that."

Ava looked up at the sky and stared at it. Finally, she was able to see the clouds without having to look through a window. She turned to Olivia. "Thank you for getting me out of there."

"I'm just glad you're safe now. So, what will you do with your freedom?"

Ava let out a sigh of relief. "Are you asking if I will stay here and remain Amish or leave and explore the *Englisher* world? I am not really sure. Technically, I am Amish, but I never really got to live the lifestyle. I guess I am stuck between your world and mine," she sighed. "Maybe I should try both and then choose."

"That's a good idea. I was raised here, but I tried both worlds. Then I chose."

"What did you choose? The *Englisher* life?"

"Yes. So I can keep on helping people like you," Olivia told her, giving a small smile.

"Seems like a good enough reason to me. I think I want to help people too. I'd like to be an author or run a shelter for women. I've read a lot of college-level books that my mother brought to me in secret. But I'd have to give up the Amish life to go to college."

"My partner says sometimes doing something you really love is worth the sacrifices you have to make," Olivia said as they reached the other remaining officers.

The revelation that Ava was very much alive jolted the entire community as if they had been struck by lightning. As she emerged, a figure of impossible survival, whispered rumors that had long since declared her dead were upended in an instant.

Maria, Liz, Anna—the names of childhood friends Ava hadn't heard in years—suddenly materialized before her, each face etched with shock and regret.

Maria, the nearest to Ava, was the first to speak. "Ava? It's really you? We... we thought you were gone forever."

Liz stepped forward, the apology in her eyes matching her words. "This is...shocking. Ava, I'm so sorry. If we had any idea of what was happening to you... I can't forgive myself for believing your father."

"I used to hear you playing outside," Ava said. "But my father told me to stay quiet and hidden."

And then, it was Anna's turn, her face a mask of regret. "Ava, we were your friends. We should've known, should've realized something wasn't right. I missed you so much, and I'm just so terribly sorry."

For Ava, who had grown used to the solitude of shadows, the sudden flood of familiar faces and the intensity of their emotions was as disorienting as it was heartening. While part of her was overjoyed to see them, another part of her recoiled, unsure how to navigate the sea of well-intentioned apologies after not speaking with anyone outside her home for years.

Before she could respond, EMTs navigated through the crowd to reach Ava. They efficiently moved her onto a stretcher and loaded her into the back of an ambulance. A quiet sense of seriousness overtook the crowd as everyone realized the gravity of Ava's condition.

With a few words of assurance to Ava that she was in good hands, the paramedics closed the ambulance doors, cutting her off from the cluster of her neighbors and onlookers. The closed doors provided a visual and symbolic barrier between her past and her uncertain future.

The ambulance took off as a moment of silence could be felt in the Amish community before Ava's transport faded into the distance. Inside, Ava lay back on the stretcher, looking out through the window at the shrinking figures of her community, now finally getting the help she needed and leaving her old life behind.

***

At the hospital, Ava underwent a battery of tests and examinations. The doctors confirmed what seemed inevitable given her prolonged confinement: her muscles had atrophied from the lack of exercise, she was dehydrated, and her body bore the tell-tale signs of malnutrition. Moreover, she had only gotten sunlight from the small windows in the basement, so her very limited exposure to sunlight had left her severely deficient in vitamin D.

While Ava began the slow process of physical recovery, hooked up to IVs and nourished back to health under careful medical supervision, her story captured the public's attention. Local news channels clamored to interview her, drawn to the harrowing account of her survival. Ava's face started to appear on television screens, her name passed between neighbors, friends, and strangers as she stared her story and her dreams of going to college in New York. She was hailed as a local hero, an embodiment of resilience and survival.

Someone set up an online account for her where people could donate money for her to use for college and living expenses, raising thousands of dollars.

As her tale continued to spread, it gained national media coverage and people donated more money. Her undaunted spirit and her eventual escape touched hearts across the country. In response to her ordeal, Ava received a victims' welfare grant, an opportunity for her to rebuild her life and pursue an education.

The swarms of reporters and the constant attention were daunting for Ava. She found the media spotlight overwhelming, so opposite from the shadows she had been confined to for so long. Yet, despite the barrage of cameras and questions, she found a purpose. Ava utilized her newfound platform to urge vigilance and compassion, reminding people of the importance of being alert to signs of others who might be silently pleading for rescue.

Grateful for her second chance, Ava embraced her role as an advocate. Her message was clear: watch carefully for the unseen cries for help, as behind them, there may be someone just like her, waiting for someone to help them.

***

After receiving the all-clear from the hospital, Ava returned to the home that had shielded her from the world—only now, it felt foreign and suffocating. It was strange to be in this house—especially upstairs—all on her own without her parents watching her every move as they often did whenever she was outside the secret room. Even her own room she'd had as a child, which the family had kept the same as if she truly had died, felt foreign.

Maybe I should move out, Ava thought, looking around at the home that she now realized was mostly filled with bad memories. There were a few good memories she had from her childhood, but mostly she remembered being afraid of her father.

Diana still technically owned the home, so she could pass the ownership on to Ava while still in prison. Ava wasn't sure her mother would do that, but maybe she would visit and ask her. Yet the thought of visiting her mother in prison filled her with anxiety. She wasn't sure she was ready to face them yet.

Not long after Ava settled in, Anna, Maria, and Liz came by, hoping to mend the fragmented ties of their past friendship.

Carrying homemade dishes filled with the comforting scents of home-cooked food, they entered Ava's space. In their gentle manner, they sought to lighten the heaviness that lingered about the house.

Ava shared stories of her hospital stay and the therapists who helped knit her back into wholeness. She spoke of the cameras and the interviews, her story laid bare for the world to see in the national spotlight.

"It's incredible that you were able to share your story with so many people," Anna said. "And to spread awareness."

"And now, well, I'm thinking about college," Ava confided, a flicker of hope and determination in her eyes. "I received a grant, so I could afford it. I want to go to college for writing. It's always been my dream to become a novelist."

Her friends exchanged warm, supportive glances. "No matter what you decide, we're here for you," Anna assured with a gentle nudge.

"*Ja*, we just want you to be happy, Ava," Maria chimed in, her voice soft and earnest.

Even Liz added, "Leaving or staying, you have our support."

"Thank you." Ava smiled.

As the day wore on, more neighbors came through her door, each visit a reminder of the life that had been ripped away from her. Although comforting, their familiar faces reflected the estrangement she felt after her long absence.

Ava knew her neighbors meant well with constantly checking in on her and offering encouragement, but with each new knock, a sense of disorientation grew within her, like she didn't belong here. The rhythm of everyday Amish life, once something she only dreamed of participating in, now felt like a garment that no longer fit. The world outside beckoned with the promise of adventure and the whisper of freedom, leaving her feeling like an outsider in her own home.

***

Ava decided to go visit her brother Ian in prison, even though she wasn't quite ready to face her mother and Samuel yet, not after what they did to her. She wasn't angry with them, but it was still too raw, and she knew the sight of her mother being detained would completely break her heart.

Ava arrived at the prison and sat in front of the glass barrier, the cold phone receiver in her hand. Her heart drummed in her chest, the weight of the years without her brother Ian hanging heavily between them. They had been close once, long ago, before their lives were torn apart by their father's violence and deceit. Now, here they were, in a prison visitation room, separated by more than just glass.

Ian, older and bearing the hardened look of someone who had seen far too much, stared back at her. The lines on his face told stories of anger, guilt, and despair.

His eyes widened in shock the moment he saw Ava, his steps faltering. It was a look she recognized—a mix of disbelief and overwhelming emotion. He had been informed that she was alive when the police rescued her, but seeing her in person for the first time since they were kids was a different reality entirely.

"Ava?" Ian's voice crackled through the receiver, raw with emotion. His eyes scanned every detail of her face, as if trying to reconcile the image of his sister now with the last memory he had of her, a six-year-old girl splashing in the pond.

"*Ja,* Ian, it's me," Ava said softly, her own voice trembling as she pressed the receiver closer to her ear. She could see the storm of emotions in his eyes—shock, relief, and pain.

"I can't believe it," he whispered, his hand shaking slightly as he gripped the phone. "All these years, I thought you were dead."

Ava's throat tightened. "I know. He lied to you, to all of us. He locked me away in the basement. I was alive, but... sometimes it felt like I wasn't really living."

Ian's face contorted with anguish. "Ava, I'm so sorry. If I had known..."

"You couldn't have known, Ian," Ava said, her voice firm but kind. "He lied to all three of you boys."

Ava took a deep breath, steeling herself for the conversation they needed to have.

"Ian," Ava began, her voice trembling slightly, "why did you do it? Why did you kill *Daed* and kidnap Jill?"

Ian's shoulders sagged, and he looked away for a moment, as if gathering his thoughts. When he spoke, his voice was rough, filled with a mix of sorrow and old rage. "I was so angry, Ava. I think you remember how abusive *Daed* was. After he told us you died, *Daed* blamed me for your death which he faked, and he punished me for years for something he knew I hadn't done. It was sick. He told me you had drowned that day at the pond and said it was my fault. I believed him because...because he was our father. We grieved your death. I thought I had lost you. I missed you so much. I just wanted you back."

Tears welled up in Ava's eyes, her heart breaking for both the lost little boy her brother had been and the broken man he had become. "Ian, I'm so sorry. I wish you had known the truth. I was alive, locked away all those years."

Ian's eyes filled with unshed tears as he leaned closer to the glass. "I did horrible things, Ava. I kidnapped Jill because she reminded me of you, Ava. She looked so much like you did when you were six. I wanted to protect her, to rewrite the past and somehow make things right. At the time, I thought you were dead, so I thought if I had Jill and I pretended she was you that I might feel less guilty, but I was wrong."

Ava pressed her hand against the glass, yearning to touch her brother, to bridge the chasm that had grown between them. "I understand why you were angry with our father. I felt the same way. When he died, I was relieved because it meant I didn't have to be afraid of him anymore. But Ian, what you did was wrong. Murder or kidnapping only create more victims."

Ian's eyes filled with tears, mirroring her own. "I know, Ava. I know I made horrible mistakes, and I've paid for them every day. Our father completely broke our family apart. Jake is dead, I'm here for the rest of my life, and now *Mamm* and Samuel are going to prison. You're the last one left with any freedom, ironically."

She nodded. "I plan to make the most of it. We can't let *Daed* win." She told him of her plans to go to college.

"I think that's incredible, Ava. I hope you find everything you're looking for and achieve all your goals. I know you'll do amazing things."

"Thank you, Ian."

"I hope Jill is doing well now. I hope she has found peace."

Ava nodded, her heart aching. "I hope so too, Ian. So, do you still consider yourself to be Amish?"

He shook his head. "No. When I left the community, I left the Amish way of life behind, and I never intend to return to it. *Daed* was the biggest hypocrite I ever met."

"You know most Amish men are not like him at all. You remember the men from our community, don't you? They were all so kind and gentle—the opposite of him."

"Because of *Daed*, I don't want anything to do with the Amish faith. I'm sorry, Ava, but I just could never do it again."

"Do you mean you don't believe in God anymore?" Ava asked.

Ian sighed. "To be honest, I've been confused. Yes, I believe in God, but I feel so distanced from Him. Like…who am I to talk to Him, you know?"

"God always wants to hear from his children, Ian. Don't lose faith. I hope we all can find some kind of peace, eventually."

As they sat there, separated by glass but connected by the fragile threads of family and shared pain, Ava felt a small glimmer of hope. This conversation, painful as it was, might be the first small step toward healing—for both of them.

Chapter Five

Ava stepped into the plain Amish church, looking around with wide eyes. On one side of the building, there were rows of backless wooden benches where services were held. This church building also doubled as the school. On the other side, there was the schoolroom with a collapsible room divider in between. There were learning charts and maps on the walls of the classrooms along with shelves of school books.

When she was a child, the last time she had gone to church with her family, services had been held in people's homes within the community.

"We are blessed to have this building. Everyone pitched in to build it years ago," Liz said, walking up to Ava. "Most Amish communities don't have a church building. How are you this morning? It must be overwhelming to see everyone all at once after..." Her voice trailed off and she shifted her feet uncomfortably.

Ava nodded. "It is, but this building is wonderful. I haven't been to church since I was six. I think the last service I went to was held in the Johnson's home. There were so many people, some had to sit outside in the summer heat," she recalled, smiling at the memory. "And we would play outside after."

"I remember," Liz said.

"Good morning, Ava," Anna said, giving Ava a hug.

Maria also joined them. "Good morning."

"I was just telling Ava about when the church was built," Liz said.

"And we all went to school here," Anna piped in, then a shadow crossed her face. "I'm sorry."

"Don't be sorry," Ava said. "My father hid me away right before I would have started school, but my mother taught me secretly." She lowered her voice. "I actually kept going beyond the eighth-grade level, and she even brought me college level books. I just wanted to keep learning as much as I could."

"That's incredible," Anna said, her eyes filled with wonder and envy. "So, you actually are more educated than any of us."

Ava gave a mirthless laugh. "I never got to put any of it to use."

"Well, maybe you will one day," Maria said, and Anna and Liz nodded in agreement.

"Let's go sit down," Liz said. "It's almost nine o'clock."

After they sat down on a backless bench in the back on the women's side of the room, the service started a few minutes later. Acapella hymns filled the air, each note a thread in the tapestry of faith she had been denied access to for so long. The only hymns she had heard in her captivity were ones her mother would sing to her, which she would then sing to herself.

Surrounded by the congregation, Ava found comfort in the rituals, recognizing what had been stolen from her in the silence of her confinement—the fellowship, the communal worship, the shared belief that coursed through the congregation.

During the service, she allowed herself to be swept up in the spiritual current, appreciating the harmonious blend of voices and the sermon that spoke of resilience and redemption. It rekindled a connection to her past, to what might have been if her father had not stolen her freedom.

Once the service concluded, the solitude she had found in worship abruptly ended. Women of all ages approached her with sympathetic eyes, nudging past one another to offer words of support and ask about her well-being.

"And how are you doing, Ava?" one would ask, her hand resting on Ava's shoulder.

"Is there anything we can do to help?" another would offer, her expression etched with concern.

The attention was suffocating. Ava felt her walls closing in, her heart racing to keep pace with the rapid-fire questions. She felt claustrophobia creep in. As Ava stood in the midst of her community, she realized she hadn't seen any of them in so long that they felt like strangers.

Excusing herself with a mumbled apology, Ava made her way outside the church for a breath of fresh air. The warmth of the outdoors offered a temporary reprieve until her eyes settled on a figure in the distance—Mr. Jonas Miller. Tensing, she watched her neighbor who had left her pleas for help unanswered.

Determined not to let the moment pass, Ava approached him. He seemed to stiffen at the sight of her.

"Mr. Miller," Ava said, her voice steady even though her insides were quaking. "I have a question for you. Did you ever see me write 'HELP' on the window? Your house is on that side of our house, so I thought maybe you might have seen it."

"I did see 'HELP' written on the window," Mr. Miller said, his confession delivered with a matter-of-fact tone. "Thought your brother was pulling a prank like he used to as a child. I decided to not get involved."

Recollections of smearing "HELP" on the grimy basement window flooded back to Ava over the years. She remembered pressing her face against the dusty pane, eyes scanning for any flicker of life from the outside world or even just someone walking by.

Ava, feeling empowered by her newfound liberation and hurt by his indifference, decided to confront him further. "You saw me asking for help. Why didn't you do anything? You should have done something, anything. You could have called the police, or told the elders or the bishop," she insisted, her voice firm despite the quiver of betrayal.

The argument between them erupted in the church parking lot as people filed out of the church.

Her words, laced with the weight of unspeakable suffering, hung heavy in the air.

Mr. Miller's response was unfeeling. "Listen here, Miss Sullivan. I'm not one to meddle. If it was something serious, I reckoned your family would handle it."

"That's just it! It was my family doing this to me," Ava retorted, her voice rising. "You should have done something. Maybe I would have been rescued years ago instead of just recently."

"I didn't have to do anything. You know it's not our way to get the police involved," Mr. Miller retorted. "I didn't do anything wrong."

"Seeing evil being done to someone and doing nothing is wrong," Ava argued.

"I didn't know evil was being done," Mr. Miller argued, his voice rising.

"You would have if you had called the police. My brothers might have been pranksters when they were younger, but do you really think a grown man would write 'HELP' on the window as a joke?" Ava cried, her voice also rising.

The onlookers listened intently as the argument simmered. Some exchanged uneasy glances, nodding in agreement with Ava, most of them agreeing that the police should have been involved earlier.

"Well..." Mr. Miller hesitated.

"You really thought it was a prank?" Ava continued, incredulous. "I was trapped, Mr. Miller. I needed help. You could have helped me. Instead, you chose to do nothing."

Mr. Miller shifted uncomfortably, the judgment of the community's gaze upon him. "This isn't my fault," he said, though the defensive edge to his voice undercut his words.

"Even if we don't involve the authorities in most matters," one bystander spoke up, "ignoring a plea for help isn't right. Mr. Miller. I think in this case, the police should have been called."

Murmurs of agreement spread through the crowd.

Chastened by the crowd and Ava's piercing words, Mr. Miller's indifference began to crack. His face, usually placid, now flushed with the heat of anger and embarrassment. He balled his hands into fists and stomped his foot.

"Well, what's done is done!" Mr. Miller barked. "I won't stand here and be lectured by all of you!"

With that, Mr. Miller turned on his heel, clenching his teeth. He climbed into his buggy and drove away.

Ava watched him go, her own mix of emotions swirling. While she felt a bitter satisfaction in holding Mr. Miller to account, her victory was hollow and would not undo the years of solitude she'd endured.

***

Ava welcomed Maria, Liz, and Anna into her home, the very walls that had echoed with the silence of her captivity now resonated with the warmth of friendship. The table was set for lunch, a simple yet thoughtful spread that spoke of new beginnings.

As they ate, the conversation meandered through light topics before Ava gathered her courage to broach the subject she knew would change everything. "I've made a decision," she started, pausing for a breath and the quiet that settled around the table. "I'm going to leave the Amish community, move to New York City, and go to college."

Her friends exchanged glances, surprise etched on their faces, quickly followed by expressions of understanding. "Oh, Ava," Anna said, reaching across the table to squeeze her hand, "We will miss you dearly."

Maria nodded, her brow furrowed in thought. "What about your house? Will you sell it?"

"I'd like to sell it, hopefully to an Amish family, but only if my mother signs it over to me. And if not, I'll hopefully be able to rent it out. I wouldn't want to live there permanently after what happened."

Liz patted Ava's arm gently. "Of course. That's completely understandable. Whatever you need, just let us know."

"Thank you so much," Ava said, thankful for the support from her friends.

Chapter Six

Ava embarked on a transformation as she prepared for college life. To get into college, she would need to take the High School Equivalency Test (HiSET) which replaced the GED in Maine, since she didn't go to high school. She studied, and a few months later, she got her HiSET certification through a local adult education program.

Preparing for city life, she used the money that people had donated to her online to purchase clothing typical of *Englishers*, such as jeans and t-shirts, items that felt foreign against her skin after a lifetime in traditional Amish attire. She also bought a laptop and a cell phone, tools that opened up a world of digital information which had previously been beyond her reach. The sales people who sold her the phone and laptop taught her the basics on how to use them, including how to use the internet and how to use the laptop for writing.

Armed with these essentials, Ava took the steps to enroll in a community college in the heart of New York City, a decision that came with the excitement and trepidation of venturing into the unknown. She would live just off campus in a tiny bachelor studio apartment, immersing herself fully in this new, bustling environment.

Ready to continue making changes in her life, she decided to let go of the long hair that she'd had her entire life. Since she would no longer be Amish, she no longer had to follow the rules regarding her hair and was now free to cut it.

Ava hesitated at the entrance to the salon, the decision weighing on her as heavily as the long hair that cascaded down to her knees when it was not tied up in a bun like it was now. To an outsider, this might have seemed a simple act of grooming, but for Ava, it signified another step away from her past, severing yet another tie to her old Amish life.

She mustered up her courage and walked into the salon. The stylist greeted her with a smile and showed her to the chair. Ava looked at her reflection in the mirror and pulled the pins and hair elastic out of her hair that had been holding it in place, removing the bun and letting her hair fall freely to the floor.

The stylist gasped. "This is the longest hair I've ever seen. It's so beautiful. Are you sure you want to cut it?"

"Yes," Ava said, her voice a mixture of resolve and nerves, "to about the middle of my back."

The stylist nodded, a glint of excitement in her eyes for the transformation she was about to undertake.

"Would you like to donate it to the foundation that makes wigs for cancer survivors?" the stylist asked.

"Oh, yes, please," Ava said, and the stylist gave her instructions on how to mail the hair.

She brushed through Ava's hair, the bristles untangling years of tradition. The stylist put Ava's hair into three braids, securing them with hair elastics at the middle of her back and again at the ends of her hair.

"This will keep your hair neat while you mail it," the stylist commented.

With a decisive snip, the scissors made their initial cut. Ava felt as though the chains of her past fell along with the strands of her hair onto the floor. Once each braid was removed, the stylist set it on the counter, then she evened out the haircut.

As the stylist worked, Ava felt a growing sense of liberation—with each portion of hair that was trimmed, she felt a release from the weight of her past. By the time the stylist had finished, Ava's hair fell in freshly cut layers to the middle of her back, bouncing lightly as she moved.

The stylist handed Ava the braids of hair, helping her put them into a plastic bag to take with her.

Ava rose from the salon chair, turning her head from side to side to appreciate the feel of her lighter, shorter hair. She thanked the stylist, paid, and walked out onto the downtown sidewalk, a new woman ready to embrace her future, her strides confident and a reflection in the salon window showing not just a changed hairstyle, but a symbol of her bold new life.

***

The time came to say goodbye to her Amish community. As she hugged her friends and neighbors, the reality of her departure brimmed in the corners of her eyes and the tightness in their embraces. With each goodbye, a thread from the fabric of her former life was gently pulled away.

Ava stood on her familiar porch, taking in the faces of Anna, Maria, and Liz—the women who had supported her through this transition.

"Your hair looks great," Anna said in a low voice. "I know we aren't supposed to comment on outward appearances, but it suits you."

"Thanks," Ava said with a smile.

"I can't believe this is it," Liz said, her voice catching slightly as she clutched Ava's hand. Her eyes shimmered with unshed tears, a testament to the bond they shared.

"New York City," Maria mused, a wistful smile on her face. "You're going to do great things, Ava. We all believe in you."

Liz stepped forward, offering a hug that enveloped Ava in a warmth that spoke louder than words. When Liz pulled away, she kept her hands on Ava's shoulders, looking into her eyes. "Just remember, no matter where you are or what you become, you'll always be a part of us. And since you were never baptized into the church, you won't be shunned. If you ever decide to come home again, we would be so happy, but we understand if you want to make your own way out there and never look back."

Ava's heart swelled, a lump forming in her throat as she absorbed the moment—the loving faces, the shared history, and the bittersweet nature of her departure. "I'm going to miss you all so much," Ava replied, her voice steady despite the emotion she felt. "You've been my anchor in a storm I thought would never end."

They all knew this was more than just a physical departure; it was Ava stepping beyond the boundary lines of everything familiar, leaving the quiet Amish community for a bustling, unfamiliar world. It was a journey Ava needed to take, a calling she could no longer ignore.

"You'll always have a home here, and good friends," Anna said, glancing at the house that had been both Ava's prison and sanctuary.

Ava nodded, a silent vow to remember where she came from but also recognizing where she was headed. She hugged each of her friends tightly, committing their faces to memory. With one last wave, Ava turned away, her bag slung over her shoulder. She walked toward the waiting car that would take her to the bus station.

It wasn't just distance she was putting between herself and her old life; it was a spectrum of dreams and hopes. As the car pulled away, Ava took a deep breath, ready to embrace her new life in the city.

At the station, Ava boarded the bus, a singular figure amongst the travelers. As it left Unity, it drew a definitive line between her past and her future. She was leaving behind everything she had known for the hope of what lay ahead.

Ava sat on the bus, her eyes fixed on the passing scenery as the miles rolled by, bringing her closer to New York City. Anticipation and anxiety churned within her, a mess of emotions difficult to untangle. She wondered if she could truly handle life in college on her own, a fresh start in a city that never slept.

Her thoughts drifted back to the years she spent locked away in her family's basement, devoid of responsibilities or exposure to the outside world. Everything she knew about life came from the books her mother had secretly provided. While these had prepared her for the academic challenges of college, nothing could have prepared her for the practical aspects of living independently.

"Am I really ready for this?" she wondered. How would she support herself?

She still had several thousand dollars left from the online donation account, but she knew that would only last so long. Living in the city was expensive, or so she heard. Rent, utilities, groceries—these were all foreign concepts. She had never used electricity or operated a cell phone, never navigated a computer, or faced the everyday tasks that came with maintaining a home, even if a small apartment was all she could find.

Despite being book smart, Ava felt the sharp sting of her inexperience in worldly matters. Yet, she knew that achieving her dream of becoming a writer required more than just intellectual prowess. An education was crucial, a stepping stone to a future she had long imagined.

I have to do this, she thought, her resolve hardening with each passing mile. *For my dreams, for my future, I have to face these challenges head-on.*

A sigh escaped her as she glanced around the bus, filled with strangers who seemed so much more familiar with the world she was only just beginning to enter. She felt a pang of isolation but also the flicker of determination.

I may stumble, she thought, clenching her hands in her lap. *But I must learn to get back up, to navigate this world on my own terms.*

As the bus neared the city, Ava felt a surge of purpose. She gripped her cell phone, still unfamiliar in her hand, and took a deep breath.

"I can do this," she whispered to herself, her voice firm. What she lacked in experience, she would gain in time. She was ready to face the unknown, driven by the same determination that had already seen her through so much. The bus rolled on, carrying her towards a new beginning.

Chapter Seven

New York City greeted Ava with its cacophony of noise, activity, and towering architecture. Stepping off the bus, her heart pounded with a mix of emotions—anticipation, fear, curiosity, and amazement. The city was a concrete and steel jungle so different from the green, open spaces she grew up in. People rushed by, each absorbed in their own worlds and preoccupied by their mobile devices as Ava stood still, taking a moment to let the reality sink in.

The skyline, that iconic mosaic of skyscrapers, both daunted and inspired her. She realized in that moment the magnitude of her journey. Ava was not just in a new place; she was at the beginning of a new life. The city's crowded streets and tall buildings were the complete opposite from the serenity and natural beauty of the Amish countryside. She drew in a deep breath, ready to face the challenge, and stepped forward into the crowd, an Amish girl in an *Englisher* world.

***

To offset her expenses, Ava took a job at a local diner, the hustle of the establishment a stark contrast to the life of monotony and boredom she had left behind. It was hard work, but the rhythm of the daily grind carried with it a sense of normalcy and independence. She felt tired but fulfilled at the end of each day. The income was modest, yet necessary to cover her basic needs, including the rent for her small apartment.

Aware that time was not on her side financially, Ava maneuvered her schedule to attend college classes in the evening. This decision allowed her to continue working during the day, serving customers and saving every penny, while nights were dedicated to her studies and the pursuit of her literary ambitions.

In Ava's first college class, the lecture hall buzzed with the excited chatter of students. She glanced nervously at her laptop, a sleek device that felt alien under her fingers. The professor began speaking, explaining the day's lesson and encouraging everyone to take notes.

Her pulse quickened when she realized she had no idea how to open the writing program. The salesperson who sold her the computer had showed her how, but now she couldn't remember. It all seemed so complicated with so many buttons. Her fingers hovered over the keyboard, aimlessly pressing keys in a futile attempt to bring up the application. Sweat beaded on her forehead as panic set in. She was so used to writing in a notebook—why hadn't she brought one with her?

Noticing her struggle, the girl sitting next to her leaned over and whispered, "Here, let me help you." With a few deft clicks, she opened the writing program, and Ava breathed a sigh of relief.

"Thank you," Ava whispered back, grateful for the girl's kindness.

However, the relief was short-lived. A group of girls sitting nearby had noticed her difficulty and were snickering among themselves. As the class came to an end, they approached Ava with smirks plastered on their faces.

One of them scoffed, "Haven't you ever used a computer before?"

Ava felt her cheeks burning with embarrassment but decided to be honest. "No, I haven't."

The girls burst into laughter. "What, are you Amish or something?" one of them sneered.

Struggling to keep her composure, Ava replied, "Actually, I was raised Amish."

Their laughter intensified, and they began snapping pictures of her with their phones, their mocking comments slicing through the air like knives. Overwhelmed, Ava gathered her things and fled the classroom, tears stinging her eyes. The sound of their laughter echoed in her ears as she ran down the hallway, her heart aching from the cruelty she had just experienced. That night she went home and cried in her tiny, empty apartment.

This was all so much harder than she'd ever expected.

Ava's life became a delicate balancing act of time management, juggling coursework, shifts at the diner, and finding time to also sleep and take care of herself. No one recognized her as the young Amish woman who had been on the news—here, in her *Englisher* clothes, she blended in and was just another face in a huge sea of people.

But Ava, determined and resilient, was no stranger to adversity. She approached each day with the same fortitude that had seen her through her time in the basement, with the belief that each step, each shift worked, each class completed, brought her closer to achieving her dream.

CHAPTER EIGHT

Officer Theo Kingsley navigated the vibrant streets of New York City, his eyes scanning the cityscape as he and his partner conducted their patrol at the end of their shift. As they were approaching the police station, the radio crackled to life with a message from dispatch, informing them that they'd need to pull an overtime shift due to an unexpected incident downtown. They were told to work an extra four hours on patrol so other officers could handle other police matters.

Theo exhaled sharply, a frown creasing his forehead. "I was supposed to meet Jennifer for our date tonight," he confided to his partner, his tone laced with disappointment. "She's going to be at the restaurant soon, expecting me."

"Sorry, man," Officer Rodriguez said. "My wife hates it when I have to work late on date night."

With a sense of urgency, Theo reached for his phone and dialed his wife's number, hoping to catch her before she became too worried. The call redirected to voicemail after several rings, and he left a message explaining the situation. There was nothing else he could do but hope she'd understand the unpredictable nature of his job.

But why wasn't she answering or calling him back? This thought nagged at him. That was unlike her.

The night pressed on, each case call pulling Theo further into his work until the late hour was the only thing consuming his attention. His patrol sergeant radioed in to tell them to come back to the police station early, which was strange.

Theo Kingsley and Officer Rodriguez concluded their patrol shift and headed back to the precinct. However, as they entered the bustling station, a hush fell over the room, a palpable shift in the air that instantly raised Theo's internal alarm. Faces that normally greeted him with nods and brief smiles now averted their gazes, somber and laden with an unspoken dread.

Officer Rodriguez cast a confused look Theo's way, but before either could question the change, their sergeant emerged from his office, his expression grim, his eyes locking with Theo's.

"Kingsley, my office, please," the sergeant's usually harsh voice carried a rare, softer tone that frightened Theo much more than if he had yelled.

Once inside the close quarters of the office, the din of the precinct muffled behind closed doors.

"There is no easy way to say this, so I'm just going to come right out and say it. There's been an accident," his sergeant began, the words measured but heavy with empathy. "Your wife, Jennifer, was involved in a hit and run while leaving a downtown restaurant tonight. She...died. I'm so sorry."

Theo heard the sergeant's words, yet his mind refused to wrap around the meaning, scrambling. The words echoed in Theo's head, refusing to find a place to settle. His wife, the love of his life, taken so suddenly, so violently—left him in a void where the pulsing life of the city around him seemed cruelly indifferent.

Officer Rodriguez's voice was somewhere in the distance, a concern muted by the thunderous silence that now enveloped Theo. His vision dimmed, the precinct walls closing in on him as he grappled with the truth.

For Theo, life as he knew it had just ended.

***

As Theo sat on the couch staring at a framed photo of his wife, his phone rang, the name "Mom" lighting up the screen. He took a deep breath to steady himself before answering, still shouldering the weight of his sorrow.

"Hey, Mom," Theo spoke, his voice softer than usual.

Carol Kingsley's voice came through, warm and tinged with concern. "Theo, honey, I've been talking to your father, and we really wish you'd consider coming back home to Maine. Your father, your sister, and I, we all miss you. We could be there for you, help you through this tough time."

Theo glanced around his New York City apartment, a space once vibrant with shared love and laughter, now reduced to silent echoes of the past. Maine—with its familiar landscapes, the community he grew up in, and the memories of a childhood long gone—seemed like a different world compared to the relentless pace of the city.

"I've been thinking about it," he admitted, the weight of his loneliness pressing down on him. "It's just, Jenny and I built a life here, you know?" His voice cracked, the mention of his wife bringing a fresh sting to his already wounded heart.

"But she's gone now, Theo," Carol whispered, a mother's intuition hearing the unspoken pain in her son's voice. "We just want to have you close, where we can take care of you. Your father and I aren't as young as we once were. It's not easy for us to get to you if you need us."

The silence stretched between them as Theo considered the possibility. New York held memories at every turn, memories that were now painful reminders of the future they'd planned but would never see. What truly kept him in the city anymore now that his wife was gone? He might miss the challenge of working in the city, but he could be a police officer anywhere.

Working was Theo's only reprieve from his sorrowful thoughts. It distracted him, offering a semblance of purpose and the chance to provide others with the protection his wife had lacked that fateful night. Yet, amidst his endless shifts and the never-ending cycle of cases, a persistent thought nagged at him: perhaps a transfer to a department in Maine was what he needed.

In a new environment, he could keep himself busy while being near his family. Maine held the promise of family dinners, shared stories, and light-hearted moments that could punctuate his days, lifting the weight of his grief, if only slightly.

A new apartment and a different bed might help him stop reaching for his wife in the middle of the night, a habit that had become a nightly agony. In Maine, every unfamiliar creak of new floors and every new shadow cast by moonlight might just help him let go, piece by piece.

He knew it wouldn't be easy, that grief wasn't something one could simply escape, but Theo saw a sliver of hope—a chance to begin healing.

"I'll look into it and see if I can get a job there," he said after a moment. It was a practical consideration, but it also felt like a small surrender to his grief—an acknowledgment that holding onto this place wouldn't bring her back.

"That's all we ask, sweetheart," Carol responded, hope evident in her tone. "Just think about it."

They said their goodbyes, and Theo ended the call. He sat there for a long time, contemplating the expanse of his life without Jenny and the potential for healing that might come from being surrounded by family. His heart ached with loss, but it ached too for comfort and familiarity, for a respite from the city that now seemed too vast and too full of ghosts.

Chapter Nine

Almost two years into her college journey, Ava found solace and inspiration in the bustling ambiance of a local coffee shop. Her fingers danced across the keys of her laptop as her heart poured out chapters of her novel—a dream that was slowly but steadily taking shape.

With her recent fifteen minutes of fame in the national spotlight, she had already received responses from interested literary agents, hoping to represent her if she wrote about her life story. Her heart ached at the mere thought. Could she write about what had happened to her, about all that time she had spent alone in the darkness? She had always wanted to finish writing her science fiction fantasy novel, but maybe writing about her life story would be the very thing she needed to heal her heart. She could write both, and hopefully many more books in the future.

She knew that writing a memoir and using her fame to her advantage, though it was short-lived, could be just what she needed to jumpstart her career.

As she focused on her narrative, a young man passed by her table. He paused, his eyes catching a glimpse of the words on her screen. Turning on a well-practiced charm, he approached Ava with a disarming smile. He appeared to be in his early thirties and wore glasses and a business suit with a tie—the look of professionalism.

"Sorry to intrude," he said with an easy graciousness that momentarily caught Ava off guard, "but I couldn't help noticing... Are you writing a book? Or is it an essay or article, maybe?"

"It's a science fiction fantasy novel," Ava said quietly. "I've been working on it for a few years."

"That's quite an accomplishment."

Ava, still a touch naïve and craving acknowledgement for her hard work, looked up and smiled tentatively. "Thank you," she replied, flattered that a stranger would take interest in her writing. "But it's not finished yet."

"I happen to be a literary agent," the man continued. "My name is Colin Monroe. I'd love to learn more about your work." He handed her a professional-looking business card.

"Really? Wow, that would be great," Ava gushed, unable to believe her luck. "I've seen you around here before, I think."

"I come here often. May I sit?" he gestured to the seat next to her.

The conversation veered into the world of publishing, with the man weaving grand tales of the authors he'd worked with, how many copies they'd sold, and the success they had achieved with book signings and movie deals. Ava listened, her heart racing with a mix of excitement and trepidation.

He proposed they set up a meeting with some publishers he knew in downtown NYC. "How about we meet up at ten o'clock on Thursday? I can introduce you to the owner of the publishing company, Mrs. Blackwell," he said confidently. "Just meet me there."

Ava was thrilled. This was the moment she had been working towards, the opportunity that could elevate her from a student to a published author. They exchanged contact details and agreed on a time and place for the meeting.

As the man left, a flicker of doubt crossed Ava's mind, but hope quickly smothered it. She returned to her writing, her mind already imagining the possibilities that awaited her, unaware of the ill intent behind the charming facade of the man who had just exited the coffee shop.

***

Ava arrived at the designated building with bubbling nerves. Colin was waiting for her in the lobby.

"Good morning, Ava," Colin said. "Glad you could make it."

He greeted her with the same polite charm as before, had her fill out an application with all her information on it for Mrs. Blackwell, and then politely began to chat. Their small talk was quickly interrupted by his phone ringing. He stepped aside to take the call, and Ava couldn't help but overhear the mention of a Mrs. Blackwell from a publishing company. However, Colin's next words dimmed her anticipation.

"She had to cancel, something came up," Colin explained after hanging up. But he quickly proposed an alternative: "Mrs. Blackwell said we can catch her on the way to her car in the parking garage. She's willing to talk there, but only for a moment. We have to hurry."

Ava hesitated, unease creeping in where excitement had thrived mere moments ago. Parking garages frightened her. They seemed so gloomy and ominous, and the concrete reminded her of the basement.

The suggestion to meet in a parking garage seemed off to her, a departure from normal professional conduct. Her intuition whispered a warning—perhaps it would be better to leave and reschedule the meeting for another day under more appropriate circumstances.

"Maybe we should just reschedule," she suggested, voicing her concern.

Colin, however, was persuasive. "This is your one opportunity," he insisted, urgency lacing his words. "Mrs. Blackwell's schedule is usually booked out for months. I only got this appointment because someone else canceled the other day. It's now or possibly not at all."

Torn between her gut feeling and the fear of missing out on a potential career breakthrough, Ava reluctantly agreed to follow Colin to the parking garage.

Their footsteps echoed in the near-empty structure, the dim lighting casting long shadows that merged with Ava's growing anxiety. "Where is Mrs. Blackwell?" she asked after a few moments had passed, and no one else was in sight.

"She'll be here. She must be grabbing a coffee on her way out of her office," Colin reassured her. But before she could inquire further, three large men emerged from the parked cars, effectively surrounding them.

Ava shrank back, but Colin didn't even flinch.

One of them stepped closer to her. He was tall and muscular with tattoos snaking over his arms, neck, and face, with a piercing between his eyebrows—something she had never seen before. He wore a backwards baseball cap, a baggy t-shirt and jeans with an expensive chain around his neck. He spoke with authority, "I'm Razor. You're with us now. What's your name? Nevermind—no one cares. Your new name is Angel."

She opened her mouth to tell him her real name, but he cut her off.

"We call you, you show up where we tell you to go. On time. Understand, Angel?" The threat was clear as Razor pressed a cell phone into her hand. "When this rings, you answer it."

Ava turned to Colin in disbelief. What was he talking about? Where was the publisher?

"There must be some mistake..." she stammered, backing away slowly.

"You belong to us now," Razor seethed, reaching forward and grabbing her arm roughly. She bit back a yelp.

Colin gave her a smug look, shaking his head slowly. "You put your name, address, and contact information on that application you filled out back there. We know where you live. I've been watching you for the past few weeks at that coffee shop, walking past you to see what you were writing, then I did my research and printed that phony business card." He laughed. "You were just too trusting."

Colin was part of this. There was no publisher. The trap had been meticulously set, and she had walked right into it.

"I don't understand," Ava cried. "What do you want from me? What do you want me to do?"

The men chuckled and snickered.

"You'll figure it out. Or your clients will tell you," Razor said.

Ava's mind swam with confusion. How had this happened? She had finally become free from her family's control and was now a prisoner once again. Devastation coursed through her veins, and she fought to remain upright as her vision blurred with tears.

To cement their control, Razor dragged Ava toward their vehicle. The back doors of the large white van swung open to reveal the lifeless form of a young woman, bloodied and bruised—a victim who had resisted their demands. Ava's blood ran cold, the image searing itself into her mind.

"This will be you if you tell anyone or fail to follow our orders. And if you go to the police, we will kill you, just like we killed her," Razor hissed into her ear, causing Ava to shudder. He was too close to her, and his cigarette breath made her want to gag.

"But if you do follow orders, we will allow you to continue going to school, write your precious book, and live your life. Just show up when we call, do what you're told, and we will let you live," Colin added—if that was even his real name.

Fear gripping her heart, Ava knew she had no choice but to comply. The threat was real, and resistance could be fatal. Numbly, she nodded her understanding, forced once more into a world of submission from which she had fought so hard to escape.

She was now their property.

Chapter Ten

After classes the next day, the shrill ring of Razor's cell phone shattered the silence of Ava's apartment, a sobering reminder of the grim reality that loomed outside her four walls. Ava froze, her breath hitched in her throat as she eyed the phone—its ringtone a siren call that signaled her handlers were reaching out with their first demand to be met.

Her hand trembled as she reached for the device, a tool not of her choosing but provided by the criminals—a leash disguised as a lifeline. She answered, the voice on the other end crisp and authoritative.

"We need you downtown in one hour at a venue where we will be holding a fashion show," Razor's voice commanded, cold, gravelly, and unyielding. "We will text you the address."

"One hour?" Ava's heart pounded with a mix of fear and resignation as she acknowledged the command. Despite her every instinct screaming against it, she couldn't refuse due to the severe consequences.

"Be there. On time." The call was disconnected.

She dressed quickly, putting on an outer zombie-like calm to mask the turmoil that raged within. The familiar streets of Manhattan no longer held the wonder and ambition they once did as she made her way to the appointed location, a picturesque venue that overlooked the sleepless energy of the city.

As she arrived, the grandeur of the venue did little to ease the dread coiled tightly in her stomach. Beyond the luxury, expectations and shadows would ensnare her. What would happen to her? She still wasn't sure what they wanted her to do. A sick feeling churned in her stomach.

Drawing a deep breath, she entered the venue, steeling herself for the night ahead, every step bringing her further into the cage her life had become.

The cool, sterile white walls of the high-end venue, which also doubled as an art gallery, stood in stark contrast to the vibrant depths of the abstract, colorful paintings adorning its walls—paintings priced beyond imagination, discussed over the clink of expensive drinkware and the hum of cultured conversation.

An older woman, harsh and direct, pulled Ava into a back room. "Come with me."

In the confines of the dressing room, there were other young women who looked as frightened as Ava did, but some of them looked completely numb, the life from their eyes drained as though they had done this a hundred times. A young woman with long black hair entered the room, looking uncertain.

"I'm Carmen," she said, her voice carrying a tremor of apprehension as she approached Ava.

"I'm Ava. This is my first...assignment. I don't really know what to expect," Ava said.

"This is also my first. I guess you could say I was recently 'recruited' too, just a few days ago."

"Me too. They told me I was meeting with a publisher."

"They told me I had a meeting with an art gallery owner who was willing to look at my portfolio," Carmen said, shaking her head. "I was an idiot to believe them."

"I also fell for it." Ava felt a kinship with Carmen. "What are we here to do? No one has really told me," she inquired, hopelessly seeking an answer she knew might unsettle her even more.

Carmen opened her mouth to speak, but before any words could spill forth, the older woman intervened. With a brusque hand, she grabbed Ava's shoulder and pushed her towards the makeup chair.

"Enough chit-chat," she snapped. "Sit down and let's get you ready. What, you don't wear makeup?"

"No," Ava admitted. She'd never worn it in her life—it was against the Amish rules.

The older woman's interruption was a harsh reminder that they were not to question their roles or the circumstances. Silenced by the woman's authoritative demeanor, Ava resigned herself to the chair.

As Ava's face was painted over with makeup, a mask to hide her true self, she stole glances at Carmen, seeing her own confusion and fear mirrored in the young woman's eyes.

The woman continued to work on Ava's hair and makeup, transforming her into something she didn't recognize—red lips, smoky eyes, and curled hair. When the woman was finished, she handed Ava a revealing, short red dress unlike anything she had worn before—certainly nothing like the modest attire of her Amish upbringing she was accustomed to.

"This is what you'll be wearing in the fashion show," the woman said flatly.

"What? I'll be in the fashion show?" Ava stammered.

"You're all in the show."

"I don't know anything about modeling," Ava said.

"It doesn't matter. Put on the dress and walk down the runway when they tell you." The woman rolled her eyes. "You'll figure the rest out."

"Why wasn't I told about this? What am I really here for?" Ava questioned, a hint of dread in her voice as she held the dress before her.

The woman laughed with a dismissive snort. "Isn't it obvious? You're what's for sale, not the dresses. The fashion show is a front for what's really happening here. And remember, use the name Razor gave you. Angel, right?"

Ava's confusion deepened, her heart pounding in alarm. "This dress is too revealing," she protested, thinking of her past—of the long dresses and aprons that she wore in her former life.

"Do I look like I care what you think? Just put it on and get backstage," the woman barked with no room for argument.

With a sinking heart, Ava obeyed, going backstage, the dress making her feel self-conscious and exposed. She tried to pull it down to cover more of her legs, but then the top came down too much, so she stopped trying to adjust it and just tried to blend in.

Carmen walked up behind Ava. "I don't really know what's going on, either, but I have a guess."

"What is it? Why do they want us here? I know it's not to model," Ava whispered.

"You," a man wearing a headset said, grabbing Ava's arm. "You're on next." He pulled her to the curtain. "When I tell you, just walk up and down the runway."

"That's it? That is all I have to do?" Ava asked, bewildered.

"Go! Now!" he said, shoving her forward. She stumbled out onto the stage and walked up and down the catwalk as loud techno music blared. She squinted in the bright lights, barely able to make out a few faces in the audience. Afterward, she waited backstage, then they were brought out to mingle with the people who had attended the show.

The wealthy patrons seemed to blur into a single entity of privilege and expectations. Then, one much older man detached from the crowd, honing in on Ava with an assessing gaze.

"What's your name?" he inquired.

"I'm Av—Angel. My name is Angel," she said, slowly backing away from him.

"What a beautiful name," he said, looking her up and down. "Almost as beautiful as that dress. I'm Mr. Roth." A charming smile played on his lips as he offered her a glass of champagne. "Here, have a drink."

"I don't drink," Ava replied. "Thank you, anyway."

The man laughed, dismissing her words as playful banter. "Are you joking?"

"No, I really don't drink," she insisted.

"Well, then, what do you think of these art pieces, Angel?" he asked with a sweeping gesture.

"I don't like any of these, really," Ava admitted, taking in the large modern, abstract paintings with bright colors and various shapes. She stared at them, trying to figure out what they looked like.

"I prefer realistic landscapes of the country...like I used to paint." A twinge of longing for her home crept in, a pang for the freedom to paint and write passionately like she used to, even though it once came from within the walls of a prison.

The man, Mr. Roth, placed a winning bid on the dress Ava was wearing. She looked at him in confusion.

"Come with me, Angel," he said, as if her accompaniment was part of the transaction.

When Ava hesitated, revealing her mother's warnings from long ago not to get into a car with a stranger, Razor stepped forward with a menacing reminder of her situation. He was dressed in a suit and tie, blending in with the other guests, despite his piercings and tattoos.

"Go with Mr. Roth, Angel," the pimp hissed.

"What do you want me to do?" she asked, her voice trembling. "I still don't know."

"Mr. Roth will tell you. Do as he says, and you'll be back home by morning."

Her objections stifled by fear, Ava nodded mutely, the realization dawning that she was being sold for the night, a chilling echo of the transactions around her. With a heavy heart and a mind fraught with trepidation, she followed Mr. Roth to his car, stepping into yet another situation where she had no control, no say—driven by the commands of others and the silent threat that kept her bound to their will.

Chapter Eleven

Theo Kingsley tightened his grip on the steering wheel, the white of his knuckles betraying the mixed emotions churning within him. The streets of Augusta, Maine were not nearly as crowded as the streets in New York City, and this picturesque town was not where one would think prostitution would exist...but Theo had learned long ago that evil can live anywhere.

His partner, a seasoned local patrol officer named Detective Barrett, glanced over with an understanding look. "How do you like living back here so far, Theo?"

Taking a deep breath, Theo replied, "I don't know. It's quieter here. Trees instead of skyscrapers, you know? But after...everything that happened," his voice faltered as he referred to the death of his late wife, "being closer to family seemed like the right move."

Detective Barrett nodded, his eyes tracing the quiet streets. "You know that evil doesn't have a zip code. It's not just a big city problem."

Theo turned to meet his partner's gaze, a wry smile touching the corner of his lips in acknowledgement. "Yeah, I'm starting to see that. Augusta may be smaller, but the shadows hold the same danger."

As they patrolled, Theo recounted tales of his experiences in NYC, the relentless pace of crime and justice, and the heartache of personal loss that shadowed his final days there. Detective Barrett listened, his expression solemn, as they shared the bond of understanding that crime knows no boundaries.

Here in Augusta, a new chapter of his life was unfolding. The Covert Police Detectives Unit had gained a determined soul, a man ready to confront the darkness.

***

In the grim world of exploitation that was now Ava's life, she kept a daily journal. It had helped her get through her years of confinement in the basement, and it was helping her cope, but she wasn't doing it just for her mental health—she was documenting evidence. She wrote down everything, especially details about clients, locations, the pimps, and anything she felt would strengthen her case. She wasn't only looking to protect herself but the other women who were victims as well. She kept the diary a secret so that no one would ever find out about it, and in case Razor and his thugs searched her apartment, she kept it hidden under a floorboard in a closet.

She grew closer to Carmen and also Carmen's roommate, Jessica, who were both going to art school.

Ava's apartment in New York City was a dimly lit sanctuary from the chaos of the life she was trapped in. One night, she sat at her small writing desk, staring blankly at the untouched manuscript. The oppressive silence was broken by a sudden, frantic knocking on her door.

Startled, Ava rushed to the door and opened it to find her friend Carmen standing there. Carmen's tear-streaked face was bruised and battered, her expression full of fear and desperation, with one eye swollen almost completely shut.

"Carmen! What happened?" Ava whispered urgently, ushering her friend inside and locking the door behind them.

Carmen collapsed onto the worn-out couch, sobbing uncontrollably. "I... I was out on the street working," she managed between sobs. "I saw a police officer in his car and I thought... I thought he could help me."

Ava's heart ached as she listened, all too familiar with the hopelessness that came from seeking help and finding none. "What happened then?"

Carmen took a deep breath, her voice trembling as she continued. "I went up to his car and told him I needed help. He told me to get in, so I did. He drove me to the police station and I thought I was finally going to be safe. I reported everything—the pimps, what they are doing to us, all of it."

Ava's eyes widened with a mixture of hope and dread. "Then what?"

Carmen's expression darkened, her hands trembling as she recounted the rest. "The officer brought me down a hallway, saying my family was there to take me home. I believed him. I was so relieved. I even thought, 'Wow, they got here really fast.' But then he opened a door to a back room, and...and Johnny Venom was there, waiting for me," she murmured, naming the name of her pimp.

Ava's blood ran cold. "The cop was dirty?"

"Oh yeah," Carmen confirmed, her voice barely above a whisper. "The officer was dirty. He took money from Venom right in front of me. They laughed together. Then Venom grabbed me and dragged me out, threw me into his car, and brought me back...and did all this to me." She gestured to the bruises all over her body. "We can't ever report this, Ava. How will we ever escape?"

Ava felt a wave of nausea and fury. The betrayal, the sheer violation, was too much to bear. She sat beside Carmen, wrapping an arm around her, trying to offer some semblance of comfort.

"I'm so sorry, Carmen," Ava said, tears streaming down her cheeks as she hugged her friend, who was also crying. "I can't believe this happened to you."

Carmen's sobs intensified. "What are we going to do, Ava? How can we survive this?"

Ava's mind raced, desperately searching for a solution, some way out of their nightmare. "I don't know, Carmen. But we have to stay strong. I promise you, we will get out of this. Somehow, some way, eventually we'll find a way to be free."

The two women clung to each other, drawing strength from their shared resolve. In that dark moment, Ava vowed to herself that she would never give up hope, and that she would fight, with every ounce of her being, to find a way out for herself, for Carmen, and for all the others trapped in their web of suffering.

***

Ava's heart pounded in her chest as she made her way to the designated alley downtown, the towering buildings of New York City casting long shadows in the darkening evening light. She slid her hand over a hidden pocket she had sewn into her pants, ensuring the small battery-operated voice recorder was securely in place, undetected. She knew she had to be cautious; this evidence could be her lifeline one day.

Carmen walked beside her, her face a mask of resolve, and a few other young women, including Jessica, trailed behind, their expressions a mixture of fear and resignation. The alley was narrow, littered with trash, and shrouded in the scent of decay. Razor, with his menacing presence, stood waiting for them under a flickering streetlight.

"You called us, and we're here, Razor," Ava said for the sake of the recording, forcing a steadiness into her voice as she met Razor's cold gaze. "What do you need us to do?"

Razor's eyes glinted with the barest hint of satisfaction. "Tonight, your client is Arnold Hoover, a wealthy businessman. It's for a bachelor party." He paused, his tone growing more threatening. "The car will be here in a minute to pick you up."

I even got the name of the client on this recording, Ava thought.

He outlined the location, giving them specific, detailed instructions, which were also good evidence for the recording. Ava listened intently, every fiber of her being focused on capturing his words. As he spoke, he leaned in closer, his voice lowering into a menacing growl. "And remember, don't tell anyone anything, or else..." He let out a string of profanities, then gestured to Carmen. "Look what Venom did to Carmen. You don't want to end up like her, do you?"

Carmen's eyes lowered to the dirty pavement. One eye was still partially swollen shut.

Ava felt a chill run down her spine, but she forced herself to remain outwardly calm. Razor's threats were harsh and explicit, and she was inwardly relieved—it meant the voice recorder was capturing every incriminating word.

Hopefully, she would survive long enough to show it to the police one day.

"Understood," Ava replied, her tone submissive and controlled, masking the turmoil inside. She glanced over at Carmen and the others, who nodded in unison, their shared fear creating an unspoken bond.

Just then, the hum of an approaching car broke the tense silence. A sleek black vehicle pulled up to the mouth of the alley, its tinted windows shielding the occupants from view.

"That's your ride," Razor said, nodding toward the car. "Get going, and remember what I said."

Ava and the other young women moved toward the car, their steps measured and unwilling. As she got into the vehicle, Ava's mind was racing with a mix of dread and a fragile sense of hope. If they could survive the night, she would have yet another piece of evidence to go along with her journal that might help her prove her innocence if they were ever arrested.

Please, God, use this evidence to set us free and imprison these criminals, she prayed. *And please help me get through tonight.*

As the car started moving, Ava whispered a silent prayer, clinging to the belief that one day, the truth would come to light, and they would all be free from Razor's grip.

The voice recorder in her pocket was a small, hidden beacon of hope. For now, they were bound to this nightmare, but Ava's determination was unwavering. She would continue gathering evidence, piece by piece, until there was enough to break the chains and expose the treachery that held them captive.

It was a dangerous risk worth taking. She was willing to do anything to escape this life, even risk her life.

Ava knew she was either going to put the nail in her pimp's coffin or get killed trying.

***

When Jessica didn't show up for a gig a few days later, Ava sensed something amiss immediately and approached Carmen.

"Have you seen Jessica lately?" Ava asked, her concern evident in her furrowed brow. "Is she sick? I didn't see her today."

Carmen's face crumpled, tears spilling over as she struggled to convey the horror of what had happened. "She's gone, Ava," she sobbed. "She didn't show up yesterday when they called after school... She must have told them she was done and that she refused to work for them anymore. She told me she was thinking about doing that, and I thought I discouraged her. I wasn't home at the time. They must have shown up at the apartment within minutes because before she could leave, they broke in and killed her, stealing her money and making a mess so it would look like a robbery gone wrong. Then they...shot her. I came home late last night and found her on the floor..." Carmen broke down into sobs, and Ava tried to comfort her with hugs, but she felt completely useless.

"Oh, no... Jessica," Ava cried, tears spilling from her own eyes at the loss of their friend.

"They called me afterward and told me if I told the police the truth, they'd do the same to me," Carmen choked out. "So, I had to lie to the police and tell them I didn't have a clue why this happened and no idea who did it. We have to do whatever they say, Ava, or that could be us."

Jessica had been murdered for her defiance. Ava was writing a journal and recording them, documenting their crimes for evidence, and she couldn't even tell Carmen about it for her own safety. If they caught Ava, surely they would kill her. Even though it caused a wave of fear to crash through her, it was still a risk she was willing to take.

She would escape somehow or die trying.

She and Carmen clung to each other, their friendship a lifeline in an ocean of despair. They spoke little of it again, the truth too grim to revisit, but the unspoken bond between them grew. They were survivors, each playing the part laid out for them by their controllers, all the while carrying the heavy burden of what they now knew. This was the second young woman that these monsters had killed that she knew about.

Ava continued to write in her journal, documenting all the details Carmen had given her. And every time she had to show up for "work," she took her voice recorder, concealing it in a hidden pocket in her pants or dress that she'd sewn. Every time she wore it on her, she knew she was risking her life.

As the days turned into months, Ava continued her double life with leaden steps. Her spirit, once vibrant and aspiring, waned under the weight of exploitation and constant dread. Yet, through the darkness, she persisted with her education and now graduation was within sight—a single flame of hope flickering in the gloom.

***

The criminals' grip on Ava's life persisted. Ava's history left her vulnerable to this form of manipulation. Her past traumas had shaped a victim mentality that made it all too easy for her to fall in line with the demands placed upon her.

She abandoned writing her novel and only continued writing her school assignments because she had to and her daily journal. She was no longer able to find the joy that had once fueled her passion. While not physically confined as she had been in her father's basement, Ava was a psychological captive.

Each assignment from Razor chipped away at her spirit. Ava moved through her days in a state of emotional detachment, the vibrancy that had once animated her now dulled to a hollow monotone.

However, she continued to gather evidence through her voice recorder, hiding the tapes in her apartment, and continued writing in her journal daily, documenting dates, names of clients, and locations.

School provided a facade of normalcy, but she wore a mask. There was no time for her to write for pleasure, and the spark that had made her dream of being a novelist once shine brightly was snuffed out by her reality. Coursework was her only outlet for writing, and it reflected the darkness that had infused her life.

Her tales were no longer about hope and happy endings; they were raw, painful, steeped in the depths of a profound distress.

Ironically, her professors saw brilliance in this anguish. Her writing, because of its intense and genuine emotion, earned her continued academic recognition and college grants.

She had earned a full academic scholarship to the local university, where she was continuing on her path toward a bachelor's degree. Ava's words and stories bled onto the page, earning her the scholarships, yet she could only receive the praise with a hollow heart.

Day by day, Ava was fulfilling her educational requirements, clinging to the structure of school as the last remnant of her aspirations. Outside of this, she felt as lifeless as the characters in her somber stories. She was no longer the hopeful writer who had longed to uplift others with her words.

Finally, graduation day arrived at school. Ava, her face a mask of calm, accepted her diploma, wondering if she would ever be able to escape this life and pursue the career she truly wanted.

Chapter Twelve

Adorned in an elegant dress that didn't match the heaviness in her heart, Ava carried herself with practiced grace through the lavish birthday party of a New York City millionaire. Carmen was there too, along with other models, all playing the roles that had been forced upon them. Each smile, each laugh was a performance; every gesture a mask hiding their sorrows within.

The birthday celebration for the wealthy millionaire was nothing short of an extravagant spectacle. Hosted in his stately mansion, the party was meticulously designed to impress and flaunt the magnitude of his financial prowess.

As guests arrived, they were greeted by the soft, harmonious tunes of a live string quartet, playing classical pieces with elegant precision. The mansion's grand ballroom was the spotlight of the evening where crystal chandeliers hung from high ceilings, casting a warm glow over the party.

The walls were adorned with artwork worthy of the finest galleries, and artfully arranged flowers were in each corner of the ballroom. There were long tables on one side of the room with flower centerpieces, covered in elegant tablecloths and an elaborate spread of catered food. Catering staff weaved through clusters of guests with silver platters, offering a selection of gourmet canapés, caviar, and other exquisite hors d'oeuvres. The sparkling champagne was served from bottles that cost more than a used car. Sky dancers dangled from the ceiling on strips of silky fabric.

In the center of it all was the man of the hour, the millionaire himself, surrounded by a group of admirers and associates. He laughed loudly, entertaining his guests with stories of his travels around the world.

Yet, amidst the pageantry and opulence, the atmosphere was tinged with an undercurrent of transaction and superficiality. Business deals were brokered with a handshake, political favors were negotiated with a wink. The "models," including Ava and Carmen, were nothing more than party decorations, their own stories of struggle and coercion hidden behind a facade of beauty and frivolity.

Ava's "date" for the evening, a well-dressed older man with a taste for younger companions, clung to her arm—his trophy for the night.

"Let's go upstairs where it will be more...quiet," the man said, tugging on her arm. She had no choice but to go with him.

As they entered the bedroom, chaos downstairs disrupted the evening's glamour. The muffled sounds quickly grew into loud shouts, then gunfire tore through the air.

The man tensed, his eyes darting toward the door, and Ava froze, her pulse racing. Fear and confusion set in as the clamor intensified. Loud footsteps thundered up the stairs, shaking the walls with urgency.

Officers in tactical gear burst through the door, shouting commands, sweeping the room with their weapons. The party, now revealed in its darkest truths, was a cocktail of illegal activities including drugs, and many of the escorts in attendance were underage, there against their will.

The police moved swiftly, making arrests. Ava and Carmen, swept up in the sudden tide of justice, found themselves being arrested in a blur of zip ties—which the police used when the handcuffs ran out—and Miranda rights.

"Ava, what's going to happen to us?" Carmen cried, tears streaming down her face as they were led outside, toward the police cars. "I don't want to go to prison."

"You didn't do anything wrong," Ava reminded her. "This isn't our fault. We were forced into this. Just tell them the truth."

"But what about Jessica? Won't that happen to us?" Carmen cried.

"They're all being arrested," Ava said, but she was still unsure. "I'm going to take that risk. Don't worry, Carmen."

Carmen and Ava were put into separate police cars and driven to the police station.

Was this the end of her captive life? Could this truly be her way out?

"Please, God, set us free," Ava whispered as they drove away.

***

Under the fluorescent lights of the police station, Ava found herself seated at a small table in a small windowless room, handcuffed, with fear and uncertainty enveloping her. The cold metal of the handcuffs was a cruel reminder of the freedom that had again been stripped from her, both by her captors and now, ironically, by the law. But for the first time, she hoped it would only be temporary until they learned the truth from her—that she was once again a victim.

Detective Reynolds entered the room, a notepad in hand, his expression unreadable. "I'm Detective Reynolds. I'm going to ask you some questions about tonight's events," he stated, sitting across from her.

Ava recoiled at him being so close at first—she was uncomfortable being around any man after what had happened to her. Hopefully, this man would help her. She nodded, feeling both hopeful and terrified at the prospect of finally speaking out.

If this went badly, she could lose her life.

"How did you find out about the party?" he began, his pen poised over the paper.

Ava's response was a mix of fear and resolve. "My pimp told me to be there. If we don't show up on time when they say, then they will beat us or even kill us. We have no choice but to do as they say. They arranged everything," she told him, her eyes meeting the officer's, pleading silently for understanding. "I have a journal documenting everything and a voice recorder documenting dozens of meetups, client names, locations, and dates. I have a lot of information. I can tell you everything I know. I want to see Razor and the other pimps put behind bars for a long time so they can't do this to anyone else. I didn't take the voice recorder with me tonight because they told us to arrive already dressed, but it's in my apartment along with the journal," she revealed, her voice shaking but insistent. "I would often hide the recorder in a secret pocket I sewed into my pants so they wouldn't notice it."

Detective Reynolds listened as Ava recounted her experience. This could be her only chance for escape, for justice. There was a chance he was a dirty cop, but that was a chance she was willing to take.

The detective didn't waste any time; after obtaining consent to search her apartment for the evidence she described and handing over her apartment key, he dispatched a team to recover the recorder and journal from Ava's apartment under the floorboards.

As they returned with the evidence, Detective Reynolds listened to Ava as she listed the names of Carmen and the other young women who had been exploited, detailing how each one was ensnared by the same people, with the same promises, the same threats. The journal and voice recorder provided invaluable information and evidence that incriminated the pimps and the clients alike.

As the pieces fell into place, the officers began to see Ava not as a suspect, but as a key witness, a survivor of a terrible ordeal whose testimony could help shut down the ring.

Encouraged by their genuine response, Ava agreed to testify in court against those who had stolen her freedom.

The prospect filled Ava with a conflicted sense of both fear and empowerment. For the first time, Ava felt the flicker of a long-extinguished hope that she might finally reclaim her life and help prevent others from enduring the horrors she had faced.

The reality of what she was about to do loomed over her. This was a decisive break from the shadows that had enveloped her existence for so long. Detective Reynolds entered the room once again.

"Ava," he began, sitting across from once more, "we've been listening to your recordings, and we're going through your journal. The details you've provided are invaluable. You've been very brave. One of the pimps, not Razor, decided to tell us what he knew, corroborating the names and operations you've given us, hoping to cut a deal and get a lesser sentence. He has even agreed to show us where one of the bodies was buried so we can pursue murder charges against the other pimps. We've also spoken to the other young women, and many of them have given us much of the same information you have, so it lines up. When they heard that you agreed to testify, many of them also agreed to testify in court as well, if necessary. We've confirmed that you and all the other young women you've named were victims and will not be going to prison."

"What happens now?" she asked, her voice steadier than it had been before. If he had been a dirty cop, she probably would have known by now, right? Hope grew within her.

"We've got a detective from a special victims' unit coming in. They'll speak with you, get more details, and walk you through what to expect in the coming months as everyone prepares for the trials."

"And what if the pimps try to kill me or the others for speaking out?" Ava asked.

"We have them in custody at this time and will be opposing any requests for bail. We're going to do everything we can to protect you and the others," Detective Reynolds assured her. "We will contact you to let you know if we hear they are being released for any reason. If you believe you are in any danger at any time, just call 911."

A sense of relief momentarily washed over Ava. For so long, she had been voiceless. Now, not only was she being heard, but her words were the lifeline to potential justice for herself and the other victims.

Detective Reynolds slid a small cup of coffee across the table to her, a quiet offering of comfort. "I'm sure it won't be easy for you, but your testimony authenticating your recordings and journal is going to make a huge difference. You're helping us take down a serious criminal enterprise."

Ava wrapped her hands around the warm cup, the steam carrying a hint of normalcy. It was a stark contrast to the cold grip of fear that had held her for so long.

The door opened once more, and a detective with a compassionate smile stepped inside the room. She introduced herself and sat down next to Ava. "We're going to discuss everything at your pace," she said softly, "We're here for you, Ava. You're no longer alone in this."

As Ava told her story to the special victims' unit detective, with each word, her spirit—which had been worn down by years of coercion and deceit—began to reclaim a small measure of power. The walls of the interview room faded into the background as she envisioned a future where her captors faced justice, and she could start the long journey of healing and rediscovering the life that had been stolen from her.

Ava paused and clasped her hands together, feeling the warmth from the coffee mug lessening as she prepared to dive back into the chilling narrative of her past. The detective across from her had opened a fresh notebook, clicked her pen, and offered Ava further nods of encouragement.

"Whenever you're ready, we can continue," the detective said. Her tone was professional, yet there was a clear thread of empathy woven through her words.

Ava took a deep breath, the oxygen filling her lungs felt like the first true breath she had taken in years. With each detail she provided, using her journal to jog her memory of each incident, she pulled at the threads that had bound her in servitude. The detective listened intently, her pen gliding over the page, while also capturing Ava's voice on a digital video recorder, the highlights repeated in ink, giving substance to the shadows. Occasionally the detective would ask for clarification or further details.

Outside the interview room, the station buzzed with increased activity. Other officers worked diligently, piecing together additional evidence, corroborating accounts from the informants and lining up the facts with Ava's story.

After what felt like hours, the detective finally closed her notebook, and with a reassuring smile, she said, "Thank you, Ava. I know that couldn't have been easy, but you've been incredibly courageous."

With the conclusion of the interview, the detective explained the next steps to Ava. The women would be assisted in moving to an apartment that they would share until the trial was over, where they could be themselves and help each other heal, if they consented, and to help ensure their safety by removing them from their previously known residence. First, with the officers present, they would go to their current residences to pack their bags and give notice to their landlords they were terminating their monthly rental agreements. Then they would stay with friends or family unknown to the pimps or get a motel room until a new apartment could be secured and rented. They were to make an application to a victims of crime program to help secure the funds to move or reimburse them.

Ava would continue to work with a victim's advocate to prepare for the trials, and the other women who had agreed to testify were doing the same.

Ava felt a weight lifting from her shoulders, replaced by a sense of purpose. The officers escorted her to an unmarked car waiting outside, where she was enveloped once more by the city—only now, she viewed every street and building through the lens of newfound freedom, similar to her view when she first arrived in New York City.

The crisp air outside the police station felt cool and calming on Ava's skin, and she was thankful to get fresh air after being cooped up in the interview room inside the police station all day.

Some of the women who had also been victimized, each carrying their own painful pasts painted on their faces, emerged from the doors of the precinct behind Ava. Carmen, with a resolve in her eyes that Ava had not seen before, approached Ava first.

"Ava," she called out. "When I heard about how brave you were, telling the police everything and agreeing to stand against Razor in court, I decided to do the same thing." She offered Ava a small but meaningful smile. "I'm going to testify in court, too."

"Yeah," another woman chimed in, "You showed us that we don't have to be afraid to speak out. That we've got power when we stand together. Even though there are more of them than us."

"I knew it was risky, but I've spent almost my entire life in captivity. I decided I'd rather die than see them get away with what they did to us," Ava told them with a strength she didn't know she had.

A chorus of agreement rippled through the group. Carmen placed her hand on Ava's shoulder, a silent gesture of solidarity. "You've started a chain reaction, Ava. You inspired all of us to speak out against them." One by one, the other women nodded, each confirming their commitment to the truth.

Ava's eyes filled with tears as she threw her arms around Carmen, starting one big group hug as they all cried tears of relief together.

Their shared understanding forged a bond stronger than the fear that had once shackled them. Together, they would face the trial not as individual victims but as a united force. The road ahead would be challenging, but they were reminded that they were no longer alone in their struggle for justice.

As the cars transporting the women pulled away from the curb, the once oppressive skyline of Manhattan was a backdrop as she whispered a vow to fight, to stand against the ones who had silenced her, and to emerge not only as a survivor, but as an inspiration for those still in captivity.

Chapter Thirteen

Ava spent months trying to rebuild a normal life for herself. But one criminal court date after another kept popping up, which required her attendance. She testified at several of the pimps' and Johns' probable cause hearings. Each of them were held over to face a criminal trial. She had supplied enough evidence to find them each guilty beyond a reasonable doubt. The court set separate jury trial dates for each defendant, again requiring her to make several more court appearances as a witness against them in the future. Several of the defendants decided to take plea bargain agreements instead of going to trial. But not Razor or Colin Monroe, though that was not his real name. Their trial dates were each rescheduled twice upon the defendants' requests for a continuance, much to Ava's frustration.

Colin Monroe's trial date finally arrived. Ava was subpoenaed to appear the second week of the trial and her testimony went on for five tiring days, but she was glad she held up under cross examination. She could see the dread and helplessness in his eyes for a change. It was empowering. And three weeks later, when the prosecutor contacted her with the guilty on all counts verdict, she felt a level of satisfaction. Only one more criminal to put away.

When the day for Razor's jury trial finally arrived, she approached the witness stand with determination. Her heart pounded like an erratic drumbeat echoing through the silent courtroom. Raymond

"Razor" DeLuca watched her from the defense table with a menacing glare that could paralyze the bravest of souls. Ava's fingers trembled slightly, betraying the composed exterior she attempted to maintain. A deep breath helped to steady her nerves as she swore to tell the truth.

The prosecutor, a stern woman with sharp features, addressed Ava, "Please state your name for the record."

Ava answered, "Ava Sullivan."

The prosecutor continued, "Do you know the man sitting at the defense table, the defendant in this case?"

"Yes, I know him."

The prosecutor proceeded, "First, please tell me how you know Raymond 'Razor' DeLuca."

Swallowing the knot of fear in her throat, Ava began recounting her ordeal in response to the prosecutor's prompts. "I... I was naïve," she started, her voice barely above a whisper, but it grew in strength as she continued. "Razor and his associate Colin Monroe, whose real name I now know is Gregory Smith, promised me a meeting with a well-known publisher. I first met him in a coffee shop where we spoke, and I told him I was writing a novel. On the day of the meeting, he said the owner of the publishing company had to cancel last minute, but we could meet her briefly in the parking garage as she walked to her car. When we got there, the defendant, Raymond De Luca, and two other men were waiting for me." She named the other pimps she had met that day. "They threatened me, saying I had to show up on time when they called or they would kill me. They showed me the body of a dead prostitute in the back of their van."

The prosecutor nodded, "And when and where did they first demand you appear?"

Ava answered, giving the details.

"What did they have you do after you showed up?" the prosecutor inquired.

"They forced me into prostitution," she declared.

"How did they obtain your cooperation?"

Through a series of questions and answers, she detailed the threats made against her, the abuse of their power, and the shadow of fear they cast over her life. "I saw the women they had killed, so I had no choice," she told them, her determined gaze locked with Razor's threatening one. In that moment, their roles reversed—he was the one in shackles, trapped by her words, and she felt the shackles of her own past begin to loosen.

"I recorded everything I could in my journal and on a voice recorder."

The prosecutor asked, holding up Ava's journal, "Do you recognize this journal?"

"Yes, that's mine," Ava said.

The prosecutor asked a few questions about when the entries were made, and she asked whether all the entries were truthful to the best of Ava's knowledge and belief. With an answer in the affirmative from Ava, she introduced the journal into evidence. She proceeded to have Ava read various entries and asked questions about them.

The prosecutor also authenticated the recordings, one by one, then entered them into evidence. She asked Ava to listen to a portion of one of the recordings. "Is this one of the recordings you made?"

"Yes," Ava replied.

"Do you recognize the man's voice on this recording?"

"Yes," Ava confirmed, "It is Raymond 'Razor' De Luca."

For one moment, she saw fear flicker in his eyes when he realized how much evidence she had compiled against him, and it was more satisfying than she ever could have imagined.

As Ava concluded three days of her testimony, including all the cross examination and redirect, an eerie silence settled briefly over the courtroom. She could feel the wave of shock and compassion for her from the jury and attendants. She gently pushed herself up from the witness stand, ready to step down, when a sudden commotion shattered the calm.

Razor, his face contorted with unchecked fury, surged from his seat. "You think you can just rat me out and walk away?!" he roared, each word poisoned with venom. The bailiff sprang into action, holding him back as he swung his arms and tried to pry his hands off him. "I'll find you, Angel! You'll pay for this! You will regret this and wish I had killed you the day we met!"

The judge's gavel hammered against the wood, demanding order, but Razor's outburst continued to echo through the courtroom. "You're dead, Angel! I'll find you and make you pay!" His lawyer was trying unsuccessfully to get his client to be quiet, and the bailiff was already restraining him.

His words chilled her, but she wouldn't let him know it. She kept her head held high, ignoring him as she walked out of the courtroom, her steps neither faltering nor quickening as she moved away from the stand and Razor's fury.

The threat was a reminder of the world she was up against—but it was met with the unspoken support from the onlookers in the gallery, the prosecutors, and most importantly, the other women who had found their voices because of her when she had decided to testify.

***

Ava's hand hovered over the doorknob of her new apartment, the adrenaline from her courtroom triumph still coursing through her veins. She turned the key, stepped inside, and let out a deep, weary sigh. The sanctuary of her newest home enveloped her, but the solace was short-lived. There, on the floor, lay a white postcard that someone had slid under the door.

Tentatively, she reached down and picked it up, only touching the corners to avoid getting her fingerprints all over it. In bold, black letters, one word screamed at her from the cardstock: "RECANT." Her hand shook slightly as she turned the postcard over, her eyes searching for a clue, a signature, anything. There was no indication of who sent it.

It had to have been one of Razor's minions. How had they found her?

She carefully placed it in a paper bag to keep it clean and prevent fingerprints from getting on it.

The message was clear. Ava's heart sank. This single word was a disguised threat, a glimpse into the darkness she thought she had just stepped out of. Razor's words from the trial reverberated in her memory, echoing the sinister promise in the postcard.

I'll find you, Angel. She could still hear his gravelly voice in the court room.

Ava clutched the postcard in her trembling hand and once again made her way to the police station. Upon arrival, she approached the front desk, her voice steady but her fear evident.

"I need to report a threat," she declared, handing over the chilling piece of paper. "Someone slid this under my apartment door."

The officer on duty took the bag with the postcard in it, his brows arching as he peered into the bag and read it. He called over a detective who was working on the cases relating to Ava. The detective escorted her into a back room and offered Ava a seat.

"Ms. Sullivan, we take this very seriously, especially in light of what happened recently in court, but we need more to go on. You're sure there's nothing else? No suspicious individuals following you? No strange phone calls?"

Ava shook her head. "No."

"We'll keep an eye out, and we'll look into this, but without a direct threat or any evidence pointing to who sent it, it's hard to take action," the detective explained gently, although the helplessness in his tone was hard to miss. "We can't do anything unless we get prints off this that we can match up or have some real evidence against the person responsible. We do know that Raymond "Razor" DeLuca could not have done this himself from prison, so maybe he hired someone, but we don't know who. We will try to find security camera footage of who delivered this, but that may be a long shot. Even if the person was on camera, they probably hid their face."

Maybe while she was getting her mail out of her numbered box, he saw her apartment number.

Ava nodded, her lips pressed into a thin line. As she left the police station, the postcard's weight seemed to grow heavier in her mind. Razor might be behind bars, but his words—a vow of retribution—had managed to slip through the cracks of the justice system and find their way to her, a sobering reminder that even the walls of a prison could not contain the dangerous influence of Razor DeLuca.

***

The city was asleep, but Ava lay wide awake in her apartment, no longer feeling safe and the events of the day replaying in her mind.

Testifying in court against Razor had taken all her courage, and now the silence of the night amplified her fears. She tried to focus on the chaotic hum of the city outside her window, seeking any distraction, hoping that even the sirens would comfort her.

Her personal phone suddenly buzzed, cutting through the stillness, causing her to jump. The screen showed an unknown number. Heart racing, she hesitated for a moment before answering.

"Hello?" she said, her voice tinged with trepidation.

There was no reply, only the sound of someone breathing on the other end of the line. The heavy, deliberate breaths sent a chill down her spine.

"Who is this?" Ava demanded, trying to muster a tone of authority but failing to mask her fear.

The breathing continued, slow and menacing, but the caller remained silent. Panic surged through her, and she quickly ended the call, her hand trembling as she set the phone down. She felt exposed and vulnerable, her earlier bravery in court now a distant memory.

Desperately trying to calm herself, Ava glanced around her dimly lit apartment, the shadows suddenly seeming more sinister.

She called the police right away, but because they couldn't trace the call, they couldn't pinpoint the caller. Since no actual threat was made, their hands were tied.

***

Ava exhaled deeply as she stepped out of the bustling city office that had become her refuge for continued therapy and recovery group sessions. The chaos of New York City's streets once seemed exciting and full of possibility to Ava when she first moved here. Lately, though, it felt as if each echo off the buildings whispered reminders of the postcard's threat.

Ava closed her eyes, allowing memories of Unity, Maine, to surface—a patchwork of peaceful green and amber fields and endless azure skies—the opposite of the concrete and incessant noise of New York City. She could almost hear the gentle rustle of cornstalks in the breeze and the carefree laughter that once echoed through the open spaces of her childhood.

Memories flickered like old film reels: the simple joys of youth, bare feet against the cool earth, and the playful chases through the endless green maze of Amish country with friends that knew her before her father had stolen her childhood and the world outside had left its mark on her. Anna, Maria, and Liz had been her closest friends. What were they doing now? She missed them so much that her heart ached.

She remembered the warmth of the community and the solid, comforting cycle of seasons and traditions.

Now, amidst a life disrupted by chaos and cruelty, those stored images promised a refuge—a return to innocence and familiarity. She envisioned her family's homestead, the soft creak of the porch swing, and the protective embrace of the tall pine and maple trees guarding the property. She longed to reclaim that sense of belonging and peace, even for a short while.

She would just have to avoid the basement at all costs. Hopefully, if she did, she wouldn't have to face her past head on, and she could focus on the few good memories she had of her childhood.

Unity, which she had fled in pursuit of broader horizons, now offered solace from the storm that had become her life. Solace sounded like exactly what she needed. Once she got there, she could find a local therapist so she could continue her healing journey.

With that, Ava made her decision. She would go back home. The house, though likely in need of a thorough cleaning and some repairs, could be a place where she could heal and gather strength for whatever lay ahead. This time, it wasn't about running away; it was about coming full circle, about finding her way back to roots that could perhaps anchor her once more.

She called to get in touch with her mother's lawyer, who told her that she had rented their home out to a couple for the past few years. They had moved in after Ava left and had moved away, then a new tenant moved in.

"The new tenant stopped paying the rent, so I had to evict them. I'm sorry to say they didn't do a good job of maintaining the property," the lawyer told Ava. "It's in desperate need of cleaning and repairs. I haven't found a new tenant yet."

Ava told the lawyer of her plans to move in temporarily to fix up the place, and she asked her to hold off on finding a new tenant and to give her the information on how to arrange a visit with her mother…even though Ava wasn't sure if she was ready to see Diana yet.

"My mother hasn't heard from me since she was arrested," Ava said. "I should go see her, but I'm not sure when I will yet."

"I'm meeting with her this week. Do you want me to give her a message?"

"Yes, please. Tell her I'm sorry I haven't been to see her yet because I was going to college in New York City, but now I'm coming home to Unity, and I am safe and well. Tell her I'll clean and fix up the house so we can rent it out, but if she wants, I can sell it for her."

"Absolutely," the lawyer said. "I'm writing all of this down. She will be glad to hear you're coming home and are doing well now. She was worried about you."

"Please tell her I wanted to get in touch, but I couldn't. It's a long story, but I'll come visit her when I'm ready and explain everything," Ava said.

"She would love to see you, and she has mentioned selling the house a few times over the past few years. I'll speak with her about it."

After getting off the phone with her mother's lawyer, it started ringing again. It was the prosecutor letting her know that Raymond "Razor" DeLuca was found guilty and sentenced to life without the possibility of parole.

It was finally over. The prosecutor thanked her again for her part in obtaining all the convictions. Ava was relieved to hear it, but knew that even though Razor would be behind bars for the rest of his life, she would never be safe from him. But this call solidified her resolve to move back to Unity, knowing she was truly done here in New York City.

"Thank You, Lord," Ava prayed as she hung up, filled with joy. "Finally, we are free!" She fell to her knees in gratitude, spending several minutes praying.

A weight lifted from her shoulders as Ava surveyed her small apartment, walls that had witnessed her recent life's turmoil. She moved mechanically, packing her few cherished belongings—a stack of well-worn novels, personal journals filled with her innermost thoughts, and her minimal wardrobe.

She sorted through clothing, kitchenware, and miscellaneous trinkets accrued over her time away from Unity. With each item set aside for donation, Ava felt lighter, as though discarding the physical weight of her possessions could somehow unburden her heart as well. She would soon donate the boxes to a local charity, hoping to help others build their lives, just as she aimed to rebuild her own. Most of the items only reminded her of the past few years of her life, and she hoped that if she got rid of those items, it might help her forget.

Or maybe that was wishful thinking. Either way, it would help others, and she wouldn't need those things in her home in Unity. While she was not planning on rejoining the Amish, she hoped to live a simpler life.

There was a knock at the door, and Ava checked who it was before opening it. Carmen stood in the doorway with an empathetic smile.

"So, this is it? You're leaving today?" Carmen asked, stepping into the room, which was already sparser than she remembered.

Ava nodded, her smile tinged with sadness. "Yes, it's time. I think the sooner I can get out of the city, the sooner I can finally start to heal. I'm going back to Unity, to my family home. I'm hoping to fix up that house and finally finish writing my novel. Maybe I can find some new inspiration there."

"That sounds wonderful. I'm sure the change of scenery and getting out of here will give you inspiration," Carmen said.

Ava asked, "And you? What's next for you?"

"I'm going home, too. Upstate New York. I'll be living with my family," Carmen answered, her eyes bright at the prospect. "I guess we're both finding our way home. I'm going to miss you so much, but I'm happy for you."

"I'm happy for you, too, Carmen. And I'm going to miss you too. Please, call me anytime." Ava's voice was sincere, her bond with Carmen strengthened by the hardships they had shared. Yet, the farewell was bittersweet.

"Of course, we'll keep in touch," Carmen assured her, embracing Ava tightly.

Ava returned the hug with equal fervor. "Of course. You've been my rock through all this," she whispered. As they pulled away, a mutual understanding passed between them: no distance would diminish the friendship they'd built within the city's confines.

Carmen said goodbye, and with the last box sealed and the apartment standing empty, Ava gave the space a final once-over. It was time to leave the chaos of the city and the darkness of her past behind.

Ava set the donations outside her door for the charity to retrieve later that day and closed and locked the door behind her. She slipped the key into the manager's drop box, leaving behind New York City and stepping forward into the familiar yet untraveled path that awaited her in Unity. Maybe there she would be able to sleep soundly at night again.

She boarded a bus, and as the skyscrapers shrank behind her, Ava's resolve to seek shelter in her past began to solidify. Unity, Maine—a place she had not thought of as home in many years—beckoned to her with the promise of anonymity and safety. Razor knew nothing of her Amish roots, a secret life that now might serve as her best camouflage.

During the long drive, Ava's mind wandered to her family, a complex tapestry of love and pain and unyielding tradition. She considered visiting her mother and Samuel for the first time since they were arrested to reconcile with the past or perhaps to seek closure and to follow up about the house. She knew she should visit Ian, too, but she knew she wasn't ready to go to the prison just yet. One step at a time.

She had no idea how bad of a condition the house was in. Maybe she would update and remodel it to make it more appealing to renters or buyers, especially if her mother agreed to sign the property over to her.

Fixing up the house would be a daunting task—a metaphor for fixing herself in many ways—but it was a challenge Ava felt compelled to take on. It would be more than just laying down new floorboards or patching up walls; it was an opportunity to rebuild her life, so distant from the city's chaos that had almost consumed her.

During the bus ride, her mother's lawyer called her.

"Hello, Miss Sullivan," the lawyer said. "I decided to go visit your mother today instead of later this week. She was overjoyed and relieved to hear you're safe, and she asked for you to come visit her soon."

Ava hesitated. "I will consider it."

"She wants to sell the house, and she wants to divide up the proceeds between you, herself, and your brother Samuel for when they are released," the lawyer explained. "She wanted to also give your brother Ian a percentage, but he is serving a life sentence, so she decided against it. She thanks you for fixing up the house and said to stay there as long as you need before selling it."

They set up a time to meet, then Ava thanked the lawyer and ended the call, surprised. Her percentage of the profits from the house sale would certainly help her rebuild her new life.

As she crossed the state line into Maine, she already felt her anxiety fade a little. Maybe, in the very place where her voice was once so tightly restricted, Ava could find the strength and freedom to weave the threads of her stolen life back together.

For now, Unity would be her haven.

Chapter Fourteen

The warm glow of the evening sun bathed his childhood home as Theo pulled into the driveway. It had been a few weeks since his last visit—his job in Augusta kept him working long hours. His parents, both retired now, loved family dinners for the chance they provided to catch everyone up with their two adult children.

He walked to the door, which opened to reveal the smiling face of his mother, Carol. "Welcome home, Theo!" she said, giving him a quick hug before he could even take off his shoes, which was her way of showing affection.

Inside, his father was setting the dinner table, and the delicious smell of food was already making Theo's stomach growl. The aroma of roasted chicken and his mother's freshly baked apple pie wafted through the air, stirring memories of simpler times.

"How was work today?" his father, Mark, asked as he came over to also give him a hug. "Do you like your job here?"

"It's not exactly like New York City, but yes, I'm liking it here so far," Theo said. "I work long hours now that I'm a detective. I'm sorry I haven't been over in a while."

He noticed that his parents exchanged knowing looks.

"Is that why you aren't dating anyone? When are we going to meet someone special in your life?" Carol asked, a twinkle of curiosity in her eye.

Theo chuckled. "Oh, Mom, I really don't have time for dating."

His father, Mark, leaned forward, "You know your mother wants grandbabies. So, don't keep her waiting."

Theo's laughter filled the room as he playfully rolled his eyes. "You're not going to get any grandbabies from me any time soon, I'm sorry to say."

Carol giggled and playfully hit him on the arm. "Oh, come on. You never know what the future holds."

Their banter was interrupted by Natalie, Theo's sister, as she walked into the room with a cup of coffee in hand. She tossed her long dark hair over her shoulder, but her usual bright smile was dulled today. Her brown eyes didn't light up like they usually did when she saw her family.

"Natalie! How was your day, sweetheart?" Carol asked, turning her attention to her daughter.

"It was good. Just needed a lot of caffeine to get through," Natalie replied, shrugging. "I was up late doing a ton of homework."

She was usually the sparkplug of these gatherings, her laughter infectious and her stories endlessly entertaining. But tonight, she carried with her a quietness that seemed out of place. She hugged their parents and then Theo, a smile on her face but not quite reaching her eyes.

Dinner was served, and the conversation flowed around updates from their parents' latest cruise to Alaska. Theo noticed the way Natalie picked at her food, contributing to the conversation when prompted but quickly retreating back into silence. He looked at her across the table and could see that her eyes lacked their usual sparkle and brightness.

"Hey, Nat, how's school going?" Theo asked, trying to start up a conversation with her. He knew that she was studying to be a dental hygienist, which was a serious career that required dedication and hard work, but he couldn't help but feel like there was more to it than what she was letting on.

Natalie shrugged nonchalantly, "It's okay, I guess. Just really busy."

Theo could tell that she wasn't herself. He had always known Natalie to be the bubbly and lively one, so her current demeanor was quite a change from what he was used to. He decided to press a little bit further to see if there was anything else bothering her.

"You don't seem like yourself lately, Nat. Is everything all right?" he asked with concern.

She sighed and looked down at her plate before meeting his gaze again, "It's just a lot of pressure, that's all. I want to do well in school and also keep working on my music, but I don't have enough time for both."

Natalie forced a smile, a look that Theo had become too familiar with over the years. It was the smile that said, I'm not okay, but I don't want to talk about it.

"Just stressed with homework and stuff. It's nothing really," she said.

Theo's heart melted as he heard her. He had known that music was a part of her life since they were young, and she had often sung to him when they were kids. He could remember the many times she would come to his room and sing him songs, her voice sweet and pure. She had won multiple local talent shows, and everyone always said how she would be famous one day.

"I'm proud of you for following your dreams, Nat," he said, trying to reassure her. "It'll be worth it in the end."

Natalie smiled a little, appreciative of his understanding. But he could see that there was still something bothering her.

Natalie's phone buzzed in her pocket, pulling her attention away from the lively dinner conversation. She quickly glanced at it and stood up abruptly, her expression changing to one of concern. "I'm sorry, but I have to go."

"Is that a new phone?" Theo asked. "I thought you still had the one you've always had, the one with music notes on the case."

"Uh, yeah, it's a new one," Natalie said.

Theo's parents, Mark and Carol, exchange worried glances. "Natalie, honey, you can't go now. Dinner isn't even over." Mark probed. "Is something wrong?"

"It's just a project I forgot I had that's due tomorrow. My classmate just reminded me."

Theo followed her to the door, his mind racing with possibilities. He could see that she was hiding something, but he couldn't put his finger on it. "Natalie, wait," he called out, his voice laced with suspicion. The police officer in him wanted to question her. "Are you sure you're okay? You seem off. Is there something going on you want to tell me?"

Natalie smiled reassuringly, but it didn't reach her eyes. "No, Theo, nothing's going on. Like I said, it's just a project. You know how important school is to me." She opened the door and turned around, ready to leave. "I'm not a victim in one of your cases, Theo. You don't have to worry about me."

"What? I'm your older brother. It's my job to worry."

Natalie gave him a quick hug and walked out the door. "Bye, Theo," she said, her voice tinged with sadness.

Theo returned to the dinner table and conversation gradually moved on, but his thoughts lingered on his sister.

The evening wound down with discussions of their next get-together and promises to not let too much time pass before the next one.

As he drove back to his apartment, Theo couldn't shake the feeling that his sister was hiding something from him, and he intended to find out what it was.

Chapter Fifteen

Ava paid the driver she'd hired to pick her up at the bus station and stepped out of the car, carrying her two bags that held everything she owned. As the car drove away, her eyes were immediately drawn to the house that had once been her childhood home and also her prison.

The lawyer was right—the tenants hadn't taken care of the property. The once vibrant yellow paint had also faded to a dull sheen, chipped and worn. The porch railing now hung broken and dangerous. The yard, where she spent countless hours playing with her siblings and friends as a young child before she was locked away was now a tangle of weeds and forgotten memories.

She walked towards the house, her footsteps heavy on the overgrown grass. The screen door creaked, a haunting sound that echoed in the silence. As she approached the house, she noticed the broken siding, the gaps in the windows, and the cracked and worn paint.

She took a deep breath, steeling herself against the wave of emotions that threatened to overtake her. She knew she had to face this place, to make it hers once again. The thought of her father still made her heart race in fear, but he was gone and she was determined to put her past behind her.

Ava came face to face with the basement door, feeling her stomach clench. She would avoid that door and the basement at all costs, knowing she was no where near ready to go down those steps again. Maybe one day, but not today.

Turning away, she took in the living room, once a warm space filled with laughter and stories read to them by their mother, now stood empty and silent, save for the dust motes dancing in the sunbeams that streamed through the grimy windows. The worn furniture still remained. Beer and soda cans were strewn across the floor, along with crumbs and dust bunnies. She would have to clean the house as soon as possible.

Her heart ached as she remembered the happy times, the family gatherings around the fireplace, the laughter that had filled this room. But there was still a heavy weight of losing those happier days after she was shut in the basement for more than half her life in this home, a sadness over losing what should have been and for what her life had become here.

In the kitchen, at least the wooden dining table and chairs her father had made still remained, though it looked more scuffed up than she remembered.

Her father hadn't been angry and violent all the time. In fact, she had many happy memories of him telling stories to her and her brothers and taking them fishing. The scariest part of him was that his moods had been so unpredictable. He could have been laughing and joking one minute and screaming with rage the next, triggered by the smallest thing.

The worn wooden floorboards creaked beneath her feet, each groan a reminder of the many times she had run outside or to her room to escape the anger that had consumed the house. She took a deep breath, trying to banish the memories of her father's furious voice and the fear that had clung to her like a second skin. But it was impossible. The scent of old wood and dust brought it all back.

Ava's eyes scanned the house, taking in filth everywhere. It was clear that no one had cared for the place since she left. Perhaps the tenants hadn't cleaned at all. Cobwebs hung like ghostly decorations from the corners of the ceiling, and the air was stale and thick with disuse. She remembered helping her mother clean this house when she was younger, the smell of soap and fresh linens lingering in the air. But now, all she could smell was the musty scent of neglect.

Ava's heart ached as she looked at the old wooden armchair in the corner, where she used to sit with her brothers, listening to their father's hunting stories. The memories of laughter and joy were there, but so were the shadows of the fear and sadness that had followed. She remembered her mother's voice, calm and soothing, as she tried to comfort her children during their father's many rampages.

Ava's eyes wandered to the kitchen, where she had spent many hours helping her mother, baking pies, cooking meals, and washing dishes before she'd been locked downstairs. But even the sight of the old woodstove and the wooden table, scarred by years of use, couldn't dispel the feeling of unease that had settled in her stomach.

She knew she had to start cleaning, had to make this place her own again, but the thought of going downstairs was too overwhelming.

No, she decided. She would not go downstairs at all. It was still too painful. She may never go down there ever again.

She walked up the creaky stairs to the second floor, where the bedrooms were located. Her old childhood bedroom, once painted a cheerful yellow, now had dirty walls and a stained carpet. The bed was bare. Once it was covered in clean sheets and the quilt her mother had made her as a child, it would seem more like home. Through the access in the hallway, she went up to the attic where she was relieved to find her quilt in a box along with boxes of their clothing and other belongings, just where she had left them before going to New York.

She had also packed up her childhood toys. Some had been brought down to the basement, but some had stayed in her bedroom while she had been locked away. Her parents had left it the way it was when she was a child, like a shrine, as if she truly had died.

She came down from the attic and ran her hand over the doorframe of her bedroom, remembering the countless times she had run into her room and shut the door to hide under her bed, hiding from her father's angry outbursts. The bed was now covered in a thick layer of dust, but still, it felt like stepping back in time.

She could hear the birds singing outside, and the wind rustling through the trees. It was a beautiful day, and she couldn't help but feel a sense of peace wash over her. She took a deep breath, trying to calm her racing heart. She had a lot of work ahead of her.

Ava's mind was a jumble of conflicting emotions as she scrubbed the furniture and dusted the shelves in her bedroom and remarkably found some clean bedding, too. She was determined to turn this house back into a home, but every creak of the wooden floorboards brought back a flood of painful memories.

She moved on to the kitchen, where she found a layer of grime on the countertops and a thick film of dust covering the old wooden table. She wiped them down, then she opened her mother's recipe box which she brought down from the attic and stared at her mother's handwriting on the faded recipe cards. She picked one up, reading the recipe for apple pie, a family favorite.

The next day, after finishing some cleaning inside the house in her bedroom and kitchen, she surveyed that weeds had overtaken the garden, choking out the flowers and vegetables she used to tend. Although she knew there was so much work remaining to be done in the house, she felt like getting outside in the quiet country sun and fixing part of the garden. She spent the afternoon digging and weeding. As she worked, she thought about her future, the choices she had to make.

Would she stay here or find a place to live nearby? She knew she should go visit her mother and brothers in prison, but she couldn't bring herself to see them just yet.

As questions swirled through her mind, she made a trip to the hardware store to buy much-needed supplies and some paint.

***

The next morning, which was a Sunday, Ava dressed in a simple and modest dress to blend in with the Amish community and walked towards the familiar church building that stood tall in the woods of Unity. The community had built it years ago, while she'd been in captivity. The sound of horses' hooves echoed from the main road, traveling up the hill to the church where several buggies were parked in the dirt parking lot. She took a deep breath and pushed open the door of the church, unsure of how people might react to seeing her again after six years.

As she stepped inside, a wave of nostalgia swept over her. The wooden backless benches and the large, plain sanctuary reminded her of when she had attended church services in her neighbors' homes as a child, before the church had been built.

She looked at the school room with envy and regret, wishing she'd had the freedom and opportunity to attend school until the eighth grade like the other children had, but her father's rage had shattered her childhood into pieces.

She took her place at the back, her eyes scanning the familiar faces. She saw some of her old friends from school, their faces now marked by the lines of hard work and simple living. She recognized Mary's freckles and rosy cheeks, Rachel's bright eyes, and Penelope's shy demeanor. But most notably, she spotted her childhood friends, Liz and Maria.

Ava made her way towards them, her heart pounding. She hoped she would be able to spend time with them soon to catch up and find out how their lives were now.

Liz's face broke into a grin when she saw Ava. "Ava! You're here!" Liz threw her arms around Ava, and Maria hurried over to join them, also hugging Ava.

"How are you? Where have you been all this time? How is your life as an *Englisher*?" Maria asked, then paused, lowering her voice. "Are you staying? Thinking of rejoining the church?"

Liz chuckled. "One question at a time, Maria."

Maria smiled, and Ava couldn't help but smile at her friends' enthusiasm.

"I'm so glad to see you both," she said, her voice trembling with a mix of excitement and nerves. "I'm not sure how long I'll be here. I'm fixing up the house. My mother has agreed to let me sell it for her."

"Oh, that's good news," Liz said.

"It's going to need a lot of work. The last tenants left it a mess."

"*Ja*, they did," Maria said.

"We tried our best to clean up the beer cans on the porch, but we didn't want to intrude and go inside," Liz said. "I'm sorry."

"Oh, thank you," Ava said. "I appreciate that."

"We're so glad you're here now," Maria said.

"I just needed to get out of the city," she replied, trying to keep the truth at bay. She hesitated, unsure of what else to say. She knew they wouldn't understand. They had never experienced the horrors that she had, as far as she knew. "My *Englisher* life there was…not what I hoped it would be."

Liz's eyes narrowed slightly. "Is everything all right? Did something happen to you?" she asked, concern etched on her face.

Ava sighed. "Something did happen to me, but it's over now. It's a long story."

Maria nodded sympathetically. "I'm sure you'll find your place here. If you ever want to talk, we are here for you."

"Thank you." Ava looked around the church. "Where is Anna? I was hoping to see her today."

Maria and Liz exchanged knowing glances, their expressions a blend of nostalgia and pride. Maria spoke, her words carrying a hint of warmth, "Anna left our Amish community to attend college, pursuing a dream of hers to become a nurse."

Liz added softly, her voice tinged with a hint of wistfulness, "We miss her dearly, but we can't deny the joy that fills us when we hear of her progress."

Ava's eyes widened. "She always had such a caring soul. I hope she's happy in her new life."

Liz nodded. "She's doing well."

Maria's voice chimed in. "Why don't we plan a day to get together and catch up on each other's lives?"

Ava hesitated. "I do want to, but I have so much work to do on the house."

Liz's face lit up. "We'll help you clean it up. It's a perfect chance to reminisce and make some new memories together."

"Yes, Ava, let us help you clean. We want to help."

Ava couldn't help but smile at the suggestion, feeling grateful for the support. "All right, let's do it. I could use your help and company tomorrow. Thank you so much."

Maria's voice rang out, "We'll be at your place bright and early tomorrow."

Ava smiled. "Thank you both."

Several Amish women approached her, smiling and welcoming her back home.

One sweet and curious young woman, Laura, asked with a twinkle in her eye, "Are you planning on staying? Or are you just visiting a short time?"

"I'm not sure. I don't have a plan yet."

"Did you go to college? What was the *Englisher* world like in New York City? Was it everything you dreamed it would be?" Laura asked, her eyes gleaming with questions.

Ava frowned, shaking her head. "I did graduate and get my degree, but sadly, life in the city was cruel. It wasn't what I expected. The grass is not always greener on the other side, as they say. You're blessed to live in this wonderful place."

"My sister says I should be thankful to live here and not dream about leaving and exploring."

"Well, never stop dreaming, but it sounds like she is just looking out for you. This is a wonderful place. The world can be more cruel than you can ever imagine."

Laura nodded in understanding, her eyes filling with realization.

"May I ask, what was it like living in the basement for so long?" Laura blurted out.

"I'm sorry, Ava," Lydia, Laura's older sister said, rushing toward them and taking Laura's arm. "Laura, you ask too many prying questions."

"It's okay," Ava said softly.

Laura smiled apologetically and let her sister lead her away.

Maria's mother, Mary, stepped forward. "It's been so long since we've had you here with us. We've missed you, Ava. I couldn't help but overhear. I am so very sorry about what happened. None of us knew you were in the basement. If my husband and I had known, we certainly would have done everything we could to help." She leaned forward and said softly. "We would have called the police."

Ava knew that not everyone here would have involved the police. "Thank you, Mrs. Mast. I do appreciate you saying that."

"Hello, Ava, how are you?" another woman asked who lived down the lane. More women joined in, greeting her.

Ava's heart swelled with emotion as the other women chimed in, sharing stories of their children and grandchildren, asking about Ava's travels, and expressing their gratitude for her presence. They welcomed her with open arms, their warmth a stark contrast to the coldness of the outside world she had grown accustomed to during her time away.

As they spoke, Maria and Liz continued to chat with the women, weaving in and out of the conversation. Ava couldn't help but feel a sense of belonging wash over her. She had missed this sense of community, this simple way of life that was deeply rooted in faith and tradition.

"Ava, this is Freya, Adam Lapp's wife," Maria said, introducing Ava to a young *Englisher* woman with red hair, holding a baby. "As you might remember, Adam grew up Amish, but he left to become a police officer, then he met Freya."

"Nice to meet you, Ava. We live just down the lane," Freya said. "We often come to church here to visit everyone, especially Adam's family."

"I remember Adam when he was a kid," Ava said.

"He's just over there," Freya said, gesturing to the young *Englisher* man across the room who was talking with some young Amish men. She made a mental note to talk to them about what it was like to live in the Amish community as *Englishers* in case she ever wanted to do that one day.

"And who is this?" she asked, referring to the red-haired baby boy Freya held.

"This is Robert," Freya said. The baby gurgled and smiled at her.

"Oh, after Adam's brother?" Ava asked. "I remember him, too."

The women suddenly looked downcast. "He passed away," Maria said solemnly. "That's a long story, though. We have a lot of catching up to do tomorrow."

"I'm so sorry to hear that." She turned to Freya. "I'd love to talk to you more about living here as an *Englisher*."

"Oh, I'd love to talk. We'll have to plan a time to get together," Freya said.

"Thank you," Ava said. "Definitely."

"We are going to Ava's house tomorrow early in the morning to help her clean up after the renters who were living there," Maria said. "Would you like to join us tomorrow?"

"Don't feel like you have to come clean," Ava said. "I know you must have your hands full."

"Actually, I'd love to. I can get there mid morning," Freya said.

"Thank you," Ava said.

"Happy to help a neighbor out," Freya said, smiling.

"We should go sit down. The service is about to start," Liz said.

As Ava took her seat on the women's side of the church, Maria and Liz flanked her, their presence a comforting anchor amidst the sea of faces. The service began, and they sang hymns together, their voices blending in harmony.

***

As he drove to a local church he attended in Augusta, Theo dialed Natalie's number. He remembered how distracted and upset she had seemed during the family dinner. It wasn't like her to be so withdrawn.

After a few rings, Natalie answered. "Hey, Theo."

"Hey, Nat," Theo replied, trying to keep his tone light. "I just wanted to check in. You seemed upset at family dinner, and I'm worried. I know it's more than just homework that's bothering you. What's wrong?"

There was a brief pause before Natalie responded. "I'm fine, really. I'm just overwhelmed with schoolwork. This is a lot harder than I thought it would be, and since I don't have time for my music anymore, it's stressing me out. I miss it."

Before Theo could respond, he heard a man's voice in the background. "Who is that on the phone?"

Natalie's voice tightened. "I have to go, Theo."

"Wait, who is that in the background?" Theo asked sharply, concern spiking through him.

"It's just my classmate," Natalie assured him. "We're doing homework together."

"On a Sunday morning?"

"Yeah, we have the huge project due, and it's crunch time, so we will be working on it all night, probably. Really, Theo, I promise I'm fine. Once I get this project and presentation done with my study partner, I'll feel so much better. I promise, okay?"

Theo took a deep breath, trying to make sense of her words. "Okay... I guess that makes sense. Maybe I'm just being overprotective."

Natalie gave a soft laugh. "You *are* being overprotective. I'll see you soon, and we can get coffee and catch up once this project is over, okay?"

"Okay," Theo said, though he was still uneasy. "Please don't stay up too late. Take care of yourself, alright?"

"Will do. Thanks, Theo. Bye."

"Bye," Theo replied, ending the call.

As drove, Theo tried to convince himself that everything was fine. Natalie said it was just schoolwork, and there was no reason to doubt her. She'd never lied to him before, not that he knew of. But despite his efforts, the nagging feeling that something was wrong wouldn't leave him. He couldn't shake the image of her drawn expression at dinner.

He told himself she was fine. Yet the unease persisted, a small knot in his stomach that refused to unravel. He would make sure they got coffee together soon, just as she'd promised.

For now, he had to trust her words and hope that she really was just overwhelmed with schoolwork. But deep down, the protective brother in him knew he wouldn't be able to rest easy until he had seen for himself that Natalie was truly fine.

Chapter Sixteen

The next morning, Ava called the number of a local therapist that had excellent online reviews and scheduled several appointments. Feeling good about her decision, she made herself a quick breakfast in preparation for a full day's work.

Ava was about to roll up her sleeves and start cleaning when she heard the crunch of gravel outside. Glancing out the window, Ava saw Maria and Liz walking down her driveway. She couldn't help but feel a surge of warmth as they approached, bringing with them memories of a simpler time.

Within moments, the trio was armed with dusters, paint scrapers, cloths, and buckets, and the silent house soon echoed with the sounds of scrubbing and laughter. They started with scraping all the old paint off the walls, sanding them, and wiping them down, then moved on to cleaning. They made small talk at first, focusing on the task at hand. As the hours passed, the house gradually began to shed its mantle of neglect, and the conversation delved deeper.

"Do you have anyone special in your life?" Maria asked Ava. "Did you have a boyfriend in the city?"

"No, I didn't have time for a boyfriend," Ava said solemnly. "What about you? Are either of you courting?"

"I'm courting Simon Hodges," Liz said. "Remember him?"

Ava smiled. "Simon? Oh, yes. He was always too afraid to climb trees."

Liz laughed out loud. "I always could climb higher than him."

Maria gave a shy smile. "I'm courting someone special," she confided, "Derek Turner." Her eyes held a twinkle as she spoke of the man who had once been a police officer, a guardian from another world who now sought peace in their own. "He came to know our way of life when he worked here to protect me from a sex trafficking ring... and we fell in love. He left the police force to join the church. I'm not sure if you knew that I was married before and my husband passed away, so my son and I are grateful for a second chance. Actually, my husband was Robert Lapp."

"You were married to Robert? And there were traffickers here?" Ava asked. "Sorry, I have so many questions right now."

"Yes, and actually, I'm glad I got to talk to you before Freya gets here, because it's a sensitive topic for all of us." She explained how Freya was escaping her abusive ex-fiancé when she accidentally hit Robert in a snowstorm with her car, killing him. "We were all devastated. Adam left to become a police officer, and she came here to tell us she was the one who killed him. I hated her at first, but I finally came around and forgave her, and now we are the best of friends. She and Adam got married, and now they have their beautiful baby boy."

"Wow. That's incredible. I mean, I'm so sorry to hear Robert passed away, but it's wonderful that something good came from such a horrible tragedy," Ava said.

"Please, tell me what happened with the traffickers? They were here, targeting you?"

Liz interjected with a sobering revelation of her own. "Maria, Anna, and I were kidnapped by traffickers—it was terrifying, but the police were able to rescue us, thanks to Maria sneaking in a cell phone that they were tracking. My sister, Anneliese, was kidnapped by a different group of traffickers later on, and I was able to help the police locate her by allowing myself to be taken."

"Wow, that's incredibly brave of you," Ava said. "That sounds terrifying."

"I was willing to do anything to find my sister," Liz said.

As the conversation unfolded, Freya arrived. "Good morning," Freya said. "It's Adam's day off, so he's on baby duty."

"Thanks so much for coming," Ava said.

"Really, I'm happy to help."

Freya picked up a cleaning cloth and joined in the conversation.

Ava realized they all shared similar experiences—danger, fear, and rescue. Encouraged by their openness, Ava took a deep breath and spoke of her own harrowing journey, of dreams turned to nightmares in the clutches of a criminal world.

"I might as well tell you what happened to me while I was gone," Ava began. "I wasn't only going to college. I was forced into prostitution for two years."

Maria and Liz glanced at each other, shocked.

"Ava, I'm so sorry," Maria said.

"We had no idea," Liz added.

"I am so sorry to hear it," Freya murmured.

Her friends listened as she told them her story, their expressions a mixture of disbelief, horror, and compassion as Ava detailed the two long years of manipulation and control that had stripped away her sense of self. Maria and Liz tried to understand what she had gone through. Yes, they had also been through a traumatic experience when they had been kidnapped, but it had been different from Ava's long-term bondage of over a decade in the basement and then the two years in New York.

"I can't even imagine what you went through," Maria said.

"It's why I came here, to get away from my past," Ava said. "It's so peaceful here. I thought I could start over and try to forget what happened to me, but I'm not sure I can ever overcome it."

"You can rebuild your life and start over," Liz said. "You might not forget, but you can overcome it, Ava."

"If I was able to do it, anyone can, and that includes you," Freya piped in.

"And we will be here for you every step of the way," Maria added.

"Right," Liz said, grabbing Ava's hand.

"And so will I," Freya included herself.

"Thank you," Ava said, her eyes filling with tears. "But I don't want anyone to know. I don't want people feeling sorry for me."

"We won't tell anyone," Liz said. "Your secret is safe with us."

Maria and Freya nodded.

"Speaking of secrets," Ava said, gesturing to the basement door. "We won't need to clean the basement, at least not for a while. I can't bring myself to go down there. I don't know when I'll be able to...or if I ever will be able to." She turned to Freya. "I'm not sure if you already heard, but my father locked me in the basement."

Freya nodded slowly. "I had heard about it after we first moved here, but I don't know the details."

Ava gave her an overview of the story. "So, that's why I don't think I'll be going downstairs any time soon."

"You should take all the time you need," Freya said. "We can handle cleaning downstairs, if you want, while you clean upstairs. Right?" She looked to Maria and Liz.

They both nodded.

"Absolutely. Take all the time you need. One step at a time. Just the fact that you've come back here is a huge step," Maria added.

"Thank you," Ava said, her voice filled with gratitude. "But we can deal with that later. Let's just focus on this floor and upstairs for now."

As the day waned and the once-abandoned house stood clean and inviting before them, the four women found solace in their rekindled bond. Maria, Liz, and Freya each extended their unwavering support to Ava, affirming that return was possible, no matter how far or how long the journey. Surrounded by her friends, Ava felt a flicker of hope.

As they continued working, Ava asked Freya, "So, what's it like living as an *Englisher* in an Amish community? I'm sure people ask you that all the time."

"Yes, they do, and we love living here. So, as you know, Adam grew up Amish, but he left when his brother died." Freya added, looked to Maria, as if silently asking if Maria had filled Ava in, and Maria nodded. "Because of what happened, he didn't want to rejoin the Amish, but he wanted to be near his family after not seeing them for so long. He's also very dedicated to his job and loves being a police officer. I also wanted to live a more simple life and be near Adam's family because I don't have a family of my own. We also want to serve God with our lives. We attend a church down the road, but we also visit the Amish church every now and then, and we visit Adam's family all the time. So, we bought a house down the lane, and now we have the best of both worlds. We love raising our son here."

"That's amazing," Ava said. "I am not sure if I would rejoin the church or not, to be honest, but I do want a simpler life. I also want to serve God. One day, I'd love to open a shelter for women who are survivors of abuse, trafficking, or prostitution."

"Wow," Freya said. "If you do, sign me up to volunteer. I'd love to give back after what happened to me. I'm guessing Maria told you about my ex. I escaped after he tried to kill me several times. I didn't have anywhere to go. I kept moving, hoping he wouldn't find me."

"Well, if I ever open one, I'll let you know how you can help."

"I would help too, of course," Liz said.

"Me too," Maria added. "I also had an abusive ex, so I know how that feels."

"Wow. So much happened while I was gone," Ava said. "I want to hear everything you feel like telling me."

They spent the rest of the afternoon cleaning as each of the women told Ava what had happened to them over the past several years, and by dinner time, she felt as if she knew them so much better than she had before.

"I can't thank you enough for coming over to help me clean," Ava said. "No one has ever done anything so kind for me before in a long time." Her eyes filled with tears of gratitude.

They rushed to her side, attempting to comfort her, telling her how glad they were to help.

"Come over to my house for dinner, Ava," Liz said. "I can't stand the thought of you spending your evening here all alone. Maria and Freya, I'd love to have you over as well."

"I have a date with Derek tonight, but thank you," Maria said. "He's taking me to the café for dinner."

"And I want to get home to see the baby, but thank you," Freya said.

"Will you come, Ava?" Liz asked.

"I don't want to impose," Ava said. "I'll be fine."

"No, I insist. You've worked enough today and could use a break. My mother and I will be making chicken and dumplings. I won't take no for an answer," Liz said, hands on her hips.

"You better go," Maria said, laughing. "She really won't take no for an answer."

"Well, that does sound nice. I haven't seen your family in a long time," Ava said.

"Let's get going then," Liz said, gathering her cleaning supplies. "We need to get dinner started."

***

The walk to Liz's house felt both foreign and familiar to Ava, the well-trodden paths of her youth now seen through the lens of years spent away. Standing at the threshold, she was greeted by a warmth that radiated from within. Liz's mother, Rachel, welcomed her with a hug that held the comfort of home, and Conrad, her father, offered a kind handshake and a gentle nod. They, along with Maria's parents, had been like an extra set of parents to her when she was a young child. Naomi and Anneliese, Liz's younger sisters, greeted Ava with shy curiosity, their faces framed by the simplicity of traditional prayer *kapps*.

As they gathered in the kitchen, the heart of the Amish home, Ava was struck by how well the women worked together. Under Rachel's practiced guidance, they began to prepare chicken and dumplings, salad, and peach cobbler for dessert. Liz and her sisters moved with an ease and expertise that Ava could only admire. The realization of what she had missed out on—the continued experiences of learning at her mother's side as she got older—came to her with a pang of envy and loss. She had only been able to cook with her mother until she was six years old, so she hadn't learned any advanced cooking skills.

"I never really learned how to cook anything advanced. I only learned as a young child with my mother," Ava confessed, a vulnerability in her voice as she watched Rachel skillfully roll out dough for the dumplings. "But I want to help, and I want to learn."

"Now is a good time to start learning," Rachel replied, her voice as comforting as the aromas beginning to fill the room. "We'll show you."

And so, under the gentle tutelage of Liz's family, Ava began to learn. She followed their movements, hesitantly at first, but with growing confidence as the steps of mixing, rolling, and shaping the dumplings became more familiar. The easy laughter and shared work connected them, and Ava found joy in the learning, her earlier envy ebbing away to gratitude for this chance to be included, to be part of something warm and loving.

A bittersweet feeling settled within her. The kitchen was a whirlwind of activity, yet every motion was infused with affection and shared purpose. The familial bonds on display were the opposite of the isolated, anguished years of her own upbringing.

The laughter and gentle teasing around her increased her sense of envy, a longing for what her childhood might have been. Instead of lighthearted kitchen mishaps with her mother, her memories were shadowed by the fear of a man who let fury dictate their lives, who tore the family fabric apart so ruthlessly. Ava yearned for the innocent times that should have been hers—times of learning, of growing within the loving circle of her family.

Yet here, amidst the flour, dough, and broth, Ava was made part of an everyday ritual she had never known. Each guiding hand on hers as she shaped dumplings, each encouraging smile quietly healed her heart just a little.

As the meal came together, they gathered to enjoy it around the handmade table. There was solace to be found in the presence of Liz's family in the love that simmered along with the chicken and dumplings on this simple Amish evening.

She was here now, surrounded by people who reached out with open hearts, offering her a seat at their table and a place in their lives. Ava realized that while she could not rewrite her past, her future was a canvas yet to be painted.

Here, with the love and acceptance of Liz and her family, she felt the first brushstrokes of hope.

Chapter Seventeen

Returning home for the day after checking out a lead on a case, Detective Theo Kingsley drove through rural landscape surrounding Unity, Maine, his eyes trailing over the serenity of the Amish farmlands through his window. It was a drastic change from the relentless pace and the crowds of New York City.

He decided to stop by and see how his Amish friends were doing. He would have called first, but he knew they didn't have phones in their homes. Some of the businesses had phones, but Conrad was probably already home from work. So, he hoped they wouldn't mind his impromptu visit.

Pulling up to the Kulp residence, Theo took a steadying breath before stepping out. He had been the investigating officer in Anneliese Kulp's kidnapping—events that had preceded his promotion to detective and had deeply affected him personally. During that case, he had seen the community come together to support Liz's family in a powerful way, and it had stuck with him. He had never seen a community come together like that before.

He moved toward the door and knocked. Moments later, he was greeted by Conrad Kulp's sturdy figure.

"Detective Kingsley, what a nice surprise! Please, come in," Conrad said cheerfully, stepping aside to welcome Theo. "Look who is here, everyone," he said, turning to his family.

The Kulps were seated around the dinner table, and Theo noticed a beautiful, young, blonde woman sitting beside Liz. She was clearly not Amish with her long hair loose around her shoulders, and she wore a long-sleeved t-shirt and jeans. Her brown eyes held a pain she tried to mask behind a shy smile. Who was she? He couldn't help but wonder.

Rachel stood from the table. "Detective Kingsley, hello! How are you?"

Liz stood up, smiling. "It's so nice to see you."

Naomi and Anneliese waved in greeting, saying hello.

"I just wanted to stop by and see how everyone is doing," Theo replied, coming into the house and shutting the door behind him. Inside, the aroma of a hearty meal filled the air. "I was in the area. I hope you don't mind my unexpected visit. I'm so sorry I'm interrupting your dinner. I can come a different time, if you'd like."

"We are happy to have you over any time," Liz said. "Please stay."

"Sit down and join us!" Rachel said, pointing to an empty chair. "Have you eaten dinner yet?"

"I haven't, but I don't want to impose," he said.

"Nonsense. Sit down. We have plenty. Here, let me get you a plate," Rachel said, hurrying into the kitchen.

"Thank you so much," Theo said looking at his watch as Rachel set a plate, glass, and fork in front of him. They all sat down.

"Theo, this is Ava. Ava, Detective Kingsley investigated Anneliese's case," Liz said, bridging the introduction with a glance between the two. She gestured to the beautiful woman sitting beside her.

Theo stood for a moment to shake her hand, extending it across the table. She looked at it, hesitating, as though she was afraid to touch him. She nervously glanced around, awkwardly reached out and briefly shook his hand, and quickly sat back down. He'd seen this before in his line of work. She was either very shy or had reservations about making any physical contact with men, such as hugging or even shaking hands. He guessed that she had probably experienced abuse from a male figure at some point in her life, but he hoped he was wrong.

"It's nice to meet you, Theo," Ava said quietly.

"The pleasure's mine, Ava," responded Theo.

Sitting around the table with the Kulps and Ava, Theo found himself enveloped in the simple pleasures of Amish hospitality. Throughout the meal, they exchanged stories and life updates.

The conversation flowed easily, and Theo inquired about everyone's well-being. Liz smiled across the table as she answered, "I've been doing well. I still work at the local greenhouse now, and Simon and I are engaged to be married in November."

"That's really great to hear, Liz," Theo said with a genuine smile. "And Anneliese? Naomi? What have you been up to?"

Anneliese beamed, "I got a part time job. I started working three hours a day, two days a week at the greenhouse with Liz."

"That is excellent news," Theo said with a smile.

Naomi chimed in from the other end of the table, "And I just started a new full-time job at the bakery in town."

Theo said, "I'm glad to hear you're all doing well."

"And how have you been doing?" Rachel asked.

"Work keeps me very busy, but I was able to have family dinner with my family recently and catch up with them. I did move here to be closer to my family, after all," he explained.

"Detective Kingsley is from Augusta, but he lived in New York City for a while and then moved back here," Liz told Ava. She turned to Theo. "Ava went to college in New York City."

"You did? What did you go to school for?" Theo asked.

"I majored in English with a minor in Creative Writing," Ava said, but then a shadow crossed her face.

"Ava is a writer," Liz said. "She even got a scholarship, and she's writing a novel."

Ava blushed, recalling how she had told her friends about her college experience earlier that day.

"She's too modest to say so," Liz said, waving her hand. "But she's a very talented writer."

Ava picked at her food distractedly, not elaborating. He decided not to pry. Maybe he could ask her more about it later.

After dinner, Ava joined Liz, Naomi, and Anneliese to help clear the table and wash up, while Theo was led into the living room by Conrad for a while where they spoke about other things that had happened in town recently. After the cleanup was done, everyone gathered in the living room to continue their conversation. Ava and Theo found themselves seated on the couch side by side, drawn together by something unspoken.

"It was quite a change coming out here from New York City for me," Theo mused. "Was it for you, too?"

Ava tucked a loose strand of hair behind her ear, her voice soft but carrying across the subtle pause in conversation. "I actually grew up in this community."

"You did? So, you were raised Amish and you left?" he asked, then paused. "Sorry. I'm prying."

"It's, uh...it's complicated," she said hesitantly. "There's a lot to that story."

Theo could see the layers of untold complexity behind her words. He could sense that she didn't want to say more and he nodded, respecting it. "It sounds like you've had quite the journey, Ava."

Her gaze held gratitude for his unspoken understanding, for him not asking for more information. Ava asked, "What about you, Theo? Why did you leave New York City?"

The question hung between them, a bridge to Theo's own loss. He looked down at the floor for a fraction of a second before meeting her eyes. "My wife was killed in a hit and run two years ago. After that, I just needed to be closer to family."

Ava's expression softened with empathy. "I can't even imagine how hard that must've been," she murmured.

"It was hard, but my family got me through it. I was a police officer in New York, and now I work at the Covert Police Detectives Unit in Augusta," he explained. "So, are you staying here?"

"I'm not sure how long I'll be in town. Right now, I'm staying in my childhood home. I'm selling it for my mother. It needs some repairs, though. The tenants left it in bad shape. Liz, Maria, and Freya helped me clean it today, but it needs a lot more work."

Theo said. "What kind of repairs does it need?"

"The sink needs fixing, the screen door needs replacing, and the siding needs to be repaired outside. The porch needs to be fixed and could use a coat of paint. That's all I know of so far. There's probably more."

As the night grew later, the room glowed with the light of the battery-operated lanterns and propane lamps on the ceilings. Ava went into the kitchen to get a drink of water while the others remained sitting in the living room.

Driven by impulse, Theo took a chance and followed her into the kitchen, hoping he didn't seem to desperate. "You know, I'm handy around the house." He also filled a glass of water for himself so that he felt less awkward about following her into the kitchen. He leaned against the counter casually, drinking the water. "Let me come by and help you this weekend. I'd be glad to do it. Then we could get a bite to eat, if you'd like."

Surprised by the sudden skip of her heartbeat at the question, Ava's eyes widened slightly. In a moment of courage, she found herself answering, "Yes. Yes, I'd like that. Thank you. I'd appreciate your help. That sounds nice."

"I'll bring my tools," Theo said, then thought to himself, *I will need to borrow Dad's tool bag. Who am I kidding? I'm no handyman. But for her, I can learn everything I can before I come back.*

He'd have to ask his dad to remind him how to fix a sink after she told him what seemed wrong with it to narrow down what kind of repair it needed. He would also need to learn how to repair a screen door and siding. He was determined to help her if it meant spending time with her and getting to know her.

"My house is just down the lane," Ava said. "It's yellow with white shutters."

"Saturday is one of my days off," he said. "Should I get there around eight in the morning?"

"That sounds good, I'll make breakfast for us," Ava said. "Thank you so much."

They returned to the living room, and Theo offering his thanks for a pleasant evening to the Kulp family. "Thank you all for dinner. It was wonderful," he said, as he edged towards the doorway. He turned to Ava, who smiled, and reluctantly turned and left.

As he made his way back to his vehicle, the cool night air offered a refreshing clarity. He pulled out his phone, pressing the call button next to 'Dad' on the screen. The line clicked after a couple of rings, and his dad's voice came through.

"Hello?" Mark said.

"Who's calling you?" Carol asked in the background.

"It's Theo," his father told his mother.

"Oh, Theo," Carol cried in the background. "How are you, dear?"

"Your mother is asking how you're doing," Mark said.

"Tell her I'm fine," Theo said. "I'm calling because—"

"He's doing fine," Mark said to Carol.

Theo rolled his eyes, chuckling. "Why don't you just put it on speaker so I can talk to both of you?"

"Speaker? How do you do that?" Carol asked. "We're still not used to these new phones."

Theo laughed. "Just look for the speaker button."

"Oh, here's the button," Mark said. "Got it. Now we can both hear you."

"So, I was actually wondering if I can borrow your tool bag, Dad?" Theo asked.

"Sure. Why? Do you need help fixing something at your apartment? Doesn't maintenance do that for you?"

Theo ran a hand through his hair, feeling somehow transparent. "It's not for my place. I'm helping someone with some repairs in their house so she can sell it."

"You don't know the difference between a screwdriver and a wrench, son. Who could possibly need your help?" Mark asked.

"I...met a girl."

Immediately, the sound of his mother's distant cheering filled the background noise of the call, her excitement palpable even through the phone. "Oh, finally! Thank the good Lord."

"Well, well. Who is she?" Mark added.

"Don't get your hopes up," Theo interjected quickly, trying to temper their enthusiasm with his level-headedness. "We've just met. But I may have given her the impression that I'm handy with fixing things around the house. I'll be watching tutorials online tonight and every day after work if I need to so I can learn as much as I can."

"Just take the tool bag, son, and be yourself—that's all you can do," his dad said warmly, the smile clear in his voice, offering support and understanding. "I know it's been a while since I've taught you how to do these things, but we can review as much as we can before you help her."

"Thanks, Dad. I'll pick it up after work tomorrow," Theo replied, a small smile gracing his lips despite the nerves beginning to bubble up within him.

"Come for dinner!" his mother called out in the background.

"Then you can tell us about what you need to fix for this nice girl you've met," Mark added.

Theo smiled. "I'd love to."

Chapter Eighteen

Ava walked the familiar path back to her house, the dimming light of dusk casting elongated shadows across the landscape.

When she'd first met Theo and shook his hand, she had hesitated to do it because she avoided all contact with men. But once she started talking to him, she quickly felt at ease with him as if she'd known him all her life. How was that possible? If he offered to shake her hand again, she knew she wouldn't hesitate a second time. She never thought she'd feel comfortable around a man ever again in her life.

She walked home and opened the door. Inside, her house was so much cleaner. Maria, Freya, and Liz had been an incredible help, but she still had so much more work and repairs to do.

She made her way to the window, gazing out at the stars, a tapestry of possibilities against the darkening sky. They were so bright here and easier to see than in New York City. The date with Theo—if fixing her house together could be called a date—might lead somewhere new, somewhere brighter, but her mind was filled with worry and doubt. Was it a date? She wasn't sure.

Theo. Just the thought of him filled her with a strange, wonderful feeling, sending her heart racing. He had been so kind, so gentle, and she found herself wanting to get to know him.

What would happen when the topic of her past emerged, as it inevitably would? The years spent hidden away, the tangle of her family tragedy, and the past two years of horror in New York City—how could she tell him the truth? Would she have the courage to tell him? Maybe not tomorrow, but the longer she kept it from him, the harder it would be to tell him.

What would he think of her when she told him she'd been a prostitute? Would he ever look at her the same way again? He was a police officer, so maybe he was used to seeing the dark side of humanity, but she was not one of his cases. Maybe he'd never personally known someone who had been lured into the crime.

Ava felt the weight of her past, yet she also knew the strength she'd found within herself to stand where she was now. Perhaps Theo, with his own story of loss and starting over, could understand the complexities of a life rebuilt from ashes.

For now, she allowed herself to sink into the quiet thrill that came with the prospect of getting to know someone new.

Tonight, she would think about the way her heart had fluttered while they'd talked at Liz's house. She'd felt an instant connection to him—something she'd never felt before. She had a sense she could trust him.

Was that crazy?

With a deep breath, she embraced the calm of her home, warmed by the idea that this might just be the first step on a path toward healing and companionship.

Ava closed her eyes, letting her heart hold onto the hope of what their time together might bring.

**

The next morning, Ava had her first therapy appointment with a lovely therapist, Doctor Wellsworth, who helped her process her move back home, how she felt about the house and the basement, and seeing old friends. Ava told her about how she was thinking about visiting her mother and brothers in prison, and by the end of the session, she knew without a doubt she wasn't ready yet. However, she felt even more confident in her decision to move back home and rebuild her life. She would be going to therapy once a week, and she left the office feeling as though a weight had been lifted off her shoulders.

Ava spent the rest of the week cleaning, scrubbing the house from top to bottom on her own and also with Maria, Liz, and Freya.

They each invited her over to their homes for dinner each night, making sure she didn't eat alone. She appreciated how much they cared for her, taking her under their wings and making her feel welcome. They taught her how to cook, told her funny stories, and played games together. She loved spending time with them and their families and was overcome with a sense of belonging.

With the help of her friends, the house gradually changed from dirty and unkept to a clean and tidy home, and Ava's heart began to mend little by little.

***

On Saturday morning, Theo pulled up to Ava's house, his eyes quickly taking in the faded siding and a porch railing that had certainly seen better days.

He had prepared as much as he could, watching tutorials on DIY repairs, and his father gave him some tips. Armed with his father's borrowed tool bag and advice, a tentative confidence in his newfound knowledge, and a box of painting brushes, rollers, and supplies, he stepped out of the car.

He knocked on the door, and Ava soon welcomed him with a warm smile, wearing a worn, white apron over her jeans and t-shirt. The scent of freshly made pancakes and eggs wafted from behind her, and she led him inside to a modest table set for two.

"I hope you're hungry," Ava said, gesturing to the plates. "It's one of the few things I can cook. The neighbors came by with their farm fresh eggs. Everyone has been so welcoming to me. I've already learned so much about cooking from Liz's family."

"I'm not surprised. Everyone here is incredibly kind and helpful, and I'm sure they're glad you're back." Theo took a seat, a friendly smile crossing his face. "This looks delicious. Thank you." Truth be told, the pancakes looked perfectly golden and the eggs looked fluffy.

Theo took a bite of the pancakes, appreciating the moment of tranquility and the surprisingly adept cooking. "These are really good," he complimented her. "I'm sure you'll learn how to cook all kinds of dishes with your friends' help."

"Thanks," Ava replied, a touch of pride in her voice.

"I also can only cook a few things, but I would like to learn more. Living alone, I have to admit I often just get takeout, but I do love going to family dinner at my parents' house. My mother is a wonderful cook. She still spoils me and my sister, Natalie." Curiosity nudged at the edges of Theo's thoughts. "So, do you live here all by yourself?" he inquired, setting down his fork and taking a sip of his coffee.

Ava nodded, "Yes, it's just me here."

"And your family?" Theo asked gently, sensing this was delicate territory.

There was a noticeable pause as Ava considered her response, a hint of shadow crossing her face. "My father was murdered, and one of my brothers also passed away. His wife killed him in self-defense when he tried to kill her," she said, acknowledging the heavy truth of her words. "And my mother and two other brothers are in prison."

He tried to hide his surprise and shock. Her mother and two of her brothers were in prison? Had they all committed a crime together? His police officer mind was flooded with questions, but now was not the time or place.

He could sense this was the tip of an emotional iceberg, a glimpse of her dark past she probably didn't want to revisit.

"I'm sorry, Ava. That must be really hard," he said sincerely, acknowledging the weight of her situation without pushing for more. "Family is...everything."

She offered a small, appreciative nod, a thin smile hinting at the resilience behind her eyes. "Yeah, it's... It's what it is," she breathed out, and it seemed to Theo as though she might have been convincing herself as much as him. She sighed, a note of sadness lacing her words. "I don't miss my father—he was a very angry and violent man. It's complicated. I do miss my mom and brothers, though."

Again, that word, "complicated." Theo noted it and wondered about the depth of her story, but he chose not to push her for more.

They continued their meal, discussing the projects they hoped to complete that day. A full day's work awaited them—a day that would bring laughter, shared tasks, and a sense of connection neither of them had expected to find.

With breakfast finished and their dishes put aside, they went outside to tackle the first task of the day. Together, they secured the porch railing back into place, Theo's careful hammer strokes matched by Ava's hand holding the wood steady. Though it had been years since his father had first taught him how to use a hammer and nails, it quickly came back to him.

They moved on to the weather-worn siding, measuring, cutting, and nailing new panels into place with a satisfying sense of progress. Laughter and light conversation filled the gaps in their work, and a sense of camaraderie began to take root.

Venturing back inside, Ava sanded and primed the kitchen walls, preparing to paint them while Theo set his sights on the screen door. After a few failed attempts, he stood back, proud to see the door swing smoothly once again.

He felt more ambitious as he tried to fix the kitchen sink, but his pride soon turned into surprise as a twist in the wrong direction sent a fountain of water spraying across the room. Ava rushed over, and they scrambled to stop the unexpected indoor geyser. They laughed as they were both sprayed, and Theo finally managed to stop the rushing water.

"I'm sorry," Theo said. "I forgot that I was supposed to turn the water off before working on the sink."

Ava couldn't remember the last time she had laughed so hard. Actually, she couldn't remember the last time she'd laughed at all.

Soaked but still chuckling, they shared a moment of unguarded joy—two people, splattered in water, finding a little bit of solace in each other's company amidst the messy business of mending what had been broken.

"You have a great laugh, Ava," Theo said, smiling. "I hope I get to hear it more."

She smiled shyly, suddenly self-conscious. Her hair and clothing were drenched. "I better go change. I'm sure my brothers still have some clothing upstairs if you want to borrow some. I took some boxes down from the attic yesterday."

Theo glanced down at his wet clothes that would take hours to dry. "I'd appreciate that, if you don't mind."

"Of course. I'll be right back." She went upstairs, and a few minutes later, she was wearing a dry t-shirt and jeans. She handed him a white men's shirt with black pants. "They were packed away for a long time, so they might be a bit dusty. Sorry."

"That's okay. Thank you," Theo said. "What do you say we go get lunch after this? Breakfast was great, but we've been getting so much done, I'm famished."

"There's a really good diner downtown that has great burgers," Ava said.

"Sounds good."

Theo went into the bathroom to change, setting the clothes on the counter. He examined them for a moment, the fabric bearing the marks of work and the gentle fray of use. Looking at the stitching and lack of tags, these were clearly homemade, expertly fashioned, probably by Ava's mother. He couldn't help but wonder about which of Ava's brothers these had belonged to.

Ava was gathering some supplies for the remainder of the day. She turned as Theo stepped out of the bathroom. She paused, her actions stilled. For a moment, she simply stared at him, a complex mix of emotions playing across her face. It was as if she was seeing more than just Theo—she was watching a ghost of times past.

"Sorry," Ava finally said, her voice catching slightly as she averted her eyes. "Those are my brother Samuel's clothes."

Theo stood still, confused, his mind swimming with unasked questions. He could tell the clothing had been worn, the threads softened by use and time, but now he also sensed the weight of history they carried for Ava. Her words hung in the air, a story half-told.

Could Samuel have left before he went to prison? Perhaps she hadn't seen him in years. Theo recognized there was a delicate fabric of family history that Ava was not yet ready to unravel.

"Thank you for letting me borrow them. I'll wash them and return them to you," he said.

Ava nodded.

Choosing to respect her privacy by steering the conversation back to their work, Theo glanced around, taking stock of what they might tackle next after lunch. He gestured to the basement door. "Is that the basement? Is there anything downstairs that needs fixing? I can take a look if there's anything that—"

"No!" Ava blurted out, a hint of fear flashing across her features so quickly that Theo almost doubted he saw it. She darted across the room, blocking the door. "Let's not go down there. There's nothing to fix. It's a big mess right now."

The intensity of her response took him aback, and he realized with sudden clarity that there was much more to it than that. It was more than just another room for her—it also held a story, a piece of her past she wasn't ready to confront or share. Perhaps every inch of this house told a story of her past that she wasn't ready to revisit yet, but the basement held the darkest secrets of all.

Theo's instinct as a detective was to delve deeper, to understand the cause of her fear, but he saw the discomfort in her eyes and knew better than to press. He wanted to help her through this more than anything, but maybe for now, that meant going to the diner and getting burgers together with some lighthearted conversation.

Quickly, he changed the subject again, hoping to ease the tension that had abruptly filled the room. "That's okay. I'm famished. Let's go eat," he said with a gentle smile, changing the subject as smoothly as he could.

Ava seemed relieved, her forced smile thanking him for the reprieve. She walked briskly to the door, a clear sign that she was ready to leave the weight of that conversation behind. Theo followed, determined to focus on the tasks at hand, all the while storing away the knowledge that Ava carried scars deeper than what could be seen on the surface.

Chapter Nineteen

The midday sun filtered through the windows of Molly's Diner as Theo and Ava slid into a booth, the red vinyl of the seat creaking beneath them. As familiar tunes buzzed softly from the jukebox in the corner, Ava's gaze landed on a 'Help Wanted' sign taped to the window of the library across the street. She bit her lip in thought, wondering if this was a town she could actually call home, at least for a while. Maybe she would apply for a job here.

When their server padded away after taking their order, Theo leaned in, "Something on your mind? You seem quiet."

Ava glanced out the window before answering, "I was thinking I might apply for a job at the library. I do love books."

"That sounds like a great idea."

"I'm just not sure how long I'll stay in this town, but I should get a job, even if I stay only a few months. I really do like it here. I was talking to Freya, an *Englisher* who lives in the community with her husband, Adam. They really love it here. Adam Lapp is a police officer. Do you know him?"

"Oh, yes! I know Adam. We work together at CPDU. They recently had a baby, right?"

"Yes, a baby boy."

"He was on leave when I was here working Anneliese Kulp's case. He told me about how he lives in the community and how he grew up Amish. He says the guys at the station used to make fun of him for being Amish. He says he took it personally at first and then realized they were just fooling around. So, you can live in the Amish community without being Amish?" Theo asked. "That's interesting."

"Yes, there are several *Englishers* who live there. It's not like it's totally closed off. It's just a large group of Amish people who live close together in one area. Anyone can live there, really."

"So, that might be something you might want to do?"

"The house has…bad memories, but I have friends here. I'm glad I'm selling the house, but I would like to live in town. I don't know where else I would go. Definitely not back to the city. I could find a smaller place nearby. I'm not sure."

He nodded in agreement, "Yeah, I couldn't do city living again after…everything." The conversation drifted naturally to lighter topics. "What do you like to write?" he asked, avoiding the topic of her mother, which he sensed was difficult for her to talk about.

"I've been working on a fantasy novel for a few years," Ava confessed, her voice dropping to a more wistful tone. "But I feel stuck. It's like the story's incomplete, and I can't figure out how to improve it. I was lacking inspiration, though I'm hoping I might find some here."

"That's understandable," Theo said, smiling encouragingly. "You'll find your way back to it. I actually love to read, when I have some time. I love reading science fiction and fantasy."

"Not thrillers or mysteries?" Ava asked.

"I only end up noticing all the things that are unrealistic in the police procedural parts of the book, so I try to avoid most of those." He chuckled. "Though some are very well written, I should add. You know, if you ever want me to read your work, I'd love to," he offered.

"Oh, it's not ready yet," Ava said shyly. "I haven't let anyone read it yet."

"I imagine that would be scary, letting people read what you wrote for the first time."

"Terrifying." She nodded.

Curiosity sparked in his eyes as he asked, "What else do you like to do for fun?"

She laughed softly, "Haven't figured that out yet."

Honestly, she hadn't had the freedom to explore new hobbies yet, but maybe here she would.

Ava looked curiously at Theo. "What about you, what do you like to do for fun? Outside of work."

Theo chuckled and glanced down at his hands briefly before sharing. "Honestly, I work a lot, and I guess it's become my life in many ways," he began. "But when I find the time," Theo continued, his eyes brightening a little, "I enjoy visiting with my family. Fishing with my dad is one of my favorite things to do. It's peaceful, not much like my day-to-day. He used to take me fishing often when I was growing up. It's our thing. And I play basketball with some guys from the station now and then. It's fun."

Ava smiled at the mention of basketball, picturing him amidst the laughter and competitive shouts of a friendly game. It was nice to hear about the aspects of his life that brought him joy, finding in his answer the common threads that connected many lives—family, relaxation, and community.

The mood grew slightly serious again as Theo added quietly, "You know, I understand if there are things you don't want to tell me...we've just met."

Her eyes met his, holding a sincerity mixed with trepidation. "There's a lot about me you don't know, and honestly, I'm scared to tell you. It's...a lot. Even in your line of work, you might still be shocked."

Theo's voice was gentle, reassuring. "When you're ready, I'm here."

Encouraged, Ava took a deep breath. "I can start by explaining why my brothers and mother are in prison. Ian, my oldest brother, killed my father. My dad was a cruel, manipulative, controlling, angry man."

"I'm sorry, Ava," Theo said, not sure what else to say. "And your mother and other brothers?"

Ava's composure wavered as she opened her mouth, her past sitting on the tip of her tongue. But then she closed her eyes briefly and shook her head. "I'm sorry. I can't revisit that right now. I thought I was ready, but I'm not."

He reached across the table and touched her hand briefly. "Take all the time you need, Ava. I'm just grateful you're here with me today."

She smiled, feeling her connection to him become even stronger.

As their food arrived, steaming burgers and crispy fries, the mood lifted. They shared a smile and turned their attention to the meal and the house repairs they hoped to finish that day.

Theo sipped his milkshake, searching Ava's face as he gauged her connection to the place where she'd grown up. "Do you ever think about rejoining the Amish community?" he asked, curiosity lacing his voice.

Ava contemplated his question, her gaze drifting outside the diner window momentarily before returning to meet Theo's eyes. "No, I don't think I could. It's my dream to be a writer, and that means needing access to things like the internet and a computer to submit my book to publishers or to self-publish online, and using the internet and computers inside the home isn't allowed in the Amish way of life. Also, I am not sure I could live the Amish lifestyle, not after everything that's happened to me," she continued, her hands wrapped around the milkshake glass. "I'm not sure. But I know I love this community; I love being close to my friends here."

Theo nodded. "When Anneliese Kulp went missing, I was so impressed how everyone came together immediately to help."

"Most people do always help each other in the Amish community. I loved growing up here."

A shadow crossed her face, so he changed the subject.

"So, how do you want to publish your book? I keep hearing about self-publishing more and more," he said.

"I don't want to go back to NYC, but I do want to publish my book. The industry has changed over the past decade; it's not necessary to move to the city for that anymore. It can all be done online. I've been weighing the options between traditional publishing and self-publishing, which is becoming more prevalent and is even putting publishers out of business. But it's a huge learning curve. I had a classmate who makes good money self-publishing her series online. She learned marketing. It was incredible to hear her story, how she built up her fanbase from nothing," Ava recalled, "but I'd be willing to learn everything I need to if it's the right path for my b ook."

Theo nodded, impressed with her knowledge and drive. "It sounds like you are willing to put in the work to become successful. And you'd have the benefit of doing it right from here, where you're comfortable," he said, reinforcing her ideas. "If that's what you want."

Ava smiled, a warmth blossoming in her chest. Theo's support, even as someone new in her life, was undeniably comforting. It felt like another piece falling into place, another reason to think she might just find the fresh start she was looking for in this place that was both familiar and full of potential.

"You like your job?" Ava asked.

"I love it," Theo said. "But I have to admit, sometimes it is extremely difficult. Cases stay with me. It's hard to believe how cruel people can be. I do love helping people, but I often feel like I'm not doing enough. I arrest the criminals, but I want to do more to help the survivors recover and rebuild their lives."

Theo could see the resolve in Ava's eyes, a determination that was rooted in both personal experience and a charitable heart. "One day," she began with a hopeful tone, "I hope to open a shelter for women and children who have been victims of crime or abuse. I'm sure you know that too often, they fall back into the cycle of violence and victimization because they don't know how to support themselves or stay safe."

"You're right," Theo said. "It's true. Women who leave their abusive partners often end up going back to them because of that. If they had a place nearby like that to go to, it would make a huge difference in so many lives."

He could sense that this was more than just an idea for her; it was her passion, forged from her own hardships and trials. Ava spoke of her vision for the shelter, a place where victims could not only find refuge but also gain the skills they needed to carve out a self-sufficient, secure life for themselves.

"I would have experts in different trades and professions come in and teach them how to earn a living legally, give them the tools they need to avoid resorting to a life of crime or getting money through dangerous, illegal means. I could teach writing. Maybe I could find people to teach cooking or budgeting or how to start a business." Her voice held the fervor of someone who had given much thought to the subject; it was personal for her, a need to give others the help she once craved. Then her voice softened as she stared out the window.

"I wish I would have had a place to go when I first left here..." Her voice trailed off, lost in the contemplation of a past that could have unfolded differently.

Theo's mind was full of questions, but most of all, he could see the pain in her eyes. But her resolve was still strong. Her desire to create a safe haven for those like her was a testament to her strength and character.

He offered a gentle smile, full of respect and empathy for her plight and her dreams. "That's a powerful goal, Ava. If you ever decide to make that happen, I think you'd do an incredible job," he said, his admiration for her clear.

Ava looked back at him, a silent gratitude in her eyes for his words of encouragement. It was a flicker of hope that with support and shared understanding, her aspirations could one day become a beacon of hope for others.

Theo's expression softened as he leaned back in the booth. "That's an amazing dream," he said, a trace of admiration in his voice. "Actually, doing something meaningful like that, it's something I'd like to be a part of one day too. I've seen so much suffering and trauma in my line of work, and I often don't get to see the victims after my work with them is complete. I'd like to also be more involved in helping them recover and get back on their feet. There's something about giving back, especially to those who've been through the worst of it," Theo said, his gaze steady on Ava. "That's what life is all about—helping others."

Ava quietly acknowledged his words with a nod, feeling a growing kinship with Theo. The understanding that they both had a desire to help others, perhaps rooted in their own painful experiences, added a layer of depth to their budding relationship. It was the kind of shared purpose that could, in time, become a strong bond and a united effort toward making that shared vision a reality.

Theo motioned for the check at the end of their meal, and when it arrived, he reached for it without hesitation. Ava, too, reached for her purse, intending to cover her share.

"Let me pay for it," she said, pulling out her wallet. "You're the one helping me fix up the house. It's the least I can do."

Theo waved her off gently, but firmly. "My parents raised me right," he said with a small smile. "They taught me that a gentleman always pays on a date. Besides, you made us breakfast."

Ava's eyebrows arched in playful surprise. "So, this is a date?" There was a lightness to her voice, but her question hung in the air.

He glanced up from his wallet, meeting her eyes. "Yes, of course, I mean... I thought it was. Is that okay?" There was a hint of vulnerability behind his confidence, a need for reassurance.

Her smile broadened as she nodded. "Yes."

They left the diner with the small thrill of mutual understanding, of something special between them. It wasn't just lunch now; it was a shared moment that marked the beginning of something more.

As they drove back to Ava's house, the air between them was lighter, filled with possibilities and the anticipation of continuing their work together—not just on the house, but perhaps on the foundations of a budding relationship.

Chapter Twenty

As the day's work wound down, Ava wiped a bead of sweat from her brow, stepping back to admire the progress they'd made together. Her hands were dirty and getting blisters, but there was satisfaction in the ache of her muscles, a gratifying exhaustion that came from a day spent doing a job well done.

Theo was collecting the last of the tools, the early evening light casting long shadows in the yard. Ava watched him for a moment, the quiet of the approaching night settling around them. They'd talked and laughed throughout the day, their easy camaraderie deepening with each shared task and story.

Finally, Theo stood straight, brushing his hands on his jeans. He took a hesitant step toward her, his expression earnest. "Ava, may I see you again?" he asked, his voice holding a hint of something more serious than the light banter of earlier.

Caught by the intensity in his gaze, Ava felt a flutter in her chest. "I'd like that," she said quietly, surprised by the quick beat of her heart.

"The connection I feel with you…it's something I haven't felt in a long time," he admitted, and there was a vulnerability hanging between them, raw and unguarded. "Sorry, maybe it's too soon for me to say that to you, but it's the truth."

Ava knew exactly what he meant; a warmth that seemed to radiate from her heart and flood her entire being. "I feel the same way," she confessed.

She never thought she'd ever be able to trust a man after what she'd been through. But she'd only known him a day, so maybe she was getting way ahead of herself.

He stepped closer, the setting sun framing him. "I can come back to help on Sunday after church. We still have a lot of painting to do, but you also deserve a break. There's a fancy Italian restaurant downtown... What do you think about going to dinner there Monday night after I get off work?"

"You don't have to keep helping me," Ava said.

"I want to, if you'll let me," Theo said. "Sunday is my day off. I can come back again next weekend on my days off, too, or on weeknights."

"Well, okay then," Ava said, her smile genuine and full of anticipation. "Thank you. I really appreciate your help, and dinner would be nice."

A surge of excitement shot through her at the prospect of spending more time in Theo's company, exploring whatever it was that was blossoming between them.

As he smiled back, there was a moment where everything else seemed to fall away: the old fears, the pain of her past, the uncertainties of the future. There was just Ava, Theo, and the promise of another day together. She agreed, and with that simple word, she felt herself stepping forward into a new chapter, hand in hand with someone who might just understand her journey more than she could have hoped.

On Sunday afternoon, the pair continued working to restore the house to its former glory, mostly painting. Ava was shocked how much faster the painting went with Theo helping than when she worked alone. With light chatter and more discussion about aligned interests and attitudes, the time passed quickly.

***

Ava walked into the local library on Monday morning, her heart pounding with a mix of hope and nervousness. The quiet, welcoming atmosphere was a stark contrast to the bustling streets of New York City she had grown somewhat accustomed to. She approached the front desk, where a friendly-looking librarian was organizing a stack of books.

"Excuse me," Ava began, her voice slightly tentative. "I saw the sign that you're looking for help. I'd like to apply."

The librarian, whose name tag read "Denise," looked up with a warm smile. "Actually, yes, we are looking to hire a librarian," she replied.

Ava's spirits lifted instantly. "Great! Can I fill out an application?"

Denise shook her head, her smile widening. "No need for that. I don't even have one. I can just interview you now. I've never seen you around town before. Did you just move here?"

"Yes, I just moved back," Ava said, nodding. "I'm living in the Amish community. I know everyone there. My name is Ava Sullivan."

"Oh, Ava," Denise said, her curiosity piqued. "I've heard about you. I remember back when you were on the news." She paused. "I was so sorry to hear what happened. But the Amish folks say you're a kind soul. What about your prior jobs? Do you have work experience?"

Ava took a deep breath. "I worked at a diner in New York City when I was going to college."

Denise's eyes sparkled with interest. "College, huh? What did you major in?"

"I got a degree in English," Ava answered, feeling a surge of pride. "I want to be a novelist. I love books."

Denise's smile broadened. "I have a good feeling about you. Besides, I really need the help. So, you're hired."

Ava felt a rush of elation wash over her. "Really? Thank you so much!"

They discussed her schedule and other details. She would work full-time, which meant she could only work on the house in the evenings and on weekends, but she needed to work full-time to support herself.

As Ava left the library, she couldn't help but feel that this job was a significant step toward something more permanent. The thought filled her with a sense of possibility and hope, making her believe that maybe, just maybe, her path was starting to become clearer.

***

Theo's car pulled up to Ava's house right on time that evening, finding her waiting on the front porch. As she descended the steps, he immediately noticed how lovely she looked in her elegant black dress. He got out of the car and opened the passenger door for her.

"You look beautiful," he said as she approached, his sincerity making her cheeks warm with a soft blush.

"Thank you."

They arrived at the restaurant which was filled with candlelight and quiet conversation. As they were escorted to their table, the gentle clinking of fine dinnerware and the hum of a violin in the background filled the space.

"This restaurant is so nice," Ava said, looking around. She appreciated him taking her here, but she suddenly felt her heart begin to race. Trying to ignore it, she walked with Theo as they followed the hostess to their table.

As the waiter took their order and drifted away, the soft clinking of silverware and glasses setting a relaxed pace to the evening, Theo turned to Ava with an easy smile.

This was a nice place, and she wanted to enjoy her evening with this wonderful man, but her anxiety was only growing. In New York, she was taken to many fancy restaurants on her assignments, and this reminded her of those times. Her mouth suddenly went dry. Maybe if she made conversation with Theo she would feel better.

"I got a job at the library," she told him. "I'll be working full-time, which means I can only work on the house in the evenings and on the weekends, but I need the work. I'm just grateful for a job."

"That's great news," he replied cheerfully.

"I'm excited. I start tomorrow, actually. I love books, so I think I'll enjoy it," Ava said, leaning forward. "Tell me about your family."

He smiled, a mixture of pride and concern lacing his expression. "My sister Natalie is incredible. She's got this dream of becoming a country singer. Her voice is amazing. And the songs she writes are wonderful...straight from the heart."

"That sounds wonderful," Ava replied, genuinely intrigued. She glanced around, suddenly feeling as if everyone was looking at her, but no one was. *Keep it together,* she told herself. "Is she pursuing it professionally?"

"Well, she's also practical. She's in school right now to become a dental hygienist. She insisted on having a 'real job' as a backup plan." He paused, chuckling, before continuing. "But the last time I saw her, I don't know, she just seemed stressed. When I asked, she chalked it up to schoolwork and she had a project due that she forgot about." He paused. "Are you okay? You seem...nervous."

"I'm fine," she said, waving her hand. Ava sensed the shift in his demeanor, the subtle furrow between his brows. "You sound worried about your sister."

Theo nodded, a small admission of his vulnerability. "I am. We've always been incredibly close, always there for each other growing up."

"It must be tough to see her stressed when she's working so hard for her dreams," Ava said, understanding the bond of siblings, even amidst her own complicated family dynamics.

He sighed, visibly appreciating Ava's empathy. "It is. I just hope she finds a balance, you know? Doesn't lose sight of that passion for her music while she's buried in textbooks. She was always so talkative and bubbly until recently."

"With a brother like you supporting her, I'm sure she'll manage both just fine," Ava said, offering reassurance. Now she couldn't ignore her hammering heart any longer. The server brought them water, saying she would be back in a moment to take their orders. Ava she gulped down the water, grateful for the distraction. Was it hot in here?

Theo looked at her with concern. "You don't seem fine, Ava. What's wrong?"

"Sorry, Theo," she said. "I've never been to this restaurant before, but it's...bringing up bad memories. I'm so sorry. I didn't realize this would happen."

"No need to be sorry. Let's go somewhere else then," Theo said, standing up.

"We're already here. I'll be fine."

"I want you to have a nice night. Come on. There's a fun pizza place down the street." He held out his hand. "How does that sound?"

"Pizza sound great." She smiled, took his hand, and they left.

They walked down the street to a casual pizza restaurant with brick walls, scratched wooden tables, and upbeat music.

"Better?" Theo asked, smiling.

"Much better." Ava smiled. "It smells delicious." She looked down at her elegant black dress. "I feel overdressed, though."

"You look amazing," Theo assured her. "Don't worry. It's laid back here. Come on, let's order. What's your favorite kind of pizza?"

Ava took a moment to think. "You know, I'm not really sure. I've only had pizza a few times in New York when I was going to college."

"My favorite is Hawaiian. A lot of people think pineapple on pizza is gross, but I've always like it."

"I've never had it, but I'll try it."

They ordered their pizza and sat down in a booth, continuing their conversation.

"Please tell me more about your family," Ava said.

"My parents just got back from this amazing Alaskan cruise," Theo shared warmly, the pride evident in his tone. "It was their way of celebrating thirty years of being married. Can you believe that? Thirty years and they are still in love."

Ava's eyes sparked with interest. "Thirty years? That's incredible. They must have seen so many changes together."

"Absolutely. They really have," Theo nodded. "My dad, he's retired from the police force. He spends a lot of his time fishing and has this hobby of making wooden birdhouses. I think he likes the peace, you know, after all those years of public service."

"That sounds lovely," Ava replied. "He must be very skilled with his hands."

"He is," Theo agreed. "And my mom, well, after years of being the secretary at the doctor's office and keeping everyone on track, she's channeling her love into quilting. She creates these beautiful, intricate designs."

"And the cruise—was it their first big trip since retiring?"

"Oh, no, not at all. They love traveling to new places." Theo chuckled lightly. "It's great to see them so happy and in love, even after all this time. I think it's what made my childhood so happy—they were always such a team, you know? I never had to worry about my parents getting divorced."

Her parents had never been that way. Had they ever been in love?

The server brought them their pizza, and as they ate, Theo told Ava more about his family. Listening to Theo, Ava felt both touched by the closeness of his family and also felt envious of the love that clearly filled every memory he had of home.

As Ava listened, a pang of longing tugged at her heart, contrasting Theo's idyllic memories with the shades of her own dark past. She envied the love and happiness that seemed to be the bedrock of his family, so starkly different from hers.

Theo's voice trailed off as he noticed the change in Ava's expression as she frowned. "What's wrong?" he asked.

Ava sighed, a single breath carrying so much of her story. "You're so blessed to have such a happy, loving family. My family...it was always broken. We went to church every week, pretending to be fine, but we never were fine. My father tore us apart with his anger and violence," she whispered, her voice resonating with remembered pain.

Theo noticed a change in Ava's demeanor as the conversation took a turn, her eyes clouding over with a mixture of memories and emotions. Gently, he prompted her, "You mentioned having siblings too, right?"

Ava nodded, taking a moment to find the right words. "Yes, three brothers. Ian and Jake... they grew up to be like our father, I'm afraid. And there was also Samuel." Her voice was steady, but there was an undercurrent of sadness.

Theo's brows knitted in concern. "Like him in what way?"

She looked down at her hands, folded neatly on her lap. "Angry and violent. They never quite escaped that part of him, even after they left home." She looked up, her face a tapestry of complex feelings.

A moment of silence passed between them.

"And Samuel?" he asked quietly, sensing there was more to her story.

Ava's lips quirked with a fond yet pained smile. "Samuel's the youngest. He's different...quiet and gentle. He stayed home with my mother, even during the weeks after my father died...until he and my mother were arrested." She exhaled slowly. "I think...he stayed to keep an eye on *Mamm*, to protect her from *Daed*."

Theo's heart ached for what Ava and her family went through. "That's an awful burden for a young man to carry," he said softly.

"It is," Ava agreed, a melancholic note in her voice. "I think Samuel never really got a chance to live his own life because he was too busy worrying about hers."

"About Jake... I told you about how my brother Ian killed my father. Jake was also violent, like my father. I mean, I know it was no excuse for them to carry on the cycle of abuse, but I wonder how my brothers would have turned out if my father had been a gentle, loving father. Jake married an Amish woman named Olivia, who he abused and almost killed several times. She killed him in self-defense. It makes me sad that my brother died, but I don't hold it against her."

"I'm so sorry, Ava," Theo said. "I'm glad you're not angry with her. I'm sure she was just trying to survive. But I'm sorry you lost your brother in such a horrible way."

Theo reached out across the table, covering her hand with his own as an offer of comfort. He was glad for her trust in him, that she could bare her soul in such a way.

"This is a bit heavy for dinner conversation, isn't it?" Ava asked softly. Rather than dwell in sadness, Ava steered the conversation toward a lighter topic—travel. "I would love to see more of the world, like your parents have," she said, her eyes brightening with the prospect of new experiences beyond the confines of her past. "I wonder what Alaska was like. It's really quite beautiful in the photos I've seen."

"They said it was absolutely incredible," he said.

Theo imagined then what it would be like to show Ava the wonders she'd missed—exotic islands or ancient ruins in Europe—the rush of seeing something for the first time through her eyes. He kept these thoughts to himself, though they warmed him with a hopeful glow.

Curious to know more about Theo's past, Ava prompted him to share stories from his childhood. He obliged, weaving tales filled with humor and mischief about him and his sister, which filled their meal with laughter and a shared understanding that the past, no matter how dark, could not overshadow the potential of their future, wherever it might lead.

"What made you want to become a police officer?" Ava asked.

Theo paused for a moment, considering Ava's question and the layers of personal history that fed into his career choice. He took a sip of his water, buying himself a moment to collect his thoughts before answering.

"My father was a cop, but that's not the only reason why. It's always been about making a difference for me," Theo began, his voice steady and reflective. "I saw things growing up—friends who made bad choices, neighborhoods that needed help. I guess I wanted to be a part of the solution, to help people find a better path."

He glanced down at his hands, turning his glass on the table. "And then, there was my dad's influence, too. He raised me with this strong sense of justice, of right and wrong. I wanted to take that to the next level."

Ava listened, seeing the sincerity on his face, understanding that for Theo, the badge was more than just a job—it was a commitment to serving the community, a way to channel his values into action.

"It's not easy, of course, and there is a ton of paperwork," he added with a rueful smile. "But at the end of the day, if I can make even a small difference in someone's life, if I can keep someone safe or steer them in the right direction, then it's worth it."

In Theo's words, Ava could hear echoes of her own desires—to mend, to heal, and to rebuild. It was another thread that connected them, a mutual yearning to contribute something meaningful to the world around them.

"I think that's wonderful," Ava said. "We both want to help people."

"I always hoped to make a difference, and once I became a police officer, I started working toward becoming a detective. I was actually promoted to detective while working on Anneliese Kulp's case. That case was life changing."

Ava watched him, seeing the dedication in his eyes, the way his hands gestured as he spoke about his work. It was a passion truly lived, not merely spoken.

He then softly added, "Bringing those responsible to justice doesn't fix the loss, but it offers a flicker of light in the darkest situation a family can face." Theo's expression turned distant for a moment as he delved into a memory, a story that clearly still held sway over him. "Actually, there's a particular moment from my childhood that made me realize I wanted to be a police officer," he said, his voice tinged with nostalgia.

Ava leaned forward, listening intently.

"When I was younger, there was this kid in the neighborhood, Lucas. We'd known each other since we were toddlers, running wild through the streets, kind of inseparable." Theo's smile was a bittersweet one as he recounted the days of his youth. "Lucas was a good kid, but he got mixed up with some troublemakers in our teen years. Before we knew it, small pranks turned into shoplifting, then into grand theft."

Ava watched Theo's face harden slightly as he continued. "One night, things went too far. They tried to break into a local store, and Lucas was caught. Everyone else ran off, leaving him behind to take the fall. I remember the night the police officer came to our door. The officer was there to tell us what had happened and because he knew we were close friends and he wanted to see if I knew anything."

He looked at Ava, his eyes earnest. "But instead of just seeing Lucas as another delinquent kid, that officer took the time with him. He talked to Lucas about choices, consequences, how one night—one choice—can change your life. He treated Lucas with respect, got him involved in community service. Lucas...well, he turned his life around after that. Now he's a youth pastor, helping kids turn their lives around if they need it."

"Wow, that's incredible," Ava said.

Theo nodded. "I saw how that police officer changed his life, and I wanted to do that, too."

Folding his napkin idly, Theo's gaze was steady. "It showed me that police work wasn't just about arrests and enforcing laws. It's also about guiding people back, giving them a second chance. That officer was a role model to me, and I wanted to be that for someone else."

Ava remained silent as she processed his story, understanding more deeply the kind of man Theo had become because of his experiences. It was not just the injustice that had driven him but witnessing the power of compassion and the impact it could have on a life gone astray.

After leaving the restaurant, the night had settled like a soft blanket around them as Theo drove Ava home. The evening had been a tapestry of laughter and confessions, of stories shared and barriers gently broken down.

When they arrived at her house, Theo turned to her with a hopeful gleam in his eyes. "I don't want the night to end just yet, at least not without the promise of another date," he said. "How about a movie the night after tomorrow? Would you like that? Or is it too soon for another date?"

A movie. Ava felt both excitement and a flutter of nervousness at the prospect. "I've... I've actually never been to a movie theater," she admitted, watching his reaction closely.

"Really? Never?" Theo was clearly surprised.

"When I was in New York, I was always so busy with school," Ava explained, but her thoughts lingered on the years that followed—years when the idea of such a simple joy like going to the movies was a freedom far beyond her reach.

She shifted in her seat, facing him more directly. "And before that, growing up, I never did because the Amish aren't allowed to watch movies. So, I've never been to a movie theater. My friends told me that sometimes Amish teens sneak out to the theater, but I..." She bent her head. "I never got that chance."

"Why not?" Theo asked.

Ava hesitated.

"Sorry. You don't have to tell me. Anyway, I'm truly honored to be the one to take you to your first movie." He smiled warmly at her, honor resonated in his voice. "How do you feel about comedies?"

They chatted for a moment about the options before settling on a title that sounded funny and lighthearted, a contrast to the deeper currents they'd navigated during dinner.

Theo drove Ava home, then they walked together to her porch. Under the soft glow of the moon, Theo took her hand in his, a comforting yet electrifying contact. "I just want to get to know you, Ava," he said, his voice tinged with a heartfelt honesty. "And I want to be honest—I really like you."

Her heart swelled, the trust and affection in his gaze mirrored by her own feelings. "I really like you too, Theo," she said, a warmth radiating from her words.

His eyes lit up. "I'm excited to see where this will go."

With a tender affection, he kissed her on the cheek, then stepped back, holding her gaze for a moment longer before he turned to leave.

Ava watched him go, her heart lighter than it had been in years. Inside, surrounded by the quiet of her home, she allowed herself to bask in the happiness of the evening, the sense of unfolding possibilities. Walking on air and twirling around in the kitchen, she held onto the budding sensation that, perhaps for the first time in her life, she might be falling in love.

Chapter Twenty-one

Ava stood at the entrance of the local library the next morning, taking a deep breath as she stepped inside for her first day on the job. The quiet hum of activity was comforting, and she felt a mix of excitement and nervousness bubbling in her chest. Denise, the head librarian, greeted her with a warm smile.

"Welcome, Ava! We're so glad to have you here," Denise said.

"Thank you," Ava replied. "I'm really excited to be here. I just love books."

Denise chuckled. "We all do. You'll love it here." She led Ava to the back room where they stored returned books. "Let's start with sorting the books. I'll show you our system."

She patiently explained the organizational system, showing Ava how to sort books by genre and author. Ava's eyes followed Denise's hands as they moved quickly and adeptly through the piles of books, feeling a bit overwhelmed but determined to learn.

"The system might seem confusing at first, but you'll get the hang of it," Denise reassured her. "And if you ever need help, just ask."

Ava nodded, absorbing the information. Denise handed her a stack of books and guided her to the main library area, where Candace, another librarian, was sorting through a cart of books.

"Candace, this is Ava," Denise introduced them. "She's starting today. Could you help show her around?"

"Of course!" Candace said with a bright smile. "Welcome, Ava. Let me show you how to check out books next."

Candace led Ava to the checkout desk and walked her through the process, explaining each step carefully. As they scanned books and interacted with patrons, Candace patiently answered all of Ava's questions, making sure she felt comfortable with the new system.

"The organizational system can be a bit tricky at first," Candace admitted with a sympathetic smile. "But don't worry, everyone needs a little time to get used to it."

Ava spent the next few hours shadowing Candace, learning the ropes of the job. As the day went on, she felt more at ease, the initial confusion slowly giving way to understanding. Being surrounded by the beloved smell of books and the gentle rustle of pages was soothing, and she appreciated the sense of purpose it brought. She enjoyed seeing children and teenagers come and check out books, eager to take them home and read them.

During a quiet moment, Ava found herself shelving a stack of historical novels. She took a deep breath, feeling a sense of accomplishment. She was starting over, making her own way. This job was a step toward rebuilding her life.

Towards the end of her shift, Denise and Candace checked in with her. "How's it going so far?" Denise asked, her tone encouraging.

"It's going well," Ava replied, smiling. "Thank you both for helping me. I'm grateful to have this job. It means a lot to me."

"We're happy to have you," Candace said warmly. "You're going to do great here, Ava."

As Ava walked back to the front desk to finish her shift, she felt the satisfaction of a full day's work. The library was more than just a job—it was a step toward a brighter future, a place where she could build a life she was proud of.

With Denise and Candace by her side, Ava knew she could overcome the challenges ahead. She was part of a community now, and that made all the difference.

Her second day of work also went well, as Ava enjoyed falling into a more comfortable routine and looked forward to her date with Theo that evening.

***

"Would you mind if we meet up with my sister after the movie for dinner?" Theo asked on the way to the movie theater the next evening. "She called earlier, sounding pretty stressed. I figured it'd be nice for her to join us so you two can meet."

"That would be wonderful. I'd love to meet Natalie," Ava replied, a smile dancing on her lips. The idea of meeting Theo's sister, the woman with a beautiful voice and dreams of being a country singer, expanded the bubble of Ava's new experiences even further.

Inside the theater, as they found their seats, Ava couldn't help but gaze around with wide, wonder-filled eyes. Theo guided her to their spots and excused himself for a moment. He returned with a large bucket of popcorn and two drinks, handing her a drink and the popcorn with a grin.

"Oh, wow!" she cried. "Thank you."

"Can't watch a movie without popcorn," he said, settling down beside her.

Ava took a handful, savoring the salty, buttery crunch as the lights dimmed and the screen came to life. The size of the moving images, the stunning clarity, and the enveloping sound captivated Ava completely. When Theo reached for her hand, she let herself be grounded by his touch, their fingers interlocking naturally and settling on the armrest. Butterflies fluttered in her stomach, and she felt safe and cherished as they held hands through the whole movie.

They laughed together at all the funny scenes, the shared joy a bridge between their worlds. Ava let herself drift into the fantasy unfolding before her.

In the back of her mind, a thought flickered, a wistful feeling—how she wished she'd met Theo a long, long time ago. But then, the warmth of his hand reminded her that what mattered was the here and now, the present moment that buzzed with laughter, connection, and a budding sense of belonging.

As the movie credits rolled and the theater lights slowly brightened, Ava blinked, still caught in the lingering magic of the film. Theo turned to her, his eyes seeking hers as the other moviegoers began to shuffle out of their seats.

"So, what did you think?" Theo asked, the anticipation clear in his voice. He appeared eager to hear her take on her very first movie theater experience.

Ava's face broke into a wide, delighted smile, her eyes still reflecting the remnants of the cinematic world she had just witnessed. "I loved it," she replied, the genuine thrill making her voice lively and vibrant. "The screen, the sounds—it's like being in a whole different universe."

"I'm really glad you enjoyed it," Theo said, his own smile mirroring her enthusiasm. They stood up together, still hand in hand, taking their time as they moved with the crowd toward the exits. The buzz of conversation around them felt distant as they shared a connection, a common joy in the simple pleasure of a good movie and good company.

***

Theo and Ava entered the casual downtown restaurant, the chatter and clinking of dishes creating a cozy ambiance. It wasn't long before Natalie, Theo's sister, came into view. Theo's face lit up with affection as he approached her, Ava trailing beside him.

Theo reached over to introduce the two women. "Nat, this is Ava," he said, but he faltered, taken aback by Natalie's downcast eyes and a forced smile—a stark contrast to her usually vibrant demeanor.

"Nice to meet you, Natalie," Ava said, extending her hand warmly.

Natalie's response was soft, a mere whisper of her usual self. "Hi, Ava. It's nice to meet you too."

As they took their seats and everyone ordered glasses of water, Ava's intuition picked up on Natalie's discomfort. She watched Natalie monitor her phone like a lifeline, on alert for the next notification. It was something Ava recognized all too well from her own past.

"Expecting a call on your new phone?" Theo asked.

"Oh, one of my classmates is going to send me notes from a class I missed," Natalie said. "We have a test coming up, so it's important."

"So, Natalie, Theo tells me you're quite the singer," Ava ventured, attempting to draw her into conversation.

Natalie's response came with a delayed nod as she managed a thin smile. "Yeah, I had an audition recently." She picked up her menu, studying it.

"That's fantastic! How did it go?" Theo chimed in, though his brows knitted together at his sister's lack of enthusiasm.

"It was...okay," Natalie murmured, checking her watch again. "Actually, I'm seeing someone now...he works in the industry. A talent recruiter. I didn't get in with that audition, but he thinks he can get me an agent and maybe a record deal."

Ava glanced at Theo. His jaw had tightened slightly, eyes sharpening with concern. He tossed a brief look Ava's way, communicating a mixture of confusion and worry without a word.

"You've seemed a bit off tonight. Is everything okay with this new guy?" Theo pressed lightly, probing for more insight. "What's his name?"

"Jason." Natalie hesitated, a flash of fear crossing her features before she composed herself. "Yes, of course. Everything is fine. I've just been...busy with school," she said, with another glance at her phone that screamed a silent alarm.

Ava observed Natalie—the way her shoulders tensed, and the way she jumped slightly with each vibration from her phone. It was a familiar dance of anxiety and control, one Ava had danced herself. She had never met Natalie before, but compared to what Theo had said about her, she did not seem like her usual self.

It was all too familiar to Ava. Her past clung to her in that moment, reflecting back in Natalie's conditioned responses. She knew the signs of someone trying desperately to keep afloat in troubled waters, and she felt a deep, binding empathy for Theo's sister.

Or was she just jumping to conclusions? She hoped she was wrong about her suspicions.

Theo glanced at Ava, his expression clouding over; he was piecing together the signs just as Ava was.

"I noticed you still have two phones," Theo said, his detective instincts kicking in.

Natalie fumbled for a response that came out too quickly, too rehearsed. "Oh, yeah...I use both sometimes. I haven't switched over all my contacts, photos, and apps yet. Such a pain. I'm too busy."

The protective brother inside Theo surged as guilt pricked at his conscience for not having noticed these changes sooner. He had been so caught up with work, he had missed opportunities to dig deeper into the subtle shifts in Natalie's character the past few weeks. He started to formulate his next inquiry carefully.

The conversation lulled into an uneasy silence when Natalie's phone vibrated yet again, prompting a reaction from her that Ava had come to recognize all too well—a flinch.

Suddenly, Natalie pushed back her chair and stood up. "I need to go. I'm sorry," she announced abruptly.

Theo's confusion was near palpable, his voice tinged with a mix of concern and frustration. "We just got here, Nat. We haven't even ordered anything yet. Why do you have to go? This happened at the last family dinner too. What's going on with you lately?"

The waiter came over at that moment. "Would you like me to come back in a moment?"

"Yes, please," Ava said, and the waiter turned and walked away.

"I'm sorry. I just have to go," Natalie insisted, her eyes darting around the restaurant, not quite meeting either of theirs. "I'm sorry, I really can't stay." Her voice carried the unmistakable tone of urgency, of a person with no other options.

Ava leaned in, her tone gentle but firm. "Natalie, are you in trouble? Can we help?"

But before Natalie could answer, a man strode into the restaurant with a proprietary air. He was tall and good-looking, in his early thirties, with dark hair and a mustache. He wore a dress shirt with black pants and an expensive silver watch. Most people wouldn't notice, but Theo detected the outline of a firearm secured to the man's side, hidden under his shirt.

As soon as Ava saw him approaching them, she immediately stiffened, sensing his malicious intentions toward women—especially Natalie.

Without proper greetings, he grabbed Natalie by the arm, his grip tight. "We need to go, Natalie. Now," he barked, his impatience evident.

Theo was out of his chair in an instant, anger flashing in his eyes. "Hey! Don't manhandle her. That's my sister. Let her go and treat her with some respect. Jason, is it?"

"Yeah. Who's asking?" Jason asked.

"I'm her brother," Theo told him firmly.

Natalie intervened with a nervous chuckle, looking up at the imposing figure. "It's all right, Theo. I'm sorry, I really do have to go. I'm holding everyone up..." Her voice trailed off. Jason's tight grasp didn't falter as Natalie added a feeble, "I deserve it for being late."

"You don't deserve to be treated like this!" Theo insisted. He turned to the brute, standing his ground, even though the other man was bigger and taller than him. "Let go of her. Back off. You can't just come in here and drag her out like that."

Jason's eyes narrowed, and his stance grew more aggressive, his grip on Natalie's arm unyielding. "Mind your own business," he sneered, a hint of a threat lacing his words. The air was charged, every patron's eyes now fixed on the escalating situation.

Theo squared his shoulders, ready to defend his sister. "She is my business. She's my sister. You don't get to treat her like that."

"What are you going to do about it?" he challenged. "Do you want to take this outside?"

Theo hesitated. There was nothing he could arrest this man for—yet. And fighting him in the parking lot would only get him in trouble, even though he knew he could take him.

"That's what I thought," Jason scoffed. "Now back off."

Theo wanted to knock this guy's lights out more than anything. He knew he could win a fight against him. For a moment, he considered it, but he didn't want to damage the restaurant, get arrested himself, or injure any of the bystanders who were close by if it turned into a full-on fist fight or worse. If he let him go now, maybe he could wait and arrest him for a much more serious crime. So, Theo restrained himself, his hands balled into fists at his sides. The man stepped closer to him, challenging him, trying to intimidate him, but Theo refused to break eye contact or back down.

But then Natalie's voice pierced the standoff, tinged with fear. "Theo, please. Just stop," she pleaded, her eyes wide with a mix of fear and desperation. "It's better if you just...let me go. It's in my best interest, believe me."

The earnestness in her plea, the way her voice shook—Theo recognized the signs all too well. He knew this was more than a simple argument; it was an abusive power dynamic at work. But with Natalie's safety in the balance, he gritted his teeth and took a reluctant step back, locking eyes with the man who'd taken a rude hold on his sister's life. He definitely did not approve of this new "boyfriend," even if Natalie was convinced he could help launch her singing career.

At this point, the manager was looking at them. "Hey, mister. Get out of here or I'm calling the police," the manager shouted, pointing at Jason.

Jason glared at Theo. "This isn't over," he growled before turning away with Natalie.

No, it wasn't over, not at all. Theo would need to resolve this later, another way. He'd also encourage Natalie to break up with him.

As the door closed behind Natalie, Theo and Ava shared a resolve between them—this was not over. Not by a long shot. They shared a look—a silent vow—they would not let this go.

"Something is definitely wrong," Ava said. "The way she was jumpy and nervous, constantly glancing at her phone, and the way

Jason intimidated her... I hate to say it, but I think that man is controlling her, forcing her to do illegal things." She glanced around nervously at the other people in the restaurant, lowering her voice. "If you know what I mean."

"I think you're right. We need to follow them, now," Theo said. "Let's go." He grabbed Ava's hand, and they hurried out of the restaurant, careful not to let Natalie and her brute boyfriend see them.

From a discreet vantage point near the front door of the restaurant, Theo and Ava watched as Natalie was pulled, almost dragged, toward an expensive car. The man's hand was a vice-like grip on her slender arm, jerking her forward whenever she struggled to match his swift, irate pace. His voice, though muffled by the distance, carried the unmistakable cadence of anger and rebuke.

"You should've been on time. You ignored my first text. How many times do I have to warn you?" he chastised with venomous sharpness, visible even in the way his jaw tensed with each word.

Natalie's head was bowed, her voice a mere wisp of sound as she attempted to placate him. "I got the times mixed up," she said, imploring for some semblance of understanding, her face hidden yet surely painted with the strain of the situation.

"The clients don't like it when we're late," the man growled.

"Clients?" Ava whispered. No, this was not good. Not good at all. "That confirms my suspicions."

Theo and Ava exchanged grim looks.

"Prostitution," Theo whispered, rage against Jason building inside him. He wanted to wring the man's neck for what he was doing to Natalie—his innocent, sweet sister.

This was anything but a typical lover's quarrel—it had the signs of control, abuse, and danger. Ava's heart ached for Natalie, her ordeal resonating with past horrors she herself had endured.

Ava's brow furrowed, mirroring Theo's scowl, as they remained concealed in the shadows. Theo's hand was a clenched fist by his side, a gesture of contained fury and helplessness, his sister's well-being his only concern.

Natalie stumbled once, faltering from the sharp tug of her captor, but she regained her footing as they neared the passenger side of the car. Without a hint of gentleness, he opened the door and practically shoved her inside before slamming it shut with a force that made Ava wince. Then, striding to the driver's side, he continued his tirade, his words now lost in the space between them but his aggressive body language still clear.

Theo and Ava dashed inside his sedan, their hearts sprinting.

"Are you going to call for backup?" Ava asked.

"I can't, really. There is no crime to report. If we show up with a bunch of police, we might make a few arrests, but will never get convictions. But if we follow them, we might be able to arrest Jason and probably a lot more clients and pimps, possibly even make some big arrests. Something appears to be going down. I'll call my partner." As the call connected, he didn't wait for the standard greetings to conclude before he spoke.

"Barrett," he said, his words quick and terse. "I need your help." He explained the situation. "I can't really call it in. There hasn't been a crime. I think we should follow them and see if I'm right about this."

"Where are you?" Barrett asked.

"We're downtown Augusta, heading south into an alley off of Stark Street between Third and Fourth Streets," he detailed, his eyes never leaving the taillights ahead. "Suspect's vehicle is a 2018 Nissan

Maxima, four-door, black sedan, Maine license plate A159 MWG." He read the license plate to them as Alpha 159 Mary William George.

"I'm on my way. Keep me updated."

"Thank you." His grip on the steering wheel tightened as he prepared to follow Natalie and the ominous figure steering her fate.

Theo's mind churned with a storm of emotions as he trailed the car ahead of him, making sure to stay back far enough so the "boyfriend" wouldn't notice. Theo's knuckles whitened on the steering wheel, a manifestation of the simmering rage that bubbled just beneath his stoic exterior. Flashes of Natalie's frightened face played in an endless loop in his mind, each replay fueling the fire of his anger.

The urge to confront that punk was a physical force, all-encompassing and fierce. Theo imagined closing the distance, pulling the man from the vehicle, showing him the price of instilling fear in his sister. The very thought of Natalie, kind-hearted and gentle, being subjected to such treatment—especially if his suspicions were correct and this man was her pimp who was controlling her—twisted a hot knife of protectiveness in his gut.

"I swear, if I get my hands on him..." Theo muttered through gritted teeth, barely audible over the car's hum. "How did this happen? How did I not realize this sooner? I was so busy the past few weeks... She seemed fine a few weeks ago. I should have noticed what was happening. I bet it all started at that so-called audition. It was probably a cover for pimps luring women into prostitution."

Ava reached over, placing a calming hand on his tense forearm. "Theo, we need to stay focused. We're doing the right thing by following and keeping them in sight."

He turned his head, meeting Ava's gaze with blazing eyes. "I'm not going to let him get away with this," Theo vowed, the words thick with fury. "Natalie's the sweetest soul; she doesn't deserve any of this.

If it's the last thing I do, I'll be the one to slap the cuffs on him and drag him to a cell where he can't hurt her or anyone else again."

Chapter Twenty-two

Ava clutched the dashboard, her knuckles white. Within her, old memories clashed, fueling her desire to help, to prevent the scene she was all too familiar with from claiming Natalie, but also making her feel sick.

They wove in and out of the downtown Portland traffic, maintaining a safe but sure distance behind Natalie's abductor. Streetlamps cast long, wavering shadows on the asphalt as Theo navigated through less-traveled roads and back alleys until their pursuit brought them to a standstill—the ominous, unlit alley where Natalie's "boyfriend" parked his car.

Theo parked a distance away so they would blend in and remain undetected. The two of them crouched low in their seats, surveying the scene unfolding before them. Shadows moved, but soon, figures became defined—other young women and even what appeared to be underage girls under the flickering glow of a distant streetlight, but it was hard to tell from this distance.

The garishness of their clothing was no match for the somberness in their eyes; they were dressed scantily, not out of choice, but necessity. High heels, overdone makeup, and short dresses were their uniforms of exploitation, but the expressions on their faces were a silent cry for help.

Ava's gaze was drawn to Natalie, her presence among them an ill-fitting piece. Her interaction with the other individuals held a hesitancy, an underlying fear that Ava knew all too well—the dance between control and survival.

The boyfriend—no, her pimp—stood by, his eyes sharp and vigilant, scanning the area. Men drove up to the curb, their hungry gazes dehumanizing, their negotiations brief and cold as the women talked to them through their open car windows. It was a marketplace of flesh and fear, an economy that thrived in the darkened corners of the city.

This was not an isolated situation, but a network, a spiderweb of criminal activity that preyed upon innocent women and girls.

And this was probably not the first time Natalie had been trapped in this web.

"This is exactly what I was afraid of," Theo said through clenched teeth, his voice a mixture of resolve and dread.

"Me too," Ava murmured. She had been clinging to her own composure, but now she felt the sharp sting of the past slice into the present. As Theo's words sank in, echoing her own dark memories, her breath hitched; anxiety pricked at the edges of her consciousness, threatening to surge forth in a tide of panic.

The world outside the car spun as her mind became a floodgate of flashbacks—fear, control, the unending sense of being trapped. It was all too much. She needed air, space—she needed to escape the confines of the car.

"I need to get out," Ava gasped suddenly, her voice thin and strained.

With no time to spare, Ava flung open the car door and sprinted to the nearest trash can on the sidewalk where the contents of her stomach churned and spilled out, the physical reaction mirroring the turmoil inside her.

Theo was right behind her, his own concerns for Natalie temporarily shelved as he focused on Ava's well-being. He held her hair back, a silent support through her ordeal.

"You okay?" he asked, keeping his voice low and even, though concern etched his features. He glanced back to make sure Natalie was still on the sidewalk a distance away. He could just barely make out her form.

Ava nodded weakly, a pale shadow of her usual self, still trembling as she attempted to regain her composure. "I'm so sorry. We are supposed to be discreet. I don't want to attract any attention."

"We are far enough away, in the shadows. They can't see us. Here, let me help you back to the car."

Theo helped her stand and gently guided her back into the car. Though the pieces of Ava's past were still vague to him, it was clear that this night had dredged up something profoundly personal and painful.

Had she also been trapped in a similar web of criminal activity? Had she been a...prostitute? He could barely form the words in his mind. Sweet, innocent Ava...he couldn't bear the thought.

Now wasn't the time to delve into those hidden depths—there was an urgent task at hand. But Theo took mental note of Ava's profound reaction; this was a wound that ran deep, a shared nightmare that somehow connected her to Natalie's situation.

"I'm sorry, I wish I had a bottle of water..." he began.

She waved her hand. "I'm fine. Don't worry about me. Just focus on Natalie."

Together, they resumed their quiet watch in the car.

Every heartbeat while they waited felt like an eternity, each tick of the clock stretching on as Ava's thoughts spiraled. The fragility of these young women and girls tugged at her heart.

Detective Barrett drove up behind him in his unmarked car, wearing plain clothes, and then Theo's phone rang.

"Hello," Theo answered his cell phone.

"Barrett, right behind you. I called in vice. You will be seeing a series of our old beater cars with undercover police 'Johns' soliciting prostitution. Tell me which one is your sister so we can try to get her out early. And let me know who her pimp is so we can try to get him to incriminate himself in the process."

"Thank goodness," Theo breathed with some relief, and then relayed the information so Barrett could pass it along to the vice squad of the CDPU.

After all the women were whisked away, allegedly for illicit sexual encounters, and as the pimps began to disperse back to their vehicles, the uniformed police officers arrived, their approach executed with a quiet urgency that did not alert the predators nor startle the prey. Vehicle barriers were placed at the only exit to this alley, trapping everyone inside, unless they were on foot. Bright beams of flashlights cut through the night as law enforcement began their intervention, voices calm but assertive as they began making arrests.

Ava noticed Theo tapping the dashboard as they waited in the car, looking conflicted as he watched the police approaching and making arrests, then glance at her with concern. She could nearly read the thoughts racing through his mind.

"Theo," Ava started, her voice stronger now, "if you want to go and arrest that man, you should."

He turned to look at her, his eyes searching for any sign of uncertainty. "Are you sure? Will you be okay here?"

She nodded with determination. "Yes. I'll be fine. Go help your sister."

With her assurance, Theo slid out of the car and quickly closed in on Natalie's "boyfriend." Even off-duty, the weight of his badge and the authority it represented never left him. He clipped it on his belt where it could be seen and had a firm grip on the handcuffs he had retrieved from his glovebox. He carried a concealed weapon, as he always did when off duty. He approached the man, aware of his surroundings. Jason was actually caught by the other officers at this point but had not yet been taken into custody.

Theo caught the thug's arm, spinning him around, and in one smooth motion secured his wrists in handcuffs and removed his weapon.

"You're going to regret hurting my sister," he whispered directly into the man's ear, quiet enough that the words were for him alone. His tone was calm, but underneath lay a cold promise, the kind that only a brother intertwined with law enforcement could make.

Satisfaction pierced through Theo's anger as he watched the realization sink into the man's eyes—the tables had turned, and now the predator had become the prey.

"Don't feel so powerful now, do you?" Theo said, steering him toward one of the marked police cars. To make sure no loopholes or police errors were made, Theo gave Jason his Miranda rights and planned to make a note of it in his report.

And while securing the handcuffs might not heal all wounds or prevent this man from hurting another woman again, it was a start—a crack in the cycle, the glint of hope in endless darkness.

A distance away, Ava observed from the car, a surge of pride warming her through the chill of her own trauma as she watched Theo handcuff that scumbag and put him in a police car.

Natalie's ordeal was far from over, but Theo had taken the first step in ensuring their abuser would face the consequences of his actions.

Once the man responsible for so much fear and manipulation was secured in the back of a police cruiser, Theo pivoted on his heel, his focus immediately shifting to his sister.

Barrett told him earlier where his sister would be taken a short distance away, before everyone was taken to the station. He headed back to Ava and his vehicle to reunite with Natalie. He knew his fellow officers would let him through the barrier when he showed them his badge.

Arriving at the location, the scene around him was one of controlled chaos—uniformed and undercover officers moving efficiently to give instructions to the women who were angry or distraught, and some were crying.

Natalie, caught in the fray, began to panic as the reality of arrest and the unknown loomed over her. Theo moved through the sea of uniforms and stopped beside her. "Natalie," he spoke, using his calmest voice to cut through her fear, "I know this wasn't your choice. Just tell them the truth; they will take your statements."

Her eyes, veiled in confusion and terror, met his. "I'll do everything I can to prove you were coerced into this," he reassured her. "Don't say anything until after you speak with your attorney."

Many of the other women's fear was palpable as they were led to marked police cars. The underage victims looked especially lost, their faces streaked with mascara-blackened tears and the dread of what jail might bring.

Across the street, Ava threw open the car door and ran toward them, her own past cascading like a torrent around her. Each step she took was heavy with the memory of her own arrest, the stark terror of facing a possible future behind bars for a crime she'd been forced to commit that her soul despised. She could still feel the snap of cold metal around her wrists, the jarring clang of a cell door, the way some of the officers had looked down on her.

She also remembered the ones who believed her and helped her.

Now, as she approached the unfolding situation, tears tracing clean paths down her cheeks, her heart ached for Natalie and all the other women caught in the trap of exploitation, afraid of what would come next.

Theo glanced over at Ava, his own eyes glistening. It was the sight of her—the realization that she may be a survivor of this same type of crime—that propelled him forward to wrap her in his arms.

As he held her, she let out a sob and cried into his chest, her shoulders shaking.

"It's okay, Ava. I'm here for you," he said over and over, rubbing her back.

As Natalie and the others were led to the police vehicles, Theo held Ava but also kept his eyes on his sister, wishing he could also give her a hug and whisper words of support. She stared at him with wide eyes through the car window, silently pleading for help he couldn't give right now. He felt his heart break for both his sister and Ava, now that he suspected what might have happened to her in her past and the secrets she'd been unable to share with him.

The police cars drove away. They would go to the station. The women would give their statements. The law would process them, but Theo and Ava both knew that justice, real justice, was a long road to walk, but Natalie wouldn't be alone. Before leaving the scene, Theo called the best criminal defense lawyer he knew and gave his credit card information to retain her to represent his sister. He would meet her at the station within the hour.

***

Theo and Ava drove to the police station in silence for the first few minutes, the weight of the evening's events pressing down upon them as the city lights streaked by. Theo glanced at Ava periodically, wrestling with the impulse to reach out to her, to offer support, wanting to let her know she could open up to him, but he was afraid that might only make her shut down.

Finally, Ava broke the silence, her voice steady but carrying an undertone that suggested the effort it took to speak. "You're probably wondering why I reacted like that back there, why I had a trauma response. I'm sure you recognize the signs of PTSD."

"Ava, you're not alone," he reminded her. "I'm here for you."

She finally turned to him, a faint but sad smile touching her lips before it fell away. "You say that now, but there are things about me you don't know—things that might change your mind."

Theo offered a quiet acknowledgment. "Nothing will change how I feel about you...but if you're not ready to tell me, I understand. But if you do want to tell me, I want you to know you can talk to me about anything."

"You've probably figured out what happened to me in New York City... The secret I wasn't ready to tell you yet," she said in a quiet voice while staring out the window.

"I have a guess, yes," he replied, his voice cautious.

Ava exhaled deeply, the sound filling the car like a prelude to confession. "Well..." She sighed. "I'm ready to tell you what happened to me."

She unraveled her entire story of what happened to her in New York City. Theo said nothing as he listened, merely tightened his hold on her hand, a silent testament to his support. Every now and then, he'd steal a look at her as he drove, eyes glistening with unshed tears—for her pain, for her strength. His heart ached at her disclosures; anger simmered underneath, a rage for justice on her behalf.

When they arrived at the station, Theo parked the car but lingered in the moment, allowing the gravity of Ava's revelation to settle between them.

"When I testified in court against my pimp, it was terrifying. His name is Raymond 'Razor' DeLuca, but everyone on the street called him Razor. He glared at me the whole time I was on the stand, and afterward, he threatened to hunt me down and make me pay whenever he gets out of prison. His sentence isn't anywhere near over, but when he gets out, I fear for my life. He even sent a postcard to me immediately after I testified saying 'RECANT', but it was not provable it was from him. Someone shoved it under my door, so he has connections, people outside of prison who will do things for him." She shuddered. Ava's voice broke as she spoke through sobs, "I understand if you never want to see me again... If you can't look at me the same anymore... If you think I'm disgusting or damaged..."

"No, that's not it at all!" Theo assured her, grabbing both of her hands. "I just hate that this happened to you, Ava. I wish I could undo it, or that I could get my hands on every man who ever hurt you..." His hand reached up to touch her cheek gently. "I'm sincerely sorry this happened to you, but in my eyes, you're a survivor, not damaged. You're beautiful, kind, ambitious, and wonderful, and I still feel the same about you. I still want to keep getting to know you."

Ava wiped at her tears, a small nod acknowledging his words. "I haven't told you all my secrets yet. I want to, but I know we need to go inside and be there for Natalie. So that can wait. But after this, I'm ready to tell you about my past... All of it."

Theo nodded solemnly. "Thank you for trusting me with what you've told me, and yes, I do want to hear more. I want to get to know you more. Thank you for being so strong, for being here for Natalie and me."

"Let's just get through tonight," Ava said.

As they exited the car and entered the bustling station, the staccato rhythm of police work surrounded them. They spotted Natalie being escorted by an officer—her gaze met theirs, an unspoken plea in her eyes.

Theo offered Ava an out, sensing the emotional toll this would have on her. "This may take a while. If you want, I can take you home. I understand if you don't want to be here...if this brings up bad memories."

But Ava shook her head, her decision firm. "No. I want to stay and see Natalie through this. I understand how terrifying being arrested is when you're innocent."

Together, they stayed, ready to provide Natalie the support she would need in the hours to come, and waited for her attorney to arrive while she was photographed, fingerprinted, and booked.

Because Natalie was his sister, Theo was not the one to interrogate her. He was off duty anyway, so he waited with Ava in the briefing room, away from the public in the lobby, and quickly jotted out his arrest report. By then, the lawyer arrived and spoke briefly to Theo before joining her client.

Ava said softly, not looking at Theo, "While we're waiting, I might as well tell you more about my past."

He turned to her. "If you're ready."

Ava's voice was just above a whisper, but every word carried the weight of the world. "When I was six years old, I saw something no child should ever see. My father...he lost his temper, and he came close to killing my mother." Her eyes clouded over with memories that would never leave her no matter how much she had tried to forget. "I told him I was going to tell the bishop what he did. He thought the best way to deal with a child who had seen too much was to lock me away. So, he put me in the basement. He built a secret room inside the basement only my mother knew about, and he told my brothers I had drowned. He even blamed them for my death, which was just cruel. He didn't have to do that."

"He was a narcissist, a sociopath," Theo observed. "So that's why you didn't want me to go down to the basement to look for repairs that first time I came over."

She nodded. "I haven't gone down since. I was locked down there for over a decade. Everyone in the community thought I was dead."

Theo felt a sharp pang in his chest as he listened. His heart ached at the thought of young Ava enduring such trauma, of the scars it must have left on her.

She went on to tell him about how her father had staged her death, the toll their secret took on her mother for all those years, how her mother and brother were finally arrested, and what it was like to be locked away for so long. "When I went to the city, I thought I was finally free, but then I fell into captivity again in the city."

"I can't even imagine what you went through," Theo said.

"The life I live in now... I've fought to build it, Theo. But the past...never really leaves you, does it?" Her eyes searched his.

Theo reached out, taking her hand in his. "Ava," he said firmly, the words falling between them like vows, "everybody has shadows in their closet, parts of their story they wish could be rewritten. But you—your past, dark as it may be, it's not who you are. And it's certainly not too much for me."

Ava's eyes glistened, the barriers around her faltering at his acceptance.

"I don't want to turn away from you because of things you couldn't control, things that hurt you. I want to be someone who helps, someone who understands," Theo continued, meaning every word. "You keep thinking your past will scare me away, but it makes me even more drawn to you. You are so remarkable. I want to get to know you more, spend more time with you—if you'll let me."

The relief was visible in Ava's face, a softening around her eyes, a release of breath she had been holding in maybe since she was that little girl in the basement.

They sat together in the police station, two people connected by a simple, powerful promise that neither of them would have to face their battles alone.

***

After signing the necessary paperwork, Natalie was finally released.

Theo quickly approached his sister, enveloping her in a protective hug. "Let's get you out of here."

Natalie nodded, her voice too choked with emotion to respond. Ava gave her a reassuring smile, gently guiding her towards the parking lot. "Come on, let's go home."

Theo drove, his focus on the road, while Ava chose to sit in the back seat, right next to Natalie. The car was filled with a heavy silence, the weight of recent events pressing down on all of them.

As they drove through the city streets, Ava turned to Natalie, her heart aching for her. "Natalie," she began softly, "I know this is hard, and I just want you to know that you're not alone. I was also forced into prostitution...for two years. I understand what you're going through."

"Two years? How did you get through it?" Natalie choked out.

"It was the darkest time of my life, and that's saying something," Ava said. "My faith in God got me through it and the hope that I'd get out and be free one day."

Natalie's eyes filled with tears. "It was only a few weeks for me, but I was so scared, Ava," she whispered, her voice trembling. "I didn't have a choice, and then being arrested... it felt like everything was hopeless."

Ava reached out, placing a comforting arm around Natalie's shoulders. "I know exactly how that feels. I was arrested too for something I was forced to do. But you have to remember, none of this was your fault. These people—they prey on vulnerability and fear. None of this is your fault."

Natalie began to weep. Ava held her close, offering a silent, steadfast presence. Theo continued to drive, glancing in the rearview mirror with concern.

"It'll be okay, Natalie," Theo said. "You have support from us and Mom and Dad."

"It may take a long time," Ava continued gently, "but you will heal. You will rebuild your life, and we will be here to help you with whatever you need. You're not alone anymore."

Through her tears, Natalie looked at Ava, a flicker of hope in her eyes. "Thank you, Ava. I don't know how I would face this without you."

Ava smiled a little.

Theo glanced in the rearview mirror, his eyes meeting Ava's. He gave a small nod, gratitude and relief evident on his face.

"I'll take you home, if that's okay, Ava," Theo said. "We need to get Natalie home and speak with my parents. I hope you understand."

"Of course, I understand." Ava nodded.

For now, they drove on, moving towards a future where hope and resilience would guide their way.

***

A few days later, when Ava arrived at the Kingsley household for dinner, there was a tangible sense of anticipation as Theo led Ava into the heart of the family home.

Theo took a breath before making the introductions. "Mom, Dad, this is Ava," he said, his voice revealing the significance he attached to the moment. "She's the one I've been telling you about."

"Ava, we've heard so much about you," Carol said, her arms opening to draw Ava into her embrace. "Thank you for being there for Natalie and Theo. We're so overjoyed to meet you," she said, her voice clear even though her eyes glistened with the threat of tears.

Ava, taken by the sincerity and love in Carol's greeting, returned the embrace with equal tenderness. "It's a pleasure to meet you, Mrs. Kingsley," she said, her words colored with the emotion of the moment.

"Please, call me Carol," Carol said.

Mark stepped up with a sturdy handshake that lingered into a caring hold. His eyes searched Ava's for a brief second; it was easy to see where Theo got his propensity for deep, silent communication. "We're just so relieved Natalie is back with us, safe," he stated earnestly. "And knowing she and Theo had someone like you by their side makes all the difference."

"I wish we were meeting under happier circumstances," Carol said. "We were so shocked and heartbroken when Theo told us what happened to our dear Natalie..." Carol pulled her daughter close as if she might disappear at any moment. "My poor girl. I never want to let you out of my sight ever again."

Natalie put her arm around her mother. "I'm not going anywhere, Mom." She turned to Ava. "I've decided to move back home for the time being while I keep going to school."

Ava nodded. "That sounds like a good idea. Family is everything," she said solemnly, meeting Theo's eyes as they communicated a silent understanding.

Mark nodded, his face etched with concern that slowly melted into relief. "It was hard to hear about what Natalie went through. I wish I could teach those thugs a lesson..." he admitted, and Ava saw the same protectiveness in him as she saw in Theo. "But we're thankful she's home safe now, and those criminals are locked away."

Natalie approached Ava with a shy but genuine smile. "Thank you for being there, for both me and Theo that night," she said, her gratitude unmistakable. "It meant the world."

Ava, feeling a connection with Natalie through their shared experiences, simply nodded and offered a warm, reassuring hug.

"You're not alone. I understand what you went through, so I am here if you ever want to talk," she replied. They now shared a bond forged by shared experiences that no one else in their lives could understand.

"Thank you," Natalie said with a grateful smile, and Ava felt their bond strengthening. Maybe as they got to know each other more, they would become good friends—at least, Ava hoped so.

Despite the dark shadows of the past, there was a clear sense that hope and resilience were paving the way forward for them all.

The mood balanced delicately between somber reflection and hopeful embrace of the future as they sat down to eat dinner together. There was comfort in knowing that the trials of the recent past had led them to a safer present where Natalie could heal and Ava could find the peace she yearned for.

Amidst it all, Ava found solace in the small acts of familial bonding, the shared stories, and the security of a close-knit circle that was opening up to embrace her. As the Kingsley family came together, bound by support and shared experiences, there was a sense of closure and the promise of a brighter future.

Chapter Twenty-three

Ava returned to her house nestled in Unity's Amish community, its tranquil farm fields and familiar faces extending a quiet welcome that brought stability into her life. For a few days, life's rhythm seemed to settle into a routine. She continued working at the library, which was a job she truly enjoyed, while fixing up the house in her spare time. She found joy in restocking books and renovating the house. It was the kind of work that made sense to her and gave her true satisfaction at the end of the day.

Later that week, Ava's tranquility was shattered by the sharp jab of Jonas Miller's voice calling across their yards. Disgruntled, he stood on the boundary of his property, glaring pointedly at Ava and Theo. Ava was repairing the garden fencing, hammering sections of the wooden slats back into place while Theo repaired a hinge on the little gate.

"Young lady, this is wholly inappropriate," Mr. Miller called out, his voice heavy with disapproval, an accusation thrown across the yard like a stone. "For an unmarried woman to be working so closely with a man—it's not decent. Especially when you're both inside the house doing Lord knows what."

Ava paused, hammer in hand, as she wiped her free hand on her mother's apron and put it on her hip, meeting Mr. Miller's scowl with a poised, yet flustered, response. "Excuse me? Theo is merely helping me with much-needed repairs, Mr. Miller. There's nothing inappropriate going on here."

Mr. Miller's lip curled as he countered, his voice cutting through the soft rustle of the surrounding greenery. "It seems to me that you don't even belong in our community. You're not Amish, not anymore. So why come back at all?"

The accusation stung, an affront to the idea that she might ever find sanctuary in Unity again. "There are several neighbors around here who aren't Amish," she retorted, her voice firm, but the hurt was evident in her eyes, as she used the hammer in her hand as a pointer. "I have as much right to live here as anyone else. I grew up here, and I want to repair my family's home."

The argument spiraled, Mr. Miller's words sharpening into a barb intended to wound. "Why did you leave in the first place, letting your family home fall into disrepair and bring down my property's value?" he demanded, his brows knitting together in a display of contempt. "If you hadn't, you wouldn't need to bring strangers in to help you repair it." He shot an accusing glare at Theo.

From the corner of his eye, Theo noted the windows of nearby homes fill with curious onlookers, their faces faint spectacles of concern and interest, and buggies were slowing down as they drove by. Ava breathed deeply, her chest rising and falling as she faced Mr. Miller, a barricade of resolve steeling her posture.

Theo tried to warn her. "Ava, I really think—" he began, but Ava continued as if she hadn't heard him.

"You don't understand. You don't know what I've been through these past few years," Ava said to Mr. Miller, her words full of sadness. "This was not my choice. I couldn't leave the city even though I wanted to." Her voice softened, a plea for even a sliver of compassion.

"If you knew what happened to me, you wouldn't say such things," she added.

"Your father would be so disappointed," Mr. Miller said, shaking his head.

"My father?" Ava shot back, her voice rising, with both hands animated and shaking, including the one with the hammer in it. "My father is the one who imprisoned me. He is the reason my family fell apart, just like this house. If you had only called the police when I wrote 'HELP' on the window, this would not be happening now. You are a big part of the reason I was imprisoned so long. You could have helped me but ignored my pleas for help." She knew what she was saying was unkind, but she was so blinded by her anger, she couldn't stop the words from tumbling out.

Before the dispute could escalate further, Theo stepped between Ava and Mr. Miller. "Let's not get carried away," he said, his voice measured but authoritative, a clear attempt to defuse the tension.

Around them, Amish friends and neighbors who had gathered on the lane and in their nearby yards stood as silent witnesses—an audience to the conflict that unfolded on what was typically a serene street. Their faces were a mix of concern and curiosity, and a few of them whispered to each other. Ava had been so absorbed in the argument that she hadn't noticed them gathering. Among the onlookers were Maria and Liz, carrying shopping bags of groceries. They looked concerned, nervously glancing around.

In this moment, Ava felt a glaring spotlight thrown upon her, exposing not only the dereliction of her childhood home but also the scars of her past. Theo recognized this vulnerability, and in a protective gesture, he placed a supportive hand on Ava's shoulder.

The tension hung in the air.

"There's nothing to see here," Theo called out. "Just a disagreement between neighbors."

The onlookers dispersed, but Ava still felt as though they were watching her.

"This isn't over," Mr. Miller huffed, then trudged back toward his house. "I'm going to speak to the bishop about this."

"Go ahead," Ava replied calmly. "As you said, I'm not Amish, so your rules don't apply to me."

He glared at her, went inside his house, and slammed the door. She flinched, feeling an ache begin to grow in her heart. For a moment, she wondered what it would be like to be Amish again, to truly be part of the community and the church. What would it be like to live in her childhood home again, on her own?

One thing was for sure—she was quite sure she wouldn't like having Mr. Miller as a neighbor. How would that work for a long-term living situation?

"Let's go inside and work on the cabinets," Theo suggested, and Ava nodded, letting him lead her inside.

Chapter Twenty-four

As early morning light crept over the quiet town two days later, Ava looked out the window to see a man knocking on Mr. Miller's door, but there was no answer, so the man turned away. He caught sight of Ava in the window, who waved and opened her front door.

"Good morning, may I help you?" she asked.

"Hello, I'm Bob Beachy. Jonas Miller works at my store. Have you seen him? He hasn't shown up at work for two days now. I'm getting worried. I thought maybe he was home sick, but he's not answering the door. This isn't like him. He hasn't missed a day of work in years."

"I saw him two days ago, but no, I haven't seen him since. I don't know where he is," she said.

"I hear his horse making some noise back in the barn, so he didn't take his buggy. I would say maybe he took a bus somewhere, but he wouldn't just leave his horse like that." Bob looked concerned.

"I'll go check on his horse right now and make sure he's watered and fed," Ava said. "Mr. Miller wouldn't just leave his horse here unattended."

"No, he wouldn't. Well, if you see him, please call my store." He handed her a business card. "Thanks."

Ava walked over to Mr. Miller's barn to check on his horse. As she did, she saw Bob asking neighbors who were walking down the lane if they had seen Mr. Miller, but no one had—not since his argument with Ava two days ago.

Ava approached Mr. Miller's barn with a sense of foreboding, each of her steps hesitant. The door groaned on its hinges as she nudged it open, a sound that seemed to echo her growing apprehension. Inside, the musty scent of hay and leather was undercut by the scent of a horse's stall that hadn't been cleaned in two days.

Her eyes adjusted to the dimness inside, and she quickly scanned the dusty interior. A shaft of light pierced the wooden slats, spotlighting whorls of dust dancing in the stillness. But it was the rhythmic stomp of a hoof that drew her attention to the far stall.

Max, Mr. Miller's chestnut horse, was restless. Ava approached slowly, murmuring softly, trying to provide some comfort with her presence. However, as she neared, she noticed the empty food trough and the nearly dry water bucket. Her heart sank, filled with guilt. If she had known, she would have come sooner.

"Poor boy. I'll take care of you," she said and set to work.

The stall bore the signs of neglect. Ava had seen Mr. Miller going into the barn often, and she knew he usually took good care of his horse. Hay was trampled underfoot, mixing with soiled bedding, and there was no fresh straw in sight. Ava glanced around, half-expecting Mr. Miller to appear with a sheepish apology for his forgetfulness, but the barn remained silent except for Max's low, distressed whinnies.

Filling a bucket with water from the nearby tap, Ava returned to Max's stall, her thoughts racing as fast as her heartbeat. She watched the animal gulp down the liquid with desperation. "Easy, boy," she whispered as Max nudged her hand gratefully, his large eyes reflecting a soulful intelligence. She filled a bucket with feed and placed it in front of him, letting him eat before taking him out to the pasture so he could get some exercise and fresh air while she cleaned his stall.

Taking care of the horse brought her a kind of solace, a distraction from the gnawing questions that churned in her mind. Where was Mr. Miller? It was unlike him to leave his horse unattended—Max was more than a pet; he was a companion, a living connection to a happier time in the old man's life when his wife had been alive, she guessed.

Ava retrieved a pitchfork and set to work cleaning the stall, her movements mechanical, but her mind far from the task at hand. She couldn't shake the worry that clung to her like the cobwebs clinging to the rafters above. People didn't just vanish, especially not sturdy, responsible types like Mr. Miller, who embodied the same work ethic and routine discipline as his prize stallion.

The barn now somewhat restored to its usual state of care, Ava leaned against the stall door, watching Max settle back into a semblance of comfort. She pledged silently to return if Mr. Miller didn't show up by nightfall. It was the least she could do for a neighbor, but her willingness to help was tinged with an unease she couldn't ignore.

Ava stepped out of the barn, pausing to look back once more. "We'll find him, Max," she said, more to herself than the horse. The warmth of the setting sun did little to ease the chill of concern that had settled deep within her bones. She hoped against all logic that Mr. Miller's absence was nothing more than an odd, uncharacteristic oversight.

Ava approached the front porch of Mr. Miller's modest house, her hand hovering before she rapped firmly, the sound of her knocking briefly breaking the quietude that enveloped the property.

"Mr. Miller?" she called out hesitantly, knowing that if he indeed was inside, he would be annoyed that she was disturbing him. She knocked again, a bit louder this time, listening intently for any movement or response from inside. Silence greeted her once more.

Most people here, including Mr. Miller, felt no need to lock their doors. Ava tried the handle, half-expecting resistance, but the door swung open smoothly at her touch.

She stepped inside. "Mr. Miller, it's Ava Sullivan. Are you home?" she ventured again with the courtesy that deep-rooted manners dictated, even when anxiety gnawed at her.

With no answer, Ava allowed herself into the kitchen, where the dirty dishes in the sink marked the last meal Mr. Miller had possibly taken in his home, and they seemed to be over two days old. Scraps of dried food clung to the plates, and the silverware was stained with residues too old to be from the previous night's meal.

She wondered if he often left his dishes undone for days at a time. Seeing how well-manicured his yard was and how well he normally took care of his horse, she guessed this also was unlike him.

Ava's presence in the quiet, expectant space felt like an intrusion, a step into a private sphere that wasn't her own.

It was clear that Mr. Miller had not been home in two days.

A twinge of distress gripped Ava's heart.

The kitchen table was bare, save for a single overturned chair, an accidental or hasty movement perhaps. Ava's gaze traveled to the hallway leading to the rest of the house, to places where the private life of Mr. Miller unfolded even further.

Steeling herself, she made her way down the corridor. "Mr. Miller, it's Ava," she announced with a courage she wasn't sure she felt. Each door opened to reveal empty rooms, perfectly made beds, and drawn curtains—a home waiting for its owner to return.

As she paced back towards the kitchen, her detective instincts kicking in, she tried to piece together the puzzle. The dirty dishes were a sign of an uncharacteristic disregard, the silent rooms a testament to a deeper story yet to be unearthed.

Ava knew it was time to expand the search. With a growing sense of urgency propelling her forward, she pulled out her cell phone, dialed Theo's number, and explained the situation.

"Theo, he's not here," she continued. "And something's not right—I can feel it. We need to find him."

"I'm on duty. I'll be right there as soon as I can, Ava," he assured her.

She hung up, casting one last glance over the quiet kitchen, the sink with its stubborn refuse of better days. Its image would haunt her until Mr. Miller was found, until the silence gave way to answers and the house could breathe life once more.

As she walked back to her own home, whispers of the onlooking neighbors intermingled with the warm breeze. A few people were looking out their windows, and people walking by on the lane glanced at her warily.

Did they suspect she had something to do with this? And now she had just left his house, which made her look even more guilty. She groaned inwardly. By looking for him, caring for his horse, and trying to help, she was only digging herself into a deeper hole.

***

Word of Jonas Miller's absence traveled through the community like a chilling breeze within only an hour. Neighbors peeked out from behind curtains and exchanged speculative glances. It wasn't like Mr.

Miller to just vanish without a word for two days and not tell anyone where he went.

Theo notified the Covert Police Detectives Unit of a possible missing person situation he was responding to. He pulled up in his unmarked police car and found Ava on the porch, eyes red with worry and tears she had been crying. They went inside, and he pulled her into his arms.

"The house was quiet, and the dishes were dirty...this isn't like him. Look at his yard. It's immaculate. He takes great pride in his property, and he loves his horse. He wouldn't just leave Max, not feeding him for two days." She hesitated, a heavy breath catching in her throat, before continuing, "I'm worried that people are starting to suspect I had something to do with Mr. Miller's disappearance."

He let go of her and looked into her eyes. "Ava," he replied, his tone firm yet reassuring, "people can think what they want, but suspicions aren't evidence. I'm going to start an investigation straight away. I'll call for the crime lab and extra patrol to look for him if I need to. We'll get to the bottom of this. I'll do everything I can to find out what really happened and clear your name in the process."

The confidence in Theo's voice provided Ava a sliver of hope, something solid to hold on to amid the uncertainty. Living under the weight of past traumas, the last thing Ava needed was a cloud of guilt by association to darken her life once more.

"Thank you, Theo. Maybe he's okay and I'm overreacting," she said.

"People often are reported missing and are then found at a friend's house or on an impulsive trip. You're right. He might have left town, even if it's not like him. Maybe he just needed to get away and forgot to tell anyone. You just lay low and keep a clear head. If you think of anything, no matter how small, that might help, let me know immediately. Okay?"

"I will, Theo. Thank you."

Though she knew she had done no wrong, the thought of being implicated in any wrongdoing after all she had overcome left a bitter taste. She resolved to keep a vigilant eye around, just as she knew Theo would be piecing together the fragments of this unsettling puzzle.

The resolve to fight this new shadow settled deep within her. And with the fading light casting long shadows across the porch, Ava knew the coming days would test the resilience that had carried her through the darkest times of her life.

***

Theo's experience in law enforcement had taught him that when a person goes missing, each second is a grain of sand slipping through the hourglass.

As was standard procedure, Theo searched Mr. Miller's property, even though Ava already had. He searched the house, seeing what she had described, then the barn. He then discovered blood in Mr. Miller's tool shed along with some boxes and tools knocked over—possible evidence of an injury, a struggle...or murder.

"What happened here?" Theo wondered aloud, his eyes sweeping over the tool shed.

Theo radioed his sergeant who told him that he would be sending a team, having non-sworn employees call local hospitals and the morgue, and to officially expand the search and start processing any possible evidence in the tool shed.

Because he had experience forming search parties in this community, Theo quickly contacted a few neighbors who committed to sweeping through their surrounding land for any sign of Mr. Miller. They navigated the woods and fields, calling his name.

Theo's partner, Detective Barrett, arrived and was briefed. Theo told him about the argument Ava had with Mr. Miller. Because Theo and Ava had a close personal relationship, Barrett suggested he talk to Ava without Theo present, and Theo agreed that was probably best.

Theo and Barrett searched Ava's yard. When they approached the shed on Ava's property, they swung open the door with an eerie creak.

There, on a wooden workbench, illuminated by the slanting rays of light that breached the small windows, was a hammer—perhaps a murder weapon. Its claw was stained with a dark brownish-red that was probably blood, and it had clumps of what appeared to be blood-soaked brown hair—the same color as Mr. Miller's hair—caught in it. Droplets of the dried substance was splattered on the bench as if the hammer had been set down hastily, carelessly, by the hands of a murderer. Bloodlike matter was also splattered around the inside of the shed, if this truly was blood.

It could be the scene of an injury…or maybe even murder.

Theo felt his gut churn. The whole situation made him feel sick to his stomach. He knew Ava hadn't harmed Mr. Miller, but the evidence before him tried to claw away at that belief. Professionalism required him to maintain composure, to preserve the scene, and to follow the protocol to the letter. Yet, he couldn't suppress the protective surge roaring within him, the refusal to allow Ava's life to be shattered again. They had to find the truth quickly.

"We better call this in," Barrett said, taking in the grim scene after a moment of silence passed. "Our sergeant will probably want to send out the rest of the homicide unit, too, in addition to the crime scene investigators and search and rescue team."

Theo's hand was already instinctively moving to his radio. They would definitely need to get a warrant and the crime lab in here. But then his partner suggested it might be better for him to contact the Covert Police Detectives Unit. The crackling voice on the other end confirmed that they were on their way.

Barrett waited, guarding the evidence with his partner until the first patrol officer arrived and took over that responsibility.

Theo's mind raced. He knew he had to inform Ava—the news would worry her. His steps were heavy as he made his way back to Ava's house, the burden of imminent grief and potential blame weighing on him.

Finding Ava pacing by the window, Theo went inside the house and shut the door. "Ava," he said gently but gravely, "We found a hammer covered in what I suspect is blood and some brown hair in your shed."

"Mr. Miller has brown hair," Ava murmured, fear rising within her. "It's a very common hair color, right? It might not be his." Even as she said the words, she doubted they were true.

"I'm sorry, Ava. I suspect Mr. Miller may have been murdered, or at least severely injured, on your property," Theo told her.

The color drained from Ava's face as Theo's words hung in the air like a chilling fog. Panic took hold, her worst fears bubbling to the surface. Tears pooled in her eyes as her lips quivered. "With the arguments I had with Mr. Miller... They'll think it was me," she whispered, her voice cracking with emotion.

Before she could spiral further, Theo was by her side, offering a shoulder to lean on. "Listen to me, Ava. I know you didn't do this. And I'll do everything in my power to prove it," he said with determination. "Right now, we need to trust the process. Trust me. We will get to the truth, and I know you are innocent, but the homicide team will probably view you as a person of interest for a while. Just tell the truth and perhaps we can get you Natalie's lawyer."

As Ava clung to Theo, sobbing as he held her, his promise an anchor in the tumultuous sea they had found themselves in. Amidst the overwhelming fear, Theo made a vow—he would find the real perpetrator.

As they waited for the homicide unit to arrive, Ava's heart raced as she reflected on the arguments she'd had with Mr. Miller. She could still feel the heat of the words they exchanged, but murder? It was absurd.

More police cruisers and unmarked units arrived, stirring up dust on the dirt lane and a further flurry of onlookers who were curious about all the commotion. Ava watched from the window as the officers moved quickly to secure the scene and began questioning the neighbors and searching for further evidence. One of the officers came to her door and served her with a search warrant. She was then asked to wait outside on her porch as they processed any evidence found in her home, expanding the search to include smaller areas where a missing person could not be found, but where other inflammatory evidence could be stashed.

The fact that Ava had not gotten along with Mr. Miller was no longer just gossip; it was potential motive.

The crime scene investigators came to photograph and perform an additional search in the shed before carefully collecting the hammer and any other evidence—no matter how small.

Theo stepped outside to for a status check with Detective Barrett. The air was thick with tension, mingling with the scent of freshly turned earth.

Barrett told Theo, due to a potential appearance of impropriety since he had a relationship with their new primary suspect, he should cease assisting with the search for further evidence at this time. Theo nodded and went inside to wait with and support Ava.

Seeing the array of police cars and the intensity of the investigation, Liz and Maria hurried over to Ava, offering silent strength simply through their presence. They offered their support, quickly making their way to where Ava sank onto the porch swing, trying to comfort the unease in her heart.

They sat beside her as Liz spoke up. "Ava, what if Mr. Miller is not dead? What if he's just missing? Maybe he had an accident with one of his tools in his shed and had to leave for the hospital in a hurry?"

"That could explain why he left his horse so abruptly," Maria added.

Ava nodded. "I had the same thought. But if that were the case, why would he go in my shed? And wouldn't he have found a way to let someone know to care for his horse? While there are no phones in the Amish homes, there are phones in many of the Amish businesses. He could have reached out by now. It's been two days; he wouldn't just abandon his horse without a word, right?"

Liz sighed, "You're right, Ava. We've known Mr. Miller a long time, and he loves that horse. It does seem out of character for him. But something urgent must have come up. Maybe he had a family emergency and hasn't been able to reach anyone yet."

"He does have family in Smyrna," Maria said. "He may have gone to see them and left quickly. Maybe he took a bus."

"Let's hold onto the hope that there's a good explanation," Ava said dejectedly. "I won't give up hope yet, but...they found my father's hammer in my shed covered in blood and someone's hair."

Liz's eyes widened.

"Let's try not to jump to conclusions," Maria murmured.

Liz said solemnly. "Let's pray. Pray that the police will find Mr. Miller in good health and that the truth will come to light."

They bowed their heads and prayed together.

As the prayer ended, however, Ava's heart was heavy with regret. "I feel terrible. The last time I talked to Mr. Miller, we argued. What if the police think that argument gives me a motive? What if they think I had something to do with his disappearance? I didn't, I would never, but...the thought alone terrifies me."

Liz and Maria glanced at each other with worry, unsure of what to say.

"Everyone here knows you would never hurt anyone," Liz said. "We all know your character. Doesn't that count for something?"

"I don't know," Ava choked out, trembling. "If they find more evidence against me...I'm afraid not even the support of everyone in town will help me."

Chapter Twenty-Five

Detective Barrett walked up to the group of onlookers that had gathered, hoping to gather witness accounts that could shed light on the events leading up to Mr. Miller's disappearance.

They approached a woman named Mrs. Johnson, an Amish neighbor known for her keen observations, Theo hung back, allowing Detective Barrett to lead the questioning. His eyes scanned the surroundings, taking in every detail, listening intently to the conversation unfolding before him.

"Good afternoon," Barrett began, offering a respectful nod. "I'm Detective Barrett. We're looking into an argument between Ava Sullivan and Jonas Miller. Did you see this argument happen?"

"*Ja*, I sure did," Mrs. Johnson said. "Several people did."

"Can you tell us what you witnessed?"

Mrs. Johnson, her expression serious and contemplative, nodded. "I've seen them have two arguments. The first one happened in the church parking lot shortly after Ava was rescued some years back. She was very upset with Mr. Miller for not calling the police when he had the chance. Ava said that if he had reported what he knew, she might have been rescued years ago."

Barrett took notes, his pen moving swiftly across the page. "And how did Ava seem during the argument two days ago?"

"She was very angry," Mrs. Johnson responded, her voice tinged with sympathy. "Her anger was understandable, given everything she'd been through and what he said to her." She recounted the things Mr. Miller had said. "Mr. Miller said it was inappropriate for Theo to be working on the house with her since they're not married. He mentioned that her father would have been disappointed in her, saying she shouldn't have left the community and let the house fall into such disrepair. Ava seemed very offended and was waving the hammer in her hand at him. I'm just telling you what happened, what I saw and heard, but I also want you to know that I think Ava is a kind young lady. She would never hurt anyone."

Barrett nodded, noting down the crucial information.

"Thank you, Mrs. Johnson," Barrett said, his tone professional but warm. "Your observations are very helpful."

Barrett gave a small nod of gratitude to Mrs. Johnson before speaking with the others who all agreed, telling the same story, which only made Ava look even more guilty. However, they all agreed that they did not think Ava was capable of hurting anyone.

***

Having been allowed to return inside her home, Ava watched as Detective Barrett again approached the house, her nerves wound tightly. He knocked on the door, and she let him in.

Detective Barrett offered a respectful nod as he entered. "Ms. Sullivan," he began as they stood in the living room, the badge on his chest reflecting the morning sun streaming through her window, "I need to ask you a few more questions alone. Is that all right with you?"

Ava braced herself, meeting Detective Barrett's eyes. "Of course. I understand," she replied, her voice betraying none of her inner turmoil.

Maria and Liz politely excused themselves to the kitchen, saying they would wait there for them to finish.

Barrett pulled out a notepad and asked, "When did you last see Jonas Miller?"

The question spun her back to the confrontation that now seemed to haunt her. "It was two days ago. We...we had an argument outside. We also argued when I was first rescued, so I know how it looks." She explained to him how she'd been imprisoned by her father and how her neighbor had ignored her signals for help. "I have to admit that during the argument, I blamed him for not calling the police to help me. I'm sure you will hear about it from the neighbors. Several people witnessed both arguments."

Barrett's pen hovered above the paper as he prompted her to continue. "So, do you believe you would have been rescued much sooner if he had called the police?"

"Well, yes. I wrote 'help' on the window several times over the years, but he ignored it, saying he didn't want to get involved."

"And during this most recent argument, were you angry with him?"

"Well...yes."

"Did you argue about anything else?"

"He thought it was inappropriate for Theo—Detective Kingsley—to be helping me with fixing up my house and spending time here together, since we aren't married," Ava explained, her hands knotting together. "Some words were exchanged. But I assure you, it was just an argument. Nothing more."

"And this argument was witnessed by others?"

Ava nodded, a resigned sigh escaping her lips. "Yes, quite a few neighbors saw it. People who live in the nearby houses and some people who were walking on the lane at the time."

Barrett made a note of this. "And you haven't seen Mr. Miller since this argument?"

"No, I haven't seen him at all. That's why I went looking for him today, after his boss reported he had not shown up to work in two days and his horse was making noise. I first went over to check on his horse and found he had no food or water, so I took care of him. I then looked in his house and his barn. I was worried," she confessed, her concern genuine and evident.

Ava then recounted the signs of Mr. Miller's absence that had drawn her deeper into worry—the unkempt state of his barn, the distress of his horse left without care, and the dirty dishes that suggested he had been missing for a couple of days. "As you can see from his house and his property, he is normally a clean and tidy person, so it seems unlike him to leave dishes undone and not feed his horse or clean the stall."

Detective Barrett listened intently, nodding as he jotted down her words, mind clearly turning over the details she provided. "Thank you, Ms. Sullivan," he said finally. "We appreciate your cooperation. If you remember anything else, even the smallest detail, please let us know immediately."

Ava watched as Barrett stepped away to confer with the other arriving officers. Theo moved to her side. His presence was both comforting and a reminder of the seriousness of the situation.

One of the officers approached her. "Ms. Sullivan," he began, "May we search your property?"

Ava nodded consent, swallowing her fear.

"It's standard procedure," Theo assured her.

"Go ahead," she managed to say, "I have nothing to hide."

The CPDU team moved through Ava's home with meticulous care, sifting through the fabric of Ava's life, seeking the tangible truth hidden in objects and dust.

Theo's presence was an odd blend of detective and protector—a man torn between his professional duties and the emotional vestiges of relationship with Ava. His keen eyes missed nothing; every scrap of paper, every personal belonging was potential evidence in this canvas of catastrophe. The perpetrator could have dropped anything nearby before, during, or after the commission of the crime. Anything from gum to gloves, cigarettes to the murder weapon, not to mention leaving behind footprints or fingerprints, possibly bloody. Many things could be potential evidence and need to be marked with their location and collected for further examination.

Theo knew this circumstantial evidence would be the crucible that tested not only investigative skill but also the resilience of trust. His relationship with Ava, the trust he had fought to build with her, was now threatened. Still, he would find the real killer and restore Ava's name, no matter the cost.

The officers brought the hammer to Ava, who was sitting at her kitchen table with Liz and Maria, her hands clasped tightly in front of her. The air was dense with accusation as the lead investigator held up a hammer from the bagged evidence using his gloved hand, the blood stain on the claw of the hammer shocking Ava.

"Ms. Sullivan, can you identify this hammer?" asked Detective Barrett, his tone professional but not unkind.

Her eyes fixed on the familiar tool, and Ava felt a cold rush of realization. "Yes, it's my hammer," she acknowledged, her voice steadier than she felt. "Well, it belonged to my father. I used it a couple of days ago to repair the loose boards on my garden fence... I was working on it when I had that argument with Mr. Miller. Theo was with me."

The silent glances between the officers didn't go unnoticed by Ava or Theo, who stood by the doorway, his arms folded and his brow furrowed.

"I understand this looks bad, the timing and all," Ava continued, her heart pounding. "I argued with Mr. Miller, and now—" She paused, swallowing back the emotion that threatened to crack her composure. "Yes, we didn't get along, but I didn't harm him. I never would." Her eyes implored them to believe her, to see the truth that lay beyond the circumstantial evidence they were piecing together.

Theo shifted, allowing his gaze to briefly meet Ava's. He knew Ava's history, the hardships she had endured, and he knew she wasn't capable of the gruesome violence that the crime scene had revealed.

A heavy silence fell among the officers as they discussed the next steps.

Any hope that Mr. Miller might simply be missing was now gone.

"What's happening now?" Liz asked.

Theo turned to Ava and her two friends, his expression grave. "My guess is they may bring in a cadaver dog to assist with the search."

Ava's brows knitted in confusion. "A cadaver dog? What is that?"

"It's a specially trained dog that helps us locate bodies," Theo explained gently.

Maria put a supportive hand on Ava's shoulder.

Ava felt sick as terror set in. "You think..."

"I'm afraid we have reason to believe Mr. Miller may have been murdered," Theo murmured.

Ava's hand flew to her mouth, her eyes widening with shock. "Oh no, poor Mr. Miller... I mean, we didn't get along, but he didn't deserve this."

Ava had an idea and approached one of the officers, her mind churning with a different possibility. "Officer, what if Mr. Miller had an accident with one of his tools in the shed and had to rush to the hospital? Maybe that's why he left his horse without any notice. Could you please call the local hospitals to see if he's there?"

The officer met Ava's gaze, nodding with a reassurance that was part empathy, part professionalism. "We haven't ruled out any possibilities. We'll definitely make calls to the local hospitals and check if he's been admitted. We want to cover all our bases."

The sound of the rumbling engine of a newly arrived vehicle outside drew their attention. Liz, Ava, and Maria shifted their gazes towards the window to see a truck open, revealing a highly trained police canine. The cadaver dog was given Mr. Miller's hat—something he wore often but didn't wash often—to smell to acquire his scent, then the canine led them across Mr. Miller's property.

The police led the dog to the shed where the blood was found, then the dog headed straight for Ava's family's property.

It wasn't long before the dog signaled by a patch of freshly turned earth in Ava's garden. Shovels pierced the soil, each scoop an invasion into the normalcy that had once been. Then, an apron—stained and forgotten—emerged from the dirt, and beneath it, the grisly discovery of Mr. Miller's body, ending all speculation in the most morbid manner. It didn't take a pathologist to see that his life had been ended by blunt force trauma to the head.

Ava stared in horror at the unearthed body on her family's property. "I didn't do this," she managed to whisper.

The lead detective on what was now confirmed as a homicide asked her if she was willing to answer some questions.

"Yes, I will do whatever you need," Ava agreed shakily.

"Is this your apron?" an officer asked, presenting the damning fabric evidence.

Ava nodded slowly, wracked with confusion and fear. "Yes, it was my mother's apron. I've been wearing it while working on the house."

As the officers documented her words and the evidence, Ava stood in the shadow of her childhood home, clinging to the truth with both hands, unwilling to let it slip through her fingers—even as the world tilted into chaos around her. Once again, she was feeling confined and trapped, but this time by damaging circumstantial evidence that pointed to her being a criminal—not a victim.

Somehow, this felt even worse.

"We appreciate your cooperation. However..." Detective Barrett's expression grew solemn. "Ms. Sullivan, given the current evidence and the fact that a serious crime has been committed, I'm placing you under arrest for the murder of Jonas Miller."

Chapter Twenty-six

Ava's heart plummeted at his words and she felt the room close in around her, a surge of fear and disbelief racing through her veins as she felt the cold grip of handcuffs around her wrists. "But I didn't do anything to him," she protested weakly, her voice tinged with the edge of panic.

Her protests were lost in the procedure and protocol as she heard the snap of handcuffs around her wrists as her Miranda rights were given to her. "Theo," she cried, looking back at him, her eyes welling with fear and pleading. "I didn't do it!"

Theo stood silent and torn, his own conflict paralyzing him. He couldn't stop them from arresting her, not with the evidence against her. As Ava was led away, Theo promised her, "I will find the truth, Ava. Hang in there. Don't answer any more questions until you get an attorney."

"I would never hurt anyone," she insisted. "I didn't kill him."

"Don't say anything, Ava," Theo told her.

As Detective Barrett led Ava out the door, Maria and Liz were outspoken in her defense, their voices rising in a chorus of indignant protest. "She didn't do it! This is a mistake!" Maria called out, her hands balled into fists.

Liz echoed her sentiments, her face showing her distress. "Ava's innocent! She would never do this. You're arresting the wrong person!"

Detective Barrett marched her out and said, "It is not my job to make the determination of her guilt or innocence. That will be up to the court to decide if, upon examination of all the evidence, there is enough to bring charges against Ms. Sullivan in the death of Mr. Miller. If that is the case, she will be tried for murder. Right now, though, we have probable cause to make the arrest. We can hold her for seventy-two hours while we make the determination whether we will be filing charges against her or releasing her."

Their words were drowned out as Ava was led to the waiting police car. The gathered neighbors watched, a ripple of murmurs passing through them like leaves in the wind.

"What's going on?"

"Is that Ava they're arresting?"

"They think she had something to do with what happened to Mr. Miller?"

The whispers swirled, the community's curiosity piqued by the drama unfolding in front of them. Ava kept her head down, the shame of being paraded in front of her friends and neighbors, handcuffed like a common criminal, igniting a flame of indignation in her chest. She hadn't done anything to her neighbor.

Arrested again. Will I be able to prove my innocence this time, with Theo's help? God, please help them see I'm innocent, she prayed.

As she was placed in the back of the police car, her eyes met Theo's for a fleeting moment. His expression was unreadable, but she saw the promise in his eyes, the unspoken assurance that this wasn't the end, that her story wouldn't close with an unjust chapter.

Detective Barrett closed the door, the solid thud shutting out the life Ava had started to rebuild. As the car pulled away, the murmur of her friends and neighbors grew fainter.

***

Inside the cold, sterile walls of the police station, Ava was photographed, checked over for injuries, fingerprinted, DNA swabbed, and ushered into an interrogation room—an environment designed to be uninviting and unyielding. Detective Barrett and another detective, a tag team of inquiry, sat across from her. The table that separated them seemed to be an ocean of doubt and accusation.

With the recorder turned on, Detective Barrett began the interrogation. "Ms. Sullivan, for the record, can you please state your name, date of birth, and repeat what happened on the day Jonas Miller disappeared?"

Ava took a deep breath, steeling herself to narrate once more the events that had catapulted her life into chaos. She decided not to hire Natalie's attorney and to just tell the truth, hoping that would be enough in the end. As she spoke, her voice was steady, though it carried the fatigue of a story retold too many times. She recounted the argument with Mr. Miller and what she'd seen in the barn and the house.

"But I swear to you, that's all there is to it. I didn't see him after the argument. I didn't do anything to him," Ava insisted, her own words starting to sound hollow in her ears.

The detectives probed, circling her story for holes and inconsistencies. They asked the same questions in different ways, but Ava's narrative remained unchanged. It was the only truth she had to offer.

As the interrogation dragged on, Ava's hope began to fray at the edges. She knew that repeating her story, true as it was, might not be enough to dispel the shadow of doubt that clung to her like an unwanted shroud. The stark reality that she was caught in the unforgiving machinery of the justice system was overwhelming.

All the while, outside the room, behind desks and doors, Theo worked tirelessly. In the battle between evidence and truth, Theo was determined to shine a light bright enough to unveil the reality of what had happened to Mr. Miller—and return Ava to the life she rightfully deserved.

The crime lab later confirmed that the blood on the hammer matched Mr. Miller's blood type, with DNA results pending. The only fingerprints were Ava's, but none were in blood or on top of the blood. Theo hadn't used her hammer but had always brought and used his father's tools.

As Ava sat alone in the cold interrogation room, she had to fight the demons of her past. She had to believe in Theo, in the fact that truth would prevail, and her newest nightmare would end.

***

Theo sat at his desk, the hum of the station around him falling away as his mind worked feverishly, seeking the thread that would unravel the knot of Ava's predicament. Then, with a flash of recollection, he remembered her words, the way her voice had faltered when she spoke of Raymond "Razor" DeLuca—the violent criminal she had bravely testified against, leading to his conviction.

DeLuca had vowed revenge in the courtroom, had promised that Ava would rue the day she took the stand against him. Theo's training had taught him that threats in the heat of a trial's moment were often just that—empty words meant to intimidate. But what if DeLuca's threat was more than mere bravado? What if he had the opportunity, means, and malice to carry it out?

His fingers moved quickly, pulling up the name Raymond DeLuca in the system. The screen switched, and Theo flinched as his worst fears took shape in the words before him: "Escaped from prison." The date was three days earlier. A supplemental report said that while he was being treated in an outside medical facility, he held a nurse at knife point with a scalpel, demanded the zip tie on his still tethered wrists be severed, then he escaped. The initial notice also included instructions to contact Ava who was a witness against him and was personally threatened.

"What?!" he yelled out loud, causing several of his colleagues to look at him with concern. He ignored them, fuming.

The realization struck Theo with the force of a blow. DeLuca was out. He could have made it to Unity within hours and had resources and connections on both sides of the prison walls. The pieces fell into a grim pattern: Ava being framed for Mr. Miller's murder and going to prison for a crime she didn't commit would be an ideal revenge, more torturous than a quick death.

Theo rose from his chair with a new urgency. He marched to his sergeant's office, his eyes blazing.

"Sarge," Theo burst in, not bothering with pleasantries, "Did you know Raymond DeLuca escaped from prison three days ago? He was Ava Sullivan's pimp who she testified against. He made threats against her. She should have been notified three days ago."

The sergeant looked up, his expression turning serious. "No."

Theo was incredulous. "And why wasn't Ava Sullivan notified by New York? Or by our department? DeLuca made a direct threat on her life in open court. She should've been the first to know, maybe even relocated for her protection."

There was a pause, the tension thick. The sergeant sighed, rubbing the bridge of his nose. "Someone dropped the ball, Theo. It might be a screw up and someone forgot to make the call, or she didn't notify them or us of her current address and phone number... I don't know.

But you're right, notification should have been made or attempted, but that does not mean she is not responsible for this murder. They may be unrelated."

Theo leaned forward, palms flat on the sergeant's desk. "I think DeLuca has found her, Sarge. He's framing her for the murder of Mr. Miller. He probably wore gloves so his prints wouldn't get on the hammer. He probably tracked Ava down—maybe even got the information from one of the other women he controlled—and witnessed the entire argument between Ava and Mr. Miller. It fits DeLuca's threat—he wanted to make her suffer for the rest of her life. What better way to do that than imprison her for a crime she didn't comm it?"

The gravity of Theo's words settled over the room. The sergeant leaned back, absorbing the implications.

"Because killing her would be too easy, right?" the sergeant said, piecing it together. "He wants her alive to live out her days behind bars, tormented by the life that's been stolen from her—all as payback for putting him in prison. He probably escaped just to do this."

Theo nodded, his jaw set. "Exactly. I need to look into this, follow the evidence. See if there are any security cameras that caught him in the area. If DeLuca is behind this, he won't stop until he's taken everything from her. If she is cleared from this murder investigation, he will try again. We can't let that happen."

The sergeant leaned forward, elbows on the desk. "All right, Theo. I'll give you the clearance to pursue this lead. But be careful. If DeLuca is in play here, you're both in danger. We'll also need to coordinate with New York to fix this lapse immediately."

Theo knew what was at stake—the innocence of a woman who had already faced too many demons in her life. The justice system had failed Ava twice already by not protecting her, and Theo wouldn't let it happen again.

***

In the interrogation room again, a place where Ava had been entangled in a web of intermittent questioning, Theo burst through the door, followed by the sergeant. Detective Barrett looked up from his notes.

The seventy-two-hour deadline to charge or release had arrived.

"Barrett, stop the questioning and uncuff her. It's time to release her," Theo said sharply, his eyes fixed on Ava with a message of silent reassurance. "Ava, we have reason to believe that Raymond DeLuca may be involved in framing you for the murder of Mr. Miller," Theo said, wasting no time. "We confirmed he has escaped from prison."

A new fear flashed in Ava's eyes, but it was replaced with realization. "Yes. It has to be him. He must have been watching me and saw the argument with Mr. Miller. It gave him the perfect opportunity to create a motive for me."

Theo nodded, his brows furrowed in thought. "It's a strong possibility he did this. The timing suggests it may be possible. And we'll have a clearer picture once the autopsy results are available to narrow down the time and manner of Mr. Miller's death. The forensic investigators have just now determined that it was likely a much taller individual that murdered Mr. Miller, due to the angle of the blow, or that he was on his knees or bent over. They are still exploring several possibilities. We are awaiting their opinions on that and several other issues now that may be exculpatory for you."

The sergeant interjected, "For now, Ava, I want you to remain in Unity, but we are working to uncover the truth."

"We need to make sure she has protection at all times, at least until DeLuca is in prison," Theo said. He turned to Ava. "DeLuca may come after you at home. Are you sure you want to go there?"

"If he comes after me at home and you or other officers are there, wouldn't that mean you might be able to catch him in the act, and that would incriminate him? If so, yes, I want to go home," Ava said.

"Do you have friends you could stay with?" Detective Barrett asked.

"Well, yes. I could stay with friends," she said.

"It would be best if you secretly move from house to house, but not let anyone see you outside or when you are transported from each location. We will have someone check outside to see if anyone is watching before you move," Theo said. "We will bring you home to get your things."

"No going outside unless it's absolutely necessary, stay away from windows, keep the curtains closed, and no going into town," Barrett added.

Ava sighed. It sounded like her life when she'd been locked in the basement. But hopefully, this wouldn't last long, and she'd be among friends.

"We are a small unit, and we need our officers investigating this case. I may be able to spare one officer to protect you part time, Ms. Sullivan," the sergeant told her.

"I will stay with her when I'm not on duty, investigating," Theo said.

"I would be happy to also protect you, Ms. Sullivan, when I'm not working and Theo is not available," Detective Barrett offered.

"Thank you, Barrett, but we may not be able to pay you. It would be a volunteer position," the sergeant said.

"I still want to do it," Detective Barrett said.

"Thank you," Ava and Theo both said at the same time.

Detective Barrett said, "Ms. Sullivan, your safety and preventing any further attempts to implicate you in any crime is our immediate concern."

"Thank you for coming with me," she said. "And I hope that if DeLuca does try to get to me there that you'll be able to arrest him."

Ava was escorted from the police station and was going home to Unity—hopefully, a safe place.

As they walked outside, each stride Theo took out of the station was driven by determination; he would find Raymond DeLuca, not just for Ava's sake but to bring closure to Mr. Miller's senseless death. It was a race against time, but he had no intention of losing.

Ava knew she might have to return if the investigation did not continue in her favor, but she had faith in Theo and God's plan.

As they settled into the unmarked car that Theo would drive to Unity, Theo kept his gaze focused on the road ahead, but his mind was locked in the intricacies of Ava's case. The streets slipped by as Detective Barrett drove in the car behind them.

"Theo, how could DeLuca have possibly figured out where I was staying?" Ava's voice was weary, the fight of the day evident in each word.

Theo glanced at her, weighing possibilities. "Did you ever tell DeLuca anything that might have led him to you? About being Amish or where you're from?"

"No, never. I didn't tell him I was Amish or anything about my past. He didn't care about where we were from."

"Could any of the other women have told him? Did you tell them about being Amish or that you were from Unity?" Theo pressed, knowing that in the intricacies of human connections often lay answers.

Ava shook her head, her lips a thin line. "No, I kept that to myself. None of the other women knew where I was from. It was a part of my life I wanted to forget, and we didn't have much time to get to know each other. A lot of them came from broken pasts and felt the same way, so we didn't really talk about where we were from."

The car hummed as Theo drove. "Did you mention going home to Unity to anyone when the pimps were arrested? Even in passing? Maybe one of the other women you were closer to?"

Ava inhaled sharply, her eyes widening as a sliver of realization cut through the fog of her troubled thoughts. "Carmen," she whispered, the name falling like a drop in still water, rippling with implication. "I only told Carmen. She was my friend."

He nodded slowly, his mind churning.

Ava looked at Theo, eyes wide. "Do you think she is in danger?"

The possibility chilled the air within the car. "Not anymore," Theo replied grimly.

"What? What is that supposed to mean? Do you think he hurt her or...that he killed her?" Her voice broke and she covered her mouth, stifling a sob.

"He may have hurt her to get her to tell him where you went. We should reach out and contact her now," Theo said, reaching for Ava's hands.

"Oh, no, Carmen!" Ava cried, her shoulders shaking as she began to sob. "This is all my fault."

"No, Ava, this is not your fault. DeLuca is a horrible person, and he is the one who did this. We need to find out if she was hurt right away. And if he did, we will bring him to justice for that, too. Do you know her last name?"

"Bernard. Her name is Carmen Bernard. She said she was going home to live with her family in upstate New York," Ava said. "But I don't know where, exactly. I'm sorry."

"That helps, Ava. New York Police may have that information. I'll find her." Theo nodded. "I'll even call several area hospitals if I hit dead ends. I'll find out if anything happened to her."

"Please tell me, no matter how bad it is," she choked out.

"I will."

The unmarked police car rolled to a stop in front of Ava's family's home.

"We should only stay here for a few minutes to pack your bag, then we need to find you a place to stay. Can you ask your friends if you can stay with one of them?" Theo asked.

"Yes, I can ask them, but they may not want to put themselves and their families in danger," she said. "And I'd understand that."

"Barrett will explain the situation to them." Theo glanced over at Ava, offering a reassuring nod as they both exited the vehicle. Behind them, Detective Barrett emerged from his car, his expression all business as he joined them.

Together, they walked to the door and entered the house. Theo and Barrett made a protective sweep of her home, exchanging a few words in hushed tones.

Turning to Ava, Theo said, "I trust Detective Barrett more than anyone else to protect you while I'm gone. I need to track down DeLuca, but you'll be safe with my partner. After my shift, we will trade places. And if there are any gaps in coverage, we will take you to one of your friend's homes that DeLuca would not know about."

Ava, her hands nervously knotted together, looking at both Theo and Barrett. "Thank you," she replied quietly.

"I think it would be a good idea for you to borrow some Amish clothing and disguise yourself. It'll help you blend in with all the other women and might throw DeLuca off just enough if he's watching from a distance."

Ava nodded. "I still have my old clothing and my mother's clothing in storage in the attic. I'll get it."

"And Barrett, I think it would also be best if you wore Amish clothing so that if DeLuca sees you, he might not realize you're protecting Ava," Theo said. He turned to Ava. "Do you have more men's clothing in storage?"

"I saw some of my father's clothing in the attic, too," Ava said in a soft voice. For some reason, her mother hadn't gotten rid of her father's clothing when he had died. It was a good thing because now they'd need it. She doubted any of her brother's clothing would fit Barrett.

"Now I need your help," Theo asked, "Can you tell me which of your neighbors are not Amish? I want to see if any of them have security cameras."

Ava pointed out a couple of houses down the road that belonged to non-Amish families.

"Thank you," he said.

She could only watch as Theo prepared to exit into the darkness that lay like a blanket over the world outside.

He turned back to her before crossing the threshold, the weight of the moment pressing down on them. In the quiet, charged air between them, there was an unspoken acknowledgment of the danger, of the dangerous path they were each about to walk. Detective Barrett stepped into the other room, giving them some privacy.

"I'll find him, Ava," Theo said, his voice a low promise that carried more than the words themselves spoke. "I'll find the truth, and I'll make sure Carmen is safe."

Ava's eyes met his. "Thank you, Theo. Be careful," she replied, her voice steady but betraying her fear.

Theo nodded, taking in the sight of her, the way her strength seemed to hold even in the face of an ever-growing storm. There was more he wanted to say, a comfort he wished he could give her with more than just words. He wanted to fold her in his arms, to reassure her with his embrace, to kiss her and promise a future that would be safe and filled with happiness.

But now was not the time for such intimacies or promises—especially since they'd only known each other for a short time. Any personal feelings had to be set aside so he could focus on what was at stake—both Ava's life and possibly Carmen's life, and more remotely, the lives of Ava's Amish friends and neighbors, especially if DeLuca already killed Mr. Miller.

So, with a final, meaningful look, Theo stepped out of the house, leaving behind the woman who had come to mean more to him than just a person he vowed to protect.

Chapter Twenty-seven

As he slowly drove down the dirt road, Theo couldn't help but notice the subtle nuances that separated the Amish homes from those of the *Englishers*. The *Englisher* homes had cars in the driveways and powerlines while the Amish homes had no powerlines or cars, of course, and they often had several loads of laundry hanging out on the clotheslines.

As he walked up the driveway to one house, he noticed a doorbell security camera. He rang the bell and waited. A middle-aged man opened the door, eyeing Theo curiously.

"Hello, sir. I'm Detective Kingsley," he said, showing his badge. "I'm working on a case and was wondering if you had any security camera footage for the past week."

The man's expression shifted to one of concern and cooperation. "Yes, we have a doorbell security camera. Is this about the commotion near the Miller place?"

"Yes, it is," Theo replied. "Would you mind sharing the footage with me? It could be crucial to the investigation."

"Of course, come in," the man said, stepping aside to let Theo in.

Inside, the man provided Theo with a USB drive containing recent recordings.

"Thank you, this could be very helpful," Theo said, shaking the man's hand firmly. He went to the other *Englisher* homes, but no one else had security cameras.

With the USB drive in hand, he drove back to CPDU to watch the footage.

***

Ava finished changing into her old Amish dress that she'd taken down from the attic. She stepped out of the hall to see that Barrett had already finished changing into her father's old clothes. Barrett didn't look anything like Bill Sullivan had, but Ava's stomach still churned when she saw the clothing on him.

"Thanks for letting me use these," Barrett said.

"Sorry if they smell a bit musty," she managed to say. He shrugged.

"No problem, really. When my shift ends, I can throw them in the wash at my house." It wasn't like they could throw them in an electric washer and dryer here. All Ava had in the house was the Maytag washer, so it would take too long to wash them and then dry on the clothesline. He needed the disguise now.

"I'll go pack," she said, quickly turning away.

She went into her room to pack her bag when she looked out the window and spotted two familiar figures hurrying toward her house in a buggy—Maria and Liz, her steadfast friends. She was just about to go ask them if she could stay with one of them to let Barrett go home to sleep, and here they were.

She answered the door and let them in.

"Ava!" Maria called out, her voice tinged with worry. "We saw the unmarked police cars nearby and hurried over to see if you were here.

Are you okay?" She looked Ava over. "Why are you wearing Amish clothing?"

"We've been so worried about you," Liz added. "Ever since we saw you being arrested…"

"I'm sure you're both wondering what's been happening," Ava started, her eyes recounting the recent turmoil in a glimpse. "Theo suspects that DeLuca framed me for the murder of Mr. Miller. They let me go. I'm wearing this to try and blend in…just in case he comes looking for me."

"I'm so sorry you're going through this," Liz said. "It's terrifying. Thank the Lord you're here now."

Maria said, "Everyone will be so relieved that you're home safe, Ava."

Ava knew she wasn't safe, but she didn't correct her friends. Her voice was quiet, laced with uncertainty. "Everyone here thinks I killed Mr. Miller, don't they?"

Maria shook her head firmly. "No, not at all. I don't know of anyone who thought you did it."

Liz added, "When we saw you being arrested, we were all just confused. It didn't make sense. We figured the police had the wrong person."

"But so many people witnessed the argument between Mr. Miller and me just before he was killed," Ava pressed, unable to shake the doubt that had settled like frost upon her spirit.

Maria shrugged, a gesture steeped in the simple logic that bonded the community of Unity. "People argue. That doesn't mean anyone thought you'd do something like that."

"Trust me, people here talk. If people thought you did it, we would have heard about it," Liz added. "You're such a sweet, kind soul. Everyone here knows you're not capable of hurting anyone."

"Really?" Ava's voice was a mix of surprise and relief. "I guess I jumped to conclusions. I assumed everyone would think I was guilty. I should have had more faith in my neighbors. I guess it's just hard for me to trust people sometimes."

"Well, that's understandable, but you know you can always trust us," Maria said. "I also used to have a hard time trusting people when I came back to rejoin the Amish. The man I dated while I was an *Englisher* was abusive and manipulative, and it took me a long time to recover. I'm still recovering."

"Oh, I trust both of you completely," Ava said. "Actually, I need to ask a favor. I need a place to stay. They want me to move from house to house so Razor is less likely to find me. Detective Barrett or Theo will be staying with me at all times to keep me safe."

Liz quickly chimed in, "You can stay with us, Ava. My family would be glad to have you."

"And you are welcome at my house, too," Maria added. "As you know, I live with my in-laws, but I'm sure they would be happy to have you over."

Ava felt a rush of gratitude. "Thank you both so much. What if I stay at your place tonight, Liz, and then at Maria's tomorrow?"

Liz nodded, her expression resolute. "That sounds like a plan. And I'm sure Freya and Adam would also have you over for a night or two. Especially since Adam is a police officer—he can protect you."

"Well, with the baby, I don't want to impose."

"This is what friends are for," Liz said. "They will want to help."

Maria added, "And my parents would probably be happy to have you over as well, if needed. We just want to make sure you're safe. Hopefully Theo can prove you're innocent before long."

With her friends beside her, Ava felt a little of the tension ease from her shoulders. She quickly packed her bags, throwing in essentials.

As she closed her suitcase, she turned to Maria and Liz, her eyes filled with determination.

"Let's go," she said with a small but firm smile.

"We can take the buggy to my house if that's okay, Detective Barrett." Liz turned to Barrett for a response, and he nodded.

"Actually, that works. I'll leave my car here. If DeLuca does show up, it might lead him to believe we are still here and possibly throw him off," he said.

The three women quickly made their way toward the buggy with Barrett following close behind. To anyone passing by, they looked like a group of Amish friends taking a ride in a buggy on a beautiful day.

When they arrived, Liz's family—Conrad, Rachel, Anneliese, and Naomi—stepped out to greet them, their faces etched with concern.

"*Mamm, Daed*, Ava needs a place to stay tonight," Liz said.

Anneliese and Naomi stood nearby, watching quietly.

"Well, before you agree, I want you to know the dangers," Ava said. She turned to Barrett. "Mr. and Mrs. Kulp, this is Detective Barrett."

Detective Barret shook their hands. "Nice to meet you. Kingsley and I will be taking turns protecting Ava." He explained the situation to them, and they listened intently.

"I understand if you don't want to put your family in danger," Ava said.

"Nonsense. We trust in the Lord. We aren't afraid," Conrad said. "We want you to stay."

"Ava, we're so sorry this is happening," Rachel said, enveloping her in a warm hug. "You're always welcome here."

Conrad nodded in agreement. "We'll do whatever we can to help you through this."

Anneliese and Naomi approached her, also hugging her.

"It'll be like a fun sleepover," Anneliese added, trying to cheer her up.

"We can try to take your mind off things, if you want," Naomi offered.

Ava nodded. "That might do me some good."

"You can have my room. I'll sleep in Anneliese's room," Liz said.

"Detective Barrett can have Naomi's room," Rachel said. "Naomi can sleep in Anneliese's room as well."

"Actually, I don't need a room. I'll stay downstairs. I won't be sleeping," Detective Barrett said.

"Very well," Rachel agreed, understanding what he was implying—he would be up all night keeping watch.

Ava felt tears well up in her eyes, touched by their kindness. "Thank you all. This means so much to me. I didn't mean for any of this to happen."

"This isn't your fault," Liz said. "What are friends for?"

They showed Ava to Liz's room, where she could store her bags and take a moment to breathe. Liz's room was cozy and inviting, a stark contrast to the police jail cell she had been in. After settling in, she joined the family downstairs.

As they sat around the table, sharing a meal and conversation, Ava felt a sense of normalcy return. Liz's family treated her not just as a guest, but as one of their own. The warmth and care in their gestures and words filled her with a semblance of peace.

***

At the station, Theo watched the footage at his desk, then he wasted no time in finding his sergeant.

"I think we have something," he announced, plugging the USB drive into the computer in his sergeant's office.

Together, they watched the footage, scanning the timeline for anything unusual. Then, there it was. DeLuca was captured walking past the neighbor's house, his demeanor suspicious. They watched as he moved towards the edge of the woods, right near Ava's house. DeLuca could be seen crouching, hiding, his gaze fixed on the house—a silent watcher. DeLuca probably hadn't even considered the possibility of security cameras in an Amish community, not realizing that some of the neighbors were not Amish.

The footage revealed another vital moment. A partially hidden figure wearing a dark hooded sweatshirt was seen watching Ava's house. By enhancing the image, they were able to see the person, who resembled Razor in height and build. The camera also caught an argument between Ava and Mr. Miller, which happened in their front yards, just at the front edge of the garden.

Later that night, a camera caught the figure again, this time sneaking onto Mr. Miller's property. The person then walked away, off camera toward the garden. After enhancing the video, they confirmed it was DeLuca.

Theo and his sergeant exchanged looks.

"This is enough to create reasonable doubt as to Ava and probable cause as to Razor," the sergeant said, nodding thoughtfully. "Even without an eyewitness to the crime, this footage shows DeLuca's presence and potential involvement and the time he was there. It will be interesting to see if it corresponds with the window of the death of Mr. Miller."

Theo felt a wave of relief wash over him. "We'll need to follow up, but this could really help Ava's case," he said, determination setting in. There was still much work to do, but for the first time, a glimmer of hope appeared on the horizon. The last known location for this suspect and prison escapee was sent out to all the units in the area.

Theo needed to find Razor and hoped to also find blood-splattered clothing or other evidence of the crime with him. The hunt for answers was on, and time was a luxury they did not have.

Chapter Twenty-eight

Theo dialed number after number, calling his former place of employment, then the local police departments in upstate New York, inquiring about any disturbances involving Carmen Bernard or her family.

Finally, a small-town officer in upstate New York shared information that lined up with Theo's inquiry.

"Yes, we did have an incident involving a Bernard here," the officer confirmed, the sound of keyboard keys clicking as he checked on his computer. "Caller was a Marcos Bernard... says his daughter, Carmen, was targeted by a man who broke into their home, a Raymond DeLuca."

Theo's grip on the phone tightened, the calm in his voice belying the storm of emotions within. "Did he say what DeLuca was after?"

"He was after the location of an Ava Sullivan, according to the report," the officer answered. "When the daughter didn't provide answers, he threatened her and the other family members with a gun. Under duress, she told him that Ava had gone home to Unity, Maine."

He steadied his voice before asking, "Was the family harmed?"

"They were shaken up, and the daughter, Carmen, she got roughed up. He hit her in the face with the gun when she wouldn't tell him where her friend was. DeLuca fled before we arrived. She's been admitted to our local hospital." The officer's tone was professional, yet it carried the unmistakable trace of empathy. "Sorry to say we didn't get the guy and were unable to find contact information for Ava Sullivan. We only sent a report with this information to the local law enforcement agency near Unity."

Relief, cold and sharp, pierced Theo's mounting dread. At least Carmen was alive, though the fact that DeLuca could have killed her was a chilling thought. And his department had received notice of this threat? What could have happened to that? Why wasn't he aware of this? Was it his own department that had dropped the ball?

"The prison guard who lost Razor should have notified everyone in a couple hours—the D.A., the police officers on the case, and any witnesses. If they had, Carmen Bernard might not have been injured," Theo spat out in indignation.

"Well, yes, but the police officer who took Carmen's report might have called, sent a teletype alert, fax, or an internet alert. Maybe the fax machine didn't have paper in it or maybe the call was missed during an overnight shift. Unfortunately, these things happens sometimes."

Theo sighed, pinching the bridge of his nose. Whatever had happened, it didn't matter now. All that mattered was keeping Ava safe. "Thank you, Officer. Your cooperation could help us stop DeLuca before he does any more harm," Theo said.

"Happy to help. Good luck to you and please notify our department if you make an arrest. We will be in line with charges of our own," the officer replied before ending the call.

Theo made a quick note as to the officer's name, number, and summary of the date, time, and what occurred for his report. With no time to waste, Theo was quick to contact Ava who was with

Detective Barrett so he could tell both of them this information himself.

The phone call connected, and the familiar yet strained voice of Ava answered. "Theo? Is everything okay? Did you find anything out about Carmen?"

He hesitated, the words catching briefly in his throat. "Ava, I've got news, put this on speaker so Detective Barrett can also hear," Once that was done, Theo began, his tone measured to deliver the update with as much care as the situation allowed. "Carmen is alive, but she was hurt. She'll be okay."

A pause hung in the air, a space filled with Ava's quickened breathing, the anticipation of further details palpable.

"Carmen was incredibly brave... She didn't give up your location, not at first," Theo continued, each word chosen to convey both the severity and the heroism of Carmen's actions. "DeLuca threatened her, but she stood her ground. It was only when he hit her in the face with his gun and threatened to kill her family that she told him you had gone to Unity."

On the other end of the line, Theo could almost feel the mix of emotions swirling within Ava as silence met his explanation. Then, with a voice carrying a tremor of both admiration and sadness, Ava responded.

"Carmen... she's always been so loyal, so protective. I can't believe she was put in such a position because of me. She could have told him right away, but she held out as long as she could. Her family was in danger. I completely understand."

Theo could hear the gratitude laced with guilt in Ava's voice—a mix of feelings that spoke to the deep bond between the two friends.

"It wasn't your fault, Ava. None of this is. Carmen made a choice to protect her family," Theo reassured her, aiming to fortify her spirit in the face of the daunting truth. "And she probably knew that if she lied, he would come back and kill them."

Ava took a deep breath, collecting herself. "Thank you for telling me, Theo. I hope she'll be okay. Can you take me to see her after this is all over?"

"Of course, I will," Theo promised, a vow etched with determination. "We're doing everything we can to find DeLuca and stop him. You and Carmen, you're both survivors, and we're here to make sure justice is served."

The promise seemed to offer Ava a fragile semblance of comfort, a light in the dark journey that lay ahead for both of them. With a few words of parting, they hung up, each left to wrestle with their realities—Ava with her growing concern for her injured friend, and Theo with the unyielding drive to bring a dangerous felon to restore the peace that both women deserved.

***

As Ava settled into the guest room, Liz, Anneliese, and Naomi came in, concern etched on their faces.

"Do you want to go to sleep, or would you like some company?" Liz asked gently. "We're so sorry about your friend, Carmen."

"Thank you. She didn't deserve that. Please, come in. There's no way I'll be able to sleep for a while, so please stay."

The three sisters immediately piled onto the bed next to her, their eyes filled with empathy and curiosity.

"Tell us about your friend, Carmen, and your time in New York," Anneliese asked softly, leaning forward. "What's the city like?"

"Unless you don't want to talk about it," Naomi added, nudging her sister.

Taking a deep breath, Ava decided to share her story. "No, it's okay. I'll tell you. Well, it was... challenging. I moved there with dreams of becoming a novelist, but things took a dark turn. I ended up under the control of some very bad people. They exploited me, and it was hard, really hard, but I met some good people too, like my friend Carmen. Carmen is a brave, sweet soul."

She kept the gruesome details out, focusing instead on the broader strokes of her journey. As she spoke, the sisters listened intently, hanging on every word.

"And then there were the years in the basement," Ava continued, her voice barely above a whisper. "I was locked away for so long. It changed me, but I'm determined to make something good out of my life now. I want to open a women's shelter and become an author."

"You're so strong," Liz said, her eyes shining with admiration. "You've been through so much, and you still have such big dreams."

Anneliese nodded. "We believe in you, Ava. You're going to do amazing things."

As the night grew later, the conversation lightened. They started sharing jokes and telling more lighthearted stories from their own lives, filling the room with laughter and giggles.

"I can't tell you how grateful I am to have such good friends who care about me and help me in my time of need," Ava said, her voice full of emotion.

The three sisters smiled, their faces radiant with the bond of friendship. "We're always here for you, Ava," Liz said, grabbing her hand.

Before finally surrendering to exhaustion, they joined hands and prayed together. "Dear Lord, please keep us safe and help Theo find the culprit. Bring justice and peace to this situation."

Soon, the three sisters dozed off, crowded together on the bed. Ava smiled at the sight, feeling a deep sense of gratitude and peace.

Gently, she rose and grabbed a quilt from the closet, wrapping it around herself as she lay down on the floor. She didn't mind the hard surface; the warmth of friendship and the hope for a better future filled her heart.

As her eyelids grew heavy, she looked at the three sisters, fast asleep on the bed, and felt incredibly blessed. Closing her eyes, she finally drifted off to sleep, comforted by the presence of true friends.

"Thank you, God," she whispered, "for the friends and family who are here for me. Please give me the strength to face what's ahead, and help us find a way to clear my name."

***

The next morning, Ava woke up with a sense of unease but also hope.

"Oh my," Liz said, stretching as she woke up. "We took over the bed!"

"Sorry, Ava. We fell asleep here and you slept on the floor," Naomi apologized.

Anneliese giggled.

"Don't worry. I actually slept fine. You all looked so peaceful, I didn't want to disturb you. Really, I didn't mind," Ava said.

They got dressed and made their way downstairs to find Detective Barrett drinking a cup of coffee, dark circles under his eyes indicating he had stayed up all night.

"Did anything happen last night?" Ava asked, her voice filled with concern.

"No, nothing worth reporting," Detective Barrett replied with a slight smile. "I kept an eye out, looking through the windows, but everything was quiet."

Relief washed over Ava, but before she could say more, there was a knock at the door. Liz opened it to find a few neighbors standing there, concern and support visible on their faces.

They stepped inside.

"How did you know I was here?" Ava asked.

"We figured you might be with either Liz or Maria. We just checked Maria's house, then came here," Mrs. Johnson explained. "Ava, I had to tell the truth when Detective Barrett questioned me, but I believe you wouldn't hurt anyone. As far as I know, everyone here believes you are innocent."

Touched by her support, Ava nodded. "Thank you, Mrs. Johnson."

More neighbors came in, each offering similar sentiments, showing their belief in her and willingness to help however they could. Soon, Maria arrived with her mother-in-law, Hannah.

"Ava," Maria started, her eyes filled with warmth, "if you need another place to stay, our home is always open to you."

Hannah nodded, smiling kindly. "We would be happy to have you."

Before Ava could respond, Freya and her husband Adam entered with their baby, Robert. Adam walked up to Ava, extending his hand. "I'm Adam Lapp. Freya and I would be glad to have you stay at our house. As a police officer, I can help protect you by rotating with Detective Barrett and Detective Kingsley. We work together, actually."

Detective Barrett, listening nearby, nodded in agreement. "That sounds like a better option. With more police in the rotation, they won't get as tired, and you'd be safer. And if Theo or the CDPU still haven't found the culprit in a day or two, you can stay with Maria, and either Theo or I will go with you."

Ava was overwhelmed by the outpouring of support. "Thank you all so much," she said sincerely, looking around at the faces of her friends and neighbors. "I can't express how grateful I am for your belief in me and your willingness to help. Truly, thank you."

"Why don't we go to my house now?" Adam asked. "It's my day off, and you'll be safer there. Detective Barrett looks like he should go home and enjoy a long nap."

"I think that's a good idea," Detective Barrett said.

Ava agreed. "I'll go pack up. Mr. and Mrs. Kulp, Liz, Anneliese, and Naomi, thank you all so much for letting me stay here last night. I really appreciate it."

Anneliese and Naomi smiled, each hugging her.

"We are happy to help," Liz said. "Please let us know if there's anything else we can do."

She felt a renewed sense of hope and determination as she went to get her things from upstairs. With her friends and community rallying around her, she felt stronger and more supported than ever. Despite the dark times, this new alliance gave her the courage to keep fighting for her innocence and future.

Even though they were putting themselves in danger, her friends were willing to shelter her. With hugs and reassurances, the group began to make plans to protect Ava—a new, unexpected Amish alliance.

Chapter Twenty-nine

The fluorescent lights of the precinct cast long shadows across the room where Theo sat that morning, surrounded by stacks of papers and open files on his desk. He'd been up all night going over files, searching for a clue. There was no time for sleep.

The air was thick with the scent of stale coffee and the tension of unsolved cases. Focused on the task at hand, Theo flipped through the pages of Raymond "Razor" DeLuca's files once more, searching for a detail he might have missed, a thread to pull in the fabric of DeLuca's elusive world. He then pored over DeLuca's social media pages for the tenth time, looking for a clue he might have missed before.

As the clock on the wall ticked steadily into the afternoon, his gaze landed on a photo that was on DeLuca's social media profile. It was an image of DeLuca standing with a broad-shouldered man who was tagged as Bruce Martin in front of a tired-looking bar. In the background, there was a sign that Theo hadn't noticed before. It was half a sign, really. It said, "The Rusty A—" The rest of the name was cut out of the picture. Theo's eyes narrowed; something about the man's smug grin seemed oddly triumphant, as if he was privy to a secret joke.

The photo was dated two weeks before DeLuca was arrested.

Theo noted the photo's location on the post, which wasn't that far from the police station. Theo did an online search for "The Rusty A" in Maine and found results for The Rusty Anchor, a bar near the Kennebec River in Augusta, Maine, and the sign matched the one in the photo, and the owner's name, a Bruce Martin. What was DeLuca doing in Maine? He must have friends or maybe even family here. He probably had connections all over New England and in New York.

Another lead. Finally. He had circumstantial evidence DeLuca was in Maine and nearby and now he discovered a possible hideout. Wasting no time, Theo grabbed his jacket and called for uniformed backup—one officer would join him, Officer Rodgers. If DeLuca was laying low, The Rusty Anchor might just be the harbor in his storm of flight. The owner of the bar was possibly hiding DeLuca. While he waited for his backup, he ran the name of the bar owner and found a minor criminal record. He also ran a CAD report (Computer Aided Dispatch) on the bar's address and discovered there were several incidents and multiple arrests that occurred there over the past several years. This seemed to support his hunch, and he couldn't wait to check it out.

The drive was a blur, his mind racing ahead to the potential confrontation.

The Rusty Anchor loomed ahead, its sign flickering half-heartedly in the dusk. The building sat near a weather-beaten harbor, where dozens of boats were docked, swaying on the Kennebec River. The building's wood-paneled exterior had aged to a soft gray over the years. Seagulls crying as they circled overhead and the creaking of the boats provided a natural symphony. The air was filled with the comforting aromas of fried foods which emanated from the kitchen vents—a siren song to hungry tourists and locals.

As Theo entered The Rusty Anchor wearing his usual business suit, the sparse crowd turned towards him with wary stares. Theo scanned the dimly lit room, his eyes searching for DeLuca or Bruce Martin.

Inside, the floorboards, worn smooth from countless shuffling feet, groaned as customers moved about. The seagulls outside could still be heard over the din of soft music, glasses clinking, and customers chatting over plates of battered fish and chips or bowls of steaming clam chowder.

There, behind the bar, wiping down glasses with a gray rag, stood Bruce Martin—easily recognizable from the photo. His large, intimidating frame was hard to miss. His gaze lifted, locked with Theo's for a second. In that instant, an unspoken understanding passed between them—Martin knew why he was here, and he wasn't going to stick around for questions.

Theo took a step forward. "Bruce Martin, I need to ask you about Raymond 'Razor'—"

But before Theo could finish, Martin threw the glass at Theo's face, but Theo dodged it just in time. Martin bolted toward the back exit of the bar. The CPDU uniformed officer on the outside leaped into action, shouting commands that he was police and to stop as they chased the fleeing bar owner.

Theo, anticipating Martin's likely escape routes, pushed through the crowd and sprinted outside through the same exit which was on the other end of the bar, near the river.

He shouted into his radio, "Heading east toward the river!" With years of training fueling his pace, he raced around the building just in time to see Martin unmooring a small motorboat.

Theo and the other officer both arrived at the harbor edge as Martin fired up the outboard motor. The uniformed office again repeated orders to stop. Without a moment of hesitation, Theo raced down the small hill, thundered down the shaking dock, and leaped into the boat just as it began to pull away from the dock.

"Bruce Martin, you're under arrest for battery," Theo announced, snapping the handcuffs onto Martin's wrists with a click that resounded over the humming of the boat's engine. He then gave Martin his Miranda rights. He fought to keep his balance and prevent Martin from falling over as the boat rocked back and forth on the waves.

Bruce Martin let out a string of colorful curse words as Theo reached over and lowered the speed of the motor. The boat swayed as Theo guided it back to the dock, where his colleague was waiting. They led a begrudging Martin to the police car. The onlookers on the dock murmured, a mix of confusion and excitement at the spectacle. Many of them took out their phones, taking photos as the locally well-known bar owner was arrested.

Back on solid ground, Theo faced Martin, who was now slumped against the police car, dejected.

"Bruce Martin, we need to know if you've had any contact with Raymond DeLuca. Think carefully—it's not just your business on the line. Aiding and abetting a fugitive is a serious charge," Theo cautioned, his tone even but firm. "If you tell the truth now and you are aiding and abetting DeLuca, we will overlook it and let you go in the interests of justice and for your cooperation."

Martin glared up at Theo, jaw clenched, then spat out onto the gravel at his feet. "I ain't saying nothing until I talk to my lawyer."

Theo nodded. They'd seen it all before. "Fine. We are taking you in."

Bruce Martin rode in the back of the uniformed police officer's car, his hands cuffed. Once they arrived, Theo's eyes followed Martin as he was taken to a holding room. He knew the process: no questioning could take place without Martin's lawyer present. Time seemed to crawl as they waited for Martin's legal counsel. The sterile ambiance of the station did nothing to alleviate Theo's impatience. Finally, the door clicked open, and in walked Martin's lawyer, a seasoned professional who took control immediately, taking a seat beside Martin.

"I need a moment alone with my client," he said, so Theo and his colleague stepped out.

When Theo and his colleague re-entered the room, the lawyer was ready. "My client is prepared to talk," he began, "but only under certain conditions. We're willing to exchange information of DeLuca's whereabouts for dropping the current charges."

Theo exchanged a glance with his partner. The offer was too compelling to ignore. After a few tense moments, all parties agreed and Bruce Martin signed a stipulation that the arrest was lawful and he was not going to be charged pursuant to a quid pro quo.

Bruce's lawyer nodded, "All right, Bruce, it's time to talk. Tell them everything you know."

Theo leaned forward. If anyone knew the whereabouts of Raymond DeLuca, it was Bruce Martin. He watched the man's every twitch, every glance, waiting for the crucial information.

"Fine," Martin said. "I'll tell you what I know."

Chapter Thirty

Ava arrived at Freya and Adam's home, a small, quaint house nestled near the Amish community. The homestead radiated warmth and welcome, its charm extending from the flower-filled garden to the cozy interiors filled with the laughter of a young family. Adam carried Ava's bag inside while Freya led her to the guest room.

"You can make yourself comfortable here," Freya said, smiling as she showed Ava the neatly made bed.

"Thank you," Ava said, placing her belongings down. She turned to Detective Barrett. "You should go home and get some sleep. You've been up all night."

Adam nodded in agreement. "I'll take over for the day. You've earned some rest."

Detective Barrett let out a tired sigh of relief. "Thanks, Ava. And thank you, Adam. I'll catch some sleep and check back later."

After Barrett went home, Ava felt a wave of gratitude and a tentative sense of peace. The day ahead promised a temporary sanctuary from her troubles. She spent the morning helping Freya take care of the baby, Robert, a chubby-cheeked delight. Ava found joy in the simple tasks—changing diapers and playing with him on the floor.

Freya watched with a tender smile as Ava played with Robert, his giggles filling the room. "Do you want kids someday, Ava?" she asked, curiosity and kindness in her eyes.

"Yes, absolutely," Ava replied without hesitation. "I would love to raise a family here in Unity. There's something special about this place."

Adam, who had been nearby, chimed in. "Theo is a great guy who loves his family. I work with him, and I've really gotten to know him. He's a very decent, honorable man. He told me about you, and it's clear he really cares about you. I haven't seen him interested in anyone since he lost his wife, so you must be very special to him."

Ava felt a blush creep up her cheeks, a mix of embarrassment and happiness. "I really like him too," she admitted shyly. "I appreciate everything he's doing to help me. It's been a tough time, but knowing he's there for me makes a big difference. He makes me laugh. We had so much fun while we were fixing up my house together. I've never felt like this before, not in my entire life." She smiled.

Freya gave her an encouraging smile. "It sounds like you two are good for each other."

"I don't think Theo would ever give up police work to join the Amish," Adam said.

"I couldn't ask him to do that. Besides, I don't think I could ever be Amish again," she said.

"Well, if you two ever got married, you could live here, near or in the Amish community as *Englishers*," Adam said.

"He could continue being a police officer, and you could open your shelter and keep writing books," Freya added.

"Well, let's not get ahead of ourselves," Ava said shyly. "I don't want to rush into anything."

"Of course not," Freya said. "But there's nothing wrong with planning ahead and thinking up possibilities." She grinned.

The day continued with a comforting sense of normalcy. Ava found herself laughing, playing with Robert and exchanging stories with Freya as they cooked together. Adam joined them as he watched out the windows, sharing light-hearted anecdotes and making sure Ava felt at home.

Later on, Maria came by to visit. "How are you doing?" she asked Ava as Freya let her inside.

"I'm okay," Ava said with a smile, holding Robert. "This little guy is keeping me busy, which helps keep my mind off things."

Robert gurgled and smiled at her, making her heart melt at the sight of his adorable, pudgy face.

"That's right," Freya said. "We've been cooking, cleaning, and staying busy all day. My house hasn't been this clean in a long time, thanks to Ava."

"It's the least I could do after you helped me clean my house," Ava said.

"Well, people have been coming to Liz and me, offering to let you stay with them. I haven't told them where you are, and I told all of them to not tell anyone else you're here in town," Maria said.

"That's good. We need to keep it quiet that Ava is here," Adam interjected.

"But everyone wants to help. They're sorry about what's happening to you, and how you were unjustly accused of killing Mr. Miller. They want to make you feel welcome and loved. People who haven't even gotten to speak to you yet since you came back from the city have offered to let you stay with them, willing to put their families at risk to help keep you safe," Maria explained, gesturing with her hands. "It's been truly remarkable. The whole community is coming together to support you."

Ava's eyes filled with tears. "Really? They'd do that for me, even though they don't know me well?"

"They don't know you well yet," Freya added. "Once this is all over, you'll be friends with everyone. Who wouldn't love you?"

"Exactly," Maria said, putting her arm around Ava's shoulders as she wiped away tears of gratitude.

"I don't know what to say. No one has ever stood up for me like this except for my mother, a long time ago." Ava sniffed. She thought of her mother who had brought her art supplies and books in secret at the risk of her father's wrath.

"Well, get used to it, because this is Unity, and here, we look after each other," Adam said with a grin.

Later on, Ava looked down at Robert, who was now peacefully asleep in his crib. She couldn't help but envision a future filled with similar moments of joy and love for herself.

Theo called her to check in on her, and she told him about her day with Adam, Freya, Maria, and baby Robert.

"Thank you for everything, Theo," Ava said. "I'm so grateful."

"I promise I'll do everything I can to find DeLuca and keep you safe, Ava," Theo said. "I promise."

***

A copy of the arrest warrant from New York was fast-tracked, and within hours, the CPDU team stood before the dilapidated motel, the heavy-duty lock securing the gate glaringly out of place in such desolation.

A few moments later, they opened the lock on the gate with the key Bruce Martin had given them. The gate creaked open.

They moved across the property, sweeping the area. Old, dead leaves skittered across the parking lot in an eerie breeze, falling into the empty, yellowed pool and gathering around the dilapidated, turquoise lawn chairs.

An undercurrent of anticipation zipped through the team as they approached the back of the motel where a room door marked 'Private' on a crooked sign suggested more secrets lay beyond.

Behind it, they could discern the muffled sounds of movement—someone was in there.

"Police! We have a warrant. Come out with your hands up!" Theo shouted. They waited, but nothing happened.

The team opened the door using the master key provided to them by the owner. They poured into the dingy space, their movements coordinated and cautious.

The officers quickly swept the main bedroom strewn with trash, dirty clothes, half-empty plates of food, and beer bottles—signs of someone recently staying here.

In the corner, one of the officers picked up a T-shirt and pants splattered in blood. He held up the shirt and pants, and there was no blood on the front where Ava's mother's apron had covered them, but it was everywhere else. Clearly, Razor had obviously worn this while murdering Mr. Miller.

Theo approached the bathroom, a narrow space that reeked of mildew and abandonment.

Suddenly, Raymond "Razor" DeLuca burst from behind the curtain with calculated fury, his gun pointed directly at Theo.

"Gun!" another officer shouted, a split second before the sharp crack of a gunshot echoed through the confined space.

Theo felt a searing heat rip through his shoulder, and he crumpled onto the cold tile floor. In the same chaotic heartbeat, the other officers fired back, DeLuca's weapon clattering uselessly away from his grasp as he too fell on the floor beside Theo. The gun was kicked away and Theo heard an officer give DeLuca his Miranda rights as he was handcuffed.

"I saw you with Ava! I know you're her boyfriend!" DeLuca hissed from where he now lay, blood pouring from his shoulder. "I told her I'd make her pay for putting me in prison, and now—I've taken you, the man she loves, away from her."

"Why, because framing her for murder didn't work?" Theo asked.

DeLuca's smug grim fell from his face.

Blood seeped through Theo's fingers as he applied pressure to the wound. "How do you know I'm her boyfriend? Were you spying on us that day Ava had the argument with Mr. Miller?" Theo's voice remained steady, incisive despite the circumstances.

One of the officers, meanwhile, came over and maintained compression on Theo's shoulder while another called in for medical assistance. The muted urgency within the bathroom contrasted starkly with the disheveled desperation of DeLuca.

Realization dawned on DeLuca's face, the consequences of his slip spilling out like the blood that now stained the floor. His sneer was now completely gone.

Theo locked eyes with DeLuca, sensing confessions ready to unravel. "I know you murdered Mr. Miller, DeLuca."

"One way or another, the truth will come out," Theo muttered, his vision tunneling into blackness and his shoulder continued to stain the old tile floor crimson. "You'll never hurt another woman again, DeLuca..." he said to the criminal before he fell into darkness.

Chapter Thirty-one

As soon as they got word of Theo's injury, Detective Barrett, who was staying with her, drove Ava to the hospital. She prayed during the entire car ride for Theo while also thanking God that DeLuca had been arrested.

She made her way to the waiting area in the hospital, where Theo's family—Mark, Carol, and Natalie—huddled together, worry and anxiety written all over their faces.

"Hi," Ava said softly, approaching them. "How's everyone holding up?"

"We're terrified," Carol admitted, her voice thin, as if stretched too far. "Ava, what happened? Who is this horrible man who shot our son? Do you know anything?"

Ava took a breath, steadying herself. "Well, Natalie knows this part about my past because we both went through similar experiences…" As she recounted the events that led to Theo's injury, his family listened intently, expressions shifting from disbelief to shock.

"Theo figured it out—that DeLuca framed me for murder," Ava explained, piecing together the elaborate puzzle Theo had solved, her voice a bridge from chaos to clarity. "Razor—Raymond DeLuca—wanted to make me pay for testifying against him in court and helping to put him in prison, so when sending me to prison didn't work, he shot Theo instead, hoping to take what matters most from me. DeLuca was watching us as Theo and I worked on the house that day, and apparently he could tell...I'm falling in love with Theo."

A small smile tugged at Carol's lips, and she looked at Mark, who still looked stunned.

"Well, that's fantastic news," Carol said. "Maybe I'll get some grandbabies after all."

Ava couldn't help but smile.

"I knew it," Natalie said. "And he's head over heels for you."

The surgeon emerged, signaling them over with a tired but reassuring smile. "Theo will make a full recovery," he said, releasing the breath the family had collectively held. "Please, follow me. He's been asking about all of you."

As they filed into Theo's room, Ava hung back, her thoughts swirling. The sight of him, bandaged but alive, sent an acute jolt of relief through her. Theo's eyes found hers, and despite the circumstance, he attempted humor.

"Turns out DeLuca was shooting to kill me," he confessed with a weak chuckle, "but he has terrible aim. Caught me in the shoulder instead."

Ava managed a smile in return, but inside, she recoiled from the "what-ifs" that haunted her. The thought of nearly losing Theo was a horrible thought she couldn't shake.

She gazed at Theo as his family enveloped him in their love and relief, and she understood then the depth of her feelings. Realization dawned on her, bright and undeniable—she was in love with him. She knew without a doubt that she would tell him, but not here, not now. His family needed time with him.

When the time was right, she would share her heart. For now, Ava was simply thankful—thankful for his survival, and for the hope that nestled in her heart.

***

With DeLuca finally arrested and Ava feeling the immense weight of relief starting to settle onto her shoulders, she knew there was one person she needed to reach out to—Carmen.

As she sat beside Theo in the hospital while he was resting, she quickly dialed Carmen's number, her fingers trembling with a mix of anxiety and hope.

The phone rang a few times before Carmen's familiar voice picked up. "Hello?"

"Carmen, it's Ava," she said, her voice shaky. "I just wanted to see if you're okay now. We thought it would be safer to wait to contact you until DeLuca was arrested, just in case he found out and tried to hurt you again. What happened? Are you okay?"

There was a brief pause on the other end, and Ava could hear Carmen take a deep breath before she spoke. "I'm okay now, but DeLuca broke into my family's home. He threatened me, demanding to know where you were. When I wouldn't tell him, he threatened my family."

Ava's heart sank, tears welling up in her eyes. "Oh, Carmen... I'm so sorry. This is all my fault. I never meant for you or your family to be in danger because of me."

"Stop, Ava," Carmen said firmly, her voice filled with unwavering support. "This isn't your fault. DeLuca is the one responsible for his actions, not you. He injured me, but I'm on the mend. As you know, I've had worse. I knew the risks, but I chose to stand by you because you're my friend, and I love you."

Ava couldn't hold back her tears any longer, the mixture of relief and guilt overwhelming her. "You're an amazing friend, Carmen.

Thank you. I'm so glad you and your family are okay. I don't know what I would do if anything happened to you or them."

"We're all safe now. The police have been very supportive, and they ensured our safety," Carmen assured her. "But Ava, don't blame yourself. You've been through enough."

Swallowing back her sobs, Ava felt a flicker of hope. "Thank you, Carmen. I don't deserve friends like you, but I'm so grateful."

"You deserve all the support and love in the world, Ava. You've been so brave through all of this," Carmen said softly. "Maybe you could come visit soon. It would be good to see you and catch up properly."

Ava nodded, though Carmen couldn't see her. "I'd love that. Let's plan something soon. I can come over in the next few days once things settle a bit more here. I'll be in touch."

"Sounds perfect," Carmen replied, her tone lifting with a hint of joy. "Take care of yourself, Ava. We'll get through this together."

Ava ended the call, feeling an overwhelming mix of emotions. She wiped away her tears, her heart heavy yet strengthened by Carmen's reassurances. The danger had passed, and although the memories still haunted her, the support and love from her friends built a new foundation of hope.

She turned to see Theo sleeping in his hospital bed, resting peacefully, and she smiled a little.

***

Once Theo was discharged from the hospital, Natalie drove them back to Unity.

"Thank you so much for driving us, Natalie," Ava said. "When I left home to move to the city, I took public transportation everywhere, and I couldn't afford a car. Traffic was terrible, anyway. So, I never got my license. I'd like to, though."

"Glad to help. Hey, Theo can teach you how to parallel park." Natalie laughed. "He's terrible at it."

"I am not," Theo shot back playfully. "Well, okay, I used to be really bad at it. But not anymore. I'd be happy to help you practice driving, Ava."

"Thanks," Ava said.

"I can help, too. Honestly, I try to stay busy as much as I can to keep my mind off...what happened," Natalie said. "I do find that if I'm alone, my mind just goes to a dark place."

"I totally understand that," Ava said.

"I have noticed I've been more tired ever since then because of the nightmares," Natalie added. "I haven't been sleeping well."

"Oh, Natalie, I'm so sorry. I understand how that is, too. It does get a little better with time," Ava said.

"Hopefully. I'm just glad to be spending more time with you both. I might need to take a nap on your couch, though. I'm beat," Natalie said, turning onto the lane that led to Ava's family home.

The sight of her childhood home brought a swell of both comfort and trepidation to Ava's heart. It still brought back bad memories, but she was also starting to create happy memories here—mostly of her fixing up the house with Theo and her friends, Maria and Liz, who were now hurrying down the lane to see her.

Ava breathed in the familiar air of Unity; it smelled of fresh air, farm fields, and a hint of manure. Theo eased out of the driver's side with his tender shoulder still on the mend.

"Ava!" Liz called. "What on earth happened? Are you okay?"

"You're hurt," Maria observed, gesturing to Theo's arm. "Did DeLuca do that to you?"

Ava explained, "Theo discovered that DeLuca framed me for the murder of Mr. Miller." She glanced over at him proudly. "He was shot while arresting DeLuca. Thanks to him, I'm safe now."

"I'm so sorry," Liz said. "But thank the Lord you're here now."

Theo spoke up. "I'll make sure everyone knows the truth. Perhaps at church tomorrow. The bishop might let us make an announcement. That way, the whole community will understand they're safe now and that the real murderer has been caught...and that Ava is innocent."

Maria and Liz nodded in earnest agreement.

"That's a good idea," Maria said. "People have been worried, and it would bring peace to hear that justice has been served."

"Who is your friend?" Liz asked, gesturing to Natalie.

"Liz, Maria, this is my sister, Natalie," Theo said.

"Hello," Maria said.

Natalie shook their hands. "Nice to meet you."

As they all went inside together, Ava felt a weight lift from her shoulders.

***

Later that evening, Liz and Maria went home and Natalie fell asleep on the couch in Ava's living room. With the quiet symphony of Unity's nature sounds playing softly in the background, Ava and Theo sat discussing how to approach the congregation.

"If you wouldn't mind, could you be the one to explain everything to the church? I'm not ready to talk about it in front of all those people," Ava said. "And... please, leave out the darker parts of my past."

"Absolutely. I'll keep it to the essentials, only what they need to know," Theo assured her, understanding in his eyes.

Ava lost herself in thought, and Theo's voice gently coaxed her back. "What are you thinking about?"

She exhaled, a flutter of vulnerability visible in her expression. "I've been so broken by the world, and sometimes... I think I just want to live a simpler life. I would like to live here in Unity, but as an *Englisher*."

The confession hung in the air, as raw and as real as anything she had said before.

Theo gave a rueful half-smile. "You know, sometimes I think the same. The job wears on me. As much as I love what I do, sometimes the thought of living a simpler life free from all this darkness sounds...incredible."

The idea seemed to hover between them, a shared dream of simplicity and peace. Ava's mind swam with questions. She didn't know where their relationship would go, but if they ever wanted to get married, would he ever join the Amish to be with her if she returned to that life?

She inwardly chided herself. Was it silly to wonder such things already?

Ava glanced toward the door leading to the basement, the gloom of her past lurking behind the wood. "Everywhere I look, especially at that basement door, I remember how I was locked away. I'll be glad when this sells so I can make a new home elsewhere in town."

Theo reached out and squeezed her hand. "I think selling this house will be a healing experience for you."

"I think so too." Ava hesitated, torn between the stubborn hurt of her past and the need to reconnect. "I wasn't ready before to visit my mother and brothers in prison...but maybe now I am. Despite everything, I miss them."

Theo offered a supportive nod. "Remember what you said before? Family is everything. You still have family, Ava. Maybe it's true, they kept you locked away out of fear, but they're your blood. They must regret what they did, right? Perhaps they need you now, just as much as you might need them."

"One day, they will be released from prison, and I keep wondering if we could be a family again when they are," Ava said.

"You could, if you wanted to. It would be nice, wouldn't it?" he asked. "Other than what happened, did you have a good relationship with them?"

"My mother and I were so close," Ava said. "She tried to make the best of a bad situation when my father was alive, always bringing me books and art supplies. My brother didn't even know until my father died, so I was never angry with him. Part of me wishes my mother had just called the police, but she was so brainwashed...I try to understand why she didn't."

"Your father probably put so much fear in her... I see it happen all the time, sadly," Theo said with a frown. "I hope one day you can all be happy, together again."

"Thanks," Ava said with a small smile. "Me too."

Eventually, Theo left to go home, and Ava was left alone with her thoughts, the conviction in his words leaving a warm imprint on her hesitant heart. By the time the night deepened further, her decision was made. She would visit her mother and brother. She would bridge the chasm her father's actions had created. They were her family, and despite the pain and the complex web of emotions, she couldn't turn her back on that.

As she stared up into the ink-black sky out her bedroom window, scattered with stars like a million promises, Ava felt a shift within. The past wouldn't hold sway over her future, not any longer. Family, in whatever fractured form, was everything—and it was time she embraced what remained of hers.

Chapter Thirty-two

The following morning brought with it a crispness that seemed to herald new beginnings. Ava and Theo, side by side, approached the humble wooden church in the woods. The Amish community of Unity gathered within, their voices a gentle hum of Sunday worship.

As they entered the church, a ripple of surprise and relief washed over the familiar faces. Ava's return carried the weight of unspoken questions, and along with Theo, she moved quietly to speak with the bishop before the service began.

With a compassionate nod, the bishop granted their request to address the congregation, understanding the importance of the truth, especially within his tight-knit flock.

When the moment came, Theo stood in front of the congregation as all eyes turned to him. "Good morning. I'm sure you all have questions about what happened to Mr. Miller, and Bishop Byler has given me permission to explain this morning." He recounted the story succinctly, sparing the gritty details of Ava's past, but leaving no room for doubt as to her innocence.

"Raymond DeLuca, a criminal from Ava's past, committed the murder of Mr. Miller and framed her for the crime. She had witnessed his criminal activity and bravely testified against him in court, and he wanted revenge on her. I can assure you, Ava is completely innocent," he stated. "And DeLuca is behind bars and will finish serving a life sentence, so now you are all safe from him. I know you've all been through so much here, so it must come as a relief."

The community absorbed his words, many people nodding and sighing in relief.

Ava stood up and joined him at the front. "I want to thank everyone for offering to let me stay in your homes before I was even proven innocent. Thankfully, DeLuca was caught quickly, but letting me stay in your homes would have put you and your families in danger. I am thankful beyond words for these new alliances and friends I have in all of you, and for your support. You had faith in me when it seemed like all hope was lost."

People approached Ava with open arms, their words a quilt of support stitched with love as her friends and neighbors expressed the hope she would stay with them permanently.

Ava truly belonged, and she looked forward to her new life defined by simplicity, peace, and serving God and other people.

Her gaze flitted to Theo—solid, reassuring, and as much an anchor as any she had known. Could he ever consider such a life?

***

In the small cemetery near the Amish church, the air was filled with the quiet murmur of the community, all gathered to pay their respects to Mr. Miller.

Ava stood near the edge of the crowd, her heart heavy with a complex mix of grief and relief. Theo stood at her side, his hand tightly clasping hers. Liz and Maria also stood close to her, offering silent support. The entire Amish community had come to show their support, not only for Mr. Miller, but for Ava.

The small wooden church behind the cemetery was a place of solace, and today it served as a backdrop for the funeral. The simple wooden casket rested near the freshly dug grave.

Bishop Byler stood at the front, staring out at the gathered congregation with a somber expression.

"Today, we gather to honor the life of Jonas Miller, a man who embodied the spirit of our community. He was a friend, a neighbor, and a brother to us all. His loss is felt deeply, and our hearts grieve together."

Ava's eyes welled with tears as she listened, her heart aching for the man wrongly taken from them. But there was also comfort in the truth that had come to light. The community knew she was innocent, and their presence was proof of their support.

"Our community is built on trust, faith in God, and forgiveness," the bishop continued. "Today, we also recognize the strength of those who have suffered unjustly. Ava, we are grateful you are safe and with us. Our prayers are with you as you continue to heal."

The community murmured their agreement, many nodding and turning to Ava with kind, encouraging smiles. She felt a surge of emotion, deeply touched by their acceptance and warmth.

As the service ended, Bishop Byler led the congregation in a hymn. The voices of the community rose in unison, a harmonious blend of sorrow and hope.

Theo gave her hand a soft squeeze, and she looked up at him, finding solace in his steady presence. Liz and Maria gave her small smiles. They would face this together, just as they had faced so much already.

As the ceremony came to a close, the Amish community encircled Ava. Women offered comforting words and embraces, while the men gave nods of solidarity and encouragement. The show of support was overwhelming yet deeply reassuring.

"We're here for you, Ava," Rachel, Liz's mother, said.

"No one should bear burdens alone. You're part of our family, now and always," Mrs. Johnson added.

Ava wiped away her tears, smiling through the overwhelming emotion. "Thank you, all of you. Your kindness means more than I can say."

She wasn't alone, and knew she never would be.

***

The prison visiting room was cold and impersonal, the harshness of the setting at odds with the emotional weight of the moment. Diana walked in wearing an orange jumpsuit looking pale and thinner, but her gray hair was still in a traditional bun and the prayer *kapp*. The prison allowed her to wear the prayer *kapp* since it was her constitutional right to practice her religion, and it did not obscure her face.

They sat across from each other, the table cold and unyielding between them. But Diana's eyes held warmth as she took in Ava's face, a mother's love transcending all else.

"You look well. You've grown up, and I'm just so happy to see you," Diana said, her voice thick with emotion. "I've missed you so much."

Ava swallowed hard, her next words laced with regret. "I'm sorry I didn't come for so long. I would have, but I...couldn't until recently. I went to New York City to go to college, and then..." She recounted the harrowing events of the past three years, the difficult journey back to Unity, and her hesitance in facing her mother. "When I got home, I had been through so much that I wasn't quite ready to visit yet... I'm sorry."

"I understand, after what I did to you," Diana acknowledged, casting her gaze downward.

A thread of pain wove through Ava's heart. "I know you were afraid, but part of me does wish you had just called the police."

"Your father told me if I ever told anyone or the police, or if I let you out, he would kill you," Diana confessed, her tone a mixture of fear and remorse. "I was misguided, but initially I was just trying to protect you. I apologize for everything. I'm so...so sorry."

Ava nodded slowly, a somber realization dawning on her. "Oh...I figured he gaslighted you, but I didn't realize he threatened me like that."

"And after Olivia married Jake and told me he was abusing her, I denied it, because I was afraid. After she killed him, I told everyone she killed him in cold blood because I didn't want anyone to know he had abused her. I regret that now. My daughter-in-law needed me, and I pretended to not believe her. No wonder she left. But she came to visit me, and she forgave me." Diana sighed, tears brimming. "And your poor brothers... They grew up thinking your death was their fault. Ian took it the hardest. That's why he left...then killed your father."

The cruelty of her father's manipulation cut deep. "Why would *Daed* do that? Why did he go that far, to blame them when I hadn't even died? He was incredibly cruel."

"He was." Diana's voice was a whisper of lost years. "When we were courting, he was so sweet and charming. He deceived me, and once we were married and I realized he was abusive, it was too late, and I was pregnant. You know the Amish don't believe in divorce. I felt trapped, but not like what we did to you, and I am so sorry. I'm also sorry that he was so cruel to you children. And that I failed to protect each of you better. I feel so much guilt and anguish over it now that I have had so much time to think about it in here."

Silence hung between them, heavy with the acknowledgment of their fractured family. Ava reached across the table, her hand seeking Diana's. "You know, I forgive you, *Mamm*."

"Thank you, my *liebling*," Diana whispered. "My darling."

"No touching!" a guard yelled, and Ava recoiled, letting go of her mother's hand.

"When you get out of here, I want us to be a family again—you, me, and Samuel. We need to make the most of it and make up for lost time."

Diana's eyes overflowed with tears. "You have no idea how much I would love that, Ava. There is so much lost time I want to make up for. I just want to spend time with you and Samuel."

They turned the conversation to the house, realizing its memories were too much for both of them.

"I'm glad you're selling it. I could never go back. I don't think Samuel would want to live there either," Diana said. "Maybe a new Amish couple will make a happy life there and rewrite its story."

Ava spoke of her plans to remain in Unity, her desire to live a simple life among her Amish friends. Diana's face lit up at the prospective future.

"I would love that. And yes," Diana softly affirmed, "I will remain Amish when I return. Despite our past and your father's actions, I've always loved our way of life. He was an anomaly—I don't know any other Amish person who was violent like him. If there are any, they must be hiding it too."

Their meeting was a bridge between the scars of the past and the hope for the future—a future they dared to shape together.

***

That same day, the visit with Samuel unfolded within another cold visiting room, punctuated by the metallic echo of distant doors clanging shut. Despite the dispassionate surroundings, the encounter was actually warm.

As they settled at the table, eyes meeting over the sterile surface, Samuel's regret was reflected in his eyes. "I'm so sorry for not letting you go after *Daed* died," he began, his voice strained with remorse. "I thought we'd end up in prison if we did—which, ironically, doesn't matter now because here I am. I was trying to protect *Mamm*, m ostly... I thought her sentence would be heavier since she kept you locked up for so much longer. It was just a guess."

"I understand, and I forgive you both," she replied, her words as much a relief for herself as they were for Samuel. She felt a weight lifted off her shoulders.

Hope flickered between them as they spoke of Samuel's upcoming court date; the possibility of early parole on good behavior was a light at the end of a long, dark tunnel they could now travel together.

She gave him the updates on the house.

"I'm so glad you're selling it," Samuel admitted. "I could never live there again either."

"*Mamm* figured," Ava said, the knots of the past slowly unraveling. "We will find a new home...we will make a new home in Unity together. *Mamm* just wants us to be a family again, and so do I."

"Me too," Samuel said.

Ava concluded her time at the prison visiting Ian by telling him about her plans to sell the house. He also agreed it sounded like a good idea, and they talked about her plans for the future. She told him about Theo and also her desire to finish writing her book and open a shelter one day. He encouraged her, telling her she'd be successful in whatever she put her mind to.

She left the prison feeling uplifted, glad she had taken the time to visit her family. Yes, they were in prison, and they'd been torn apart, but they were still family.

***

The car ride to upstate New York was quiet, the hum of the highway a soothing cadence beneath the weight of their thoughts. Natalie drove them, since Theo's arm was still in a sling, and Ava didn't have a driver's license yet.

Next to Theo in the back seat of the car, Ava seemed lost in reflection, her gaze often drifting to the passing scenery. When they finally arrived in the small, serene town where Carmen lived, a sense of solace embraced them—a stark contrast to the tumult of the trial and the shadows of their recent pasts.

Carmen's family home was a quaint, white two-story house with a welcoming porch and an aroma of home-cooked meals wafting through the open windows. Soon Carmen and her parents stood in the doorway, smiling, their warm presence dissolving the last of Ava's apprehensions.

Ava made the introductions. They were greeted with tender hugs and ushered inside the cozy living room, where family photos adorned the walls and comfortable furniture invited intimate conversation. Carmen's bruise, a stark reminder of harsher realities, did little to diminish her spirit as her eyes brightened at seeing Ava.

"How are you holding up?" Ava asked, concern lacing her words.

"I'm recovering, thanks," Carmen replied with a small, resilient smile. "Each day is a little better." She turned to Theo. "Ava told me all about how you found Razor. Thank you for putting that monster away."

"I'm just glad he's behind bars," Theo said with a nod.

Ava's eyes shimmered with unshed tears, guilt and gratitude mingling in her voice as she spoke to Carmen and her family. "I'm so sorry that DeLuca threatened you all because of me. You were so brave, trying to hold out as long as you did. I can't tell you how awful I feel that he put your family in danger."

Carmen reached out, taking Ava's hand. "I'm sorry I told him where you were. I regret it so much now. And to learn the police did not warn you like I requested. He could have killed you."

Ava shook her head firmly, squeezing Carmen's hand in reassurance. "He threatened your family; I completely understand, and you have nothing to be sorry for. Family is everything. I'm just thankful that you're safe—that all of you are."

There was a silence as Ava glanced around the loving home, a wistful look crossing her face. "I wish I still had two loving parents like you. My father is gone, and now my mother and brothers are in prison." She sighed, a faraway expression clouding her eyes. "Maybe when they get out, we can be something like a family again... but I don't know."

"Maybe you can," Natalie offered.

"You all deserve a second chance. I'm sure they miss you terribly," Carmen said.

Theo nodded in agreement.

As bitter as some of the past chapters of their lives had been, this moment, here with Carmen and her family, was a testament to the enduring strength of human connections and to the healing power of unity.

Ava said gently, "I'm just so thankful I have the chance to see you again and to make sure you're okay, Carmen. That means everything to me."

In the warmth of the gathering, the future didn't seem quite so uncertain.

Chapter Thirty-three

The local covered bridge, with its weathered timbers and years of stories, provided a picturesque backdrop for Theo and Ava's date. Theo led her to a picnic basket that was sitting on a blanket on the grass near the bridge.

"Oh, wow!" Ava cried in delight. "You did this for me?"

"I had some help," he said with a small smile.

Ava marveled at the spread as they opened the basket—fresh fruit, an assortment of sandwiches on homemade bread, lemon bars, and jars of pink lemonade—the colors vibrant against the picnic blanket. "This is wonderful," she exclaimed, touched by the thoughtful gesture. "So, who helped you?"

"My mother and sister," Theo said. "Well, they did most of it and told me what I could do to help." He chuckled. "Then they told me to get out of the way, saying it needed to be perfect and I'd only mess it up."

Ava chuckled. "I'll have to thank them."

They settled on the grass as they put food on their plates. Ava sighed, contented and relieved as she looked around at the beautiful nature around them. The leaves were just starting to turn orange and red, but the weather was still warm as summer came to an end. Soon, trees all over town would be decorated in the fiery colors of fall. She remembered how beautiful it was from when she was a child.

"I'm so glad this is all over. Now we can be free to spend time together, without fear. When you were shot," she confessed, "the thought of losing you was too much to bear. I knew right then I had to tell you as soon as possible that..." She took in a deep breath.

He finished her sentence. "I love you."

She smiled, joy overflowing in her heart. "I love you."

Theo reached out with his good arm, cradling Ava's hand in his. The memory of coming so close to death—an echo of gunshots, pain, and the shadow of loss—was now faded by the light in her eyes.

Ava finally felt like she could conquer the pain of her past—at least, she felt like she could finally put it behind her and start to heal more each day.

"I'm so grateful for each moment we have," she replied earnestly. "You're a reminder of how much light there is, even after the darkest days. It gives me strength, knowing we have each other."

With the flowing stream beneath the old covered bridge providing a gentle soundtrack, Theo gazed at Ava, his eyes searching hers for an unspoken permission.

Ava met his gaze, a silent conversation passing between them, the kind that only eyes can convey. Slowly, as if drawn by an invisible thread, she leaned in and he followed her lead, the world around them fading to a quiet hum.

Their lips touched softly at first, a tentative brush like the flutter of a butterfly's wing. It was a kiss filled with the promise of new beginnings, a silent vow they'd yet to speak aloud. They pulled away with a tender reluctance, Theo's hand finding Ava's, their fingers entwining—a silent affirmation of a connection that had quietly bloomed in the midst of darkness.

In the tranquil haven beside the covered bridge, the pair sat in a bubble of newfound dreams and the hope of a brighter future.

"I have a confession to make. When I first met you, I told you I was handy around the house. The truth is, I had to watch online tutorials and ask my dad for help in preparation for that first day I showed up to help you. I had no idea what I was doing. That's why the sink exploded," he confessed.

Ava laughed out loud. "Really?"

"I just wanted to get to know you so badly. I was so drawn to you that first night we met."

"Me too." She smiled. "I think that's...sweet."

"I know we haven't known each other long, but I hope I don't scare you when I say that I can see us getting married, starting a new life together," Theo said.

"That doesn't scare me at all." She gave a nervous laugh. "It makes me happy." Tears of joy rimmed Ava's eyes as a profound peace washed over her. His words were a balm, dissolving any fleeting doubt. "Because I... I want to marry you one day too," she whispered, her voice a fusion of love and resolve.

"I thought about rejoining the Amish, but I don't think it's the right choice for me because I want to publish books and run a women's shelter one day. I want to live a simple life, and I want to live in Unity and give my life to serving God, just not as a member of the Amish church."

"I feel the same way. I want to continue helping people in the police force, and I wouldn't be able to do that if I were Amish," Theo said. "And one day, I hope I can help you run the shelter."

She grinned, the thought of working with him side by side filling her with joy. "I would love that. And I see us living our lives in Unity, together, living a simple life in the Amish community, but as *Englishers*. I can picture us raising our family here. Do you?"

"I do," he responded, his tone firm and full of promise. "I see us raising our family in Unity. We will have the best of both worlds, and I know the best is yet to come."

They kissed again, the air around them alive with the hum of the future—a future in which they would weave their days with the threads of tradition, love, and togetherness. Ava's heart was overflowing with joy, a joy that echoed across the bridge and into the life they would build together in Unity.

***

Ava invited Maria and Liz over to her house, and the living room was filled with the aroma of freshly brewed tea. She had something important to share, and her closest friends' support meant everything to her. As they settled into their seats, their faces filled with curiosity, Ava took a deep breath.

"I've made a decision," Ava began, her voice steady but tinged with excitement. "I've decided not to become Amish again. I want to live a simple life and stay in the Amish community, among the Amish, but as an *Englisher*, like Freya and Adam."

Maria and Liz exchanged glances but remained quiet, allowing Ava to explain further.

"My dream is to become an author and also open a shelter for women. I know that being Amish wouldn't let me follow my dreams to their full extent. I want to live simply while still serving God and devoting my life to Him," Ava continued. "I plan to attend the Amish church, knowing they welcome *Englishers*, until I find a church home."

The room was silent for a moment as her words sank in. Then Maria broke into a smile. "Ava, that sounds wonderful. I'm so glad you're staying nearby. We can see each other often."

Liz nodded in agreement, her eyes shining with support. "Absolutely. We fully support your decision, Ava. It's important to follow your heart and dreams."

Ava felt a surge of gratitude for her friends' unwavering support. "Thank you. I'm planning to sell my family's house and rent a place nearby until I can buy a house of my own."

"Or until you get married, perhaps?" Liz, ever the curious one, leaned forward. "And how are things going with Theo?"

Ava blushed, laughter bubbling up. "We are in love. Maybe it's too soon, but I hope one day we can get married and live and raise our family right here in Unity."

Maria and Liz exchanged knowing smiles. "Theo's a good man," Maria said. "It sounds like you're building a beautiful life for yourself, Ava."

Ava felt a warmth spread through her chest, a mix of hope and certainty. With her dreams laid out before her and the support of her friends, she felt ready to take on whatever the future held.

The conversation shifted to plans and possibilities, laughter and shared moments filling the room. In that small, comforting space, surrounded by friends, Ava felt the first true sense of belonging she had experienced in a long time. It was the beginning of a new chapter, one filled with love, dreams, and the simple, fulfilling life she yearned for.

***

The sun had started its climb in the sky when Theo and Ava pulled up to the gates of the local prison. They had been waiting in the car, filled with an anxious energy that comes with reunion and change. Samuel was being released today, and neither Theo nor Ava could wait to start anew with him.

As the gates opened and Samuel stepped out, a free man in his traditional Amish attire of black pants, suspenders, and a white shirt, Ava leaped out of the car, unable to contain her joy, and Theo also got out.

"Samuel!" she called out, her voice cracking with emotion.

Samuel's eyes found his sister, a broad smile carving through the years of hardship on his face. They embraced tightly, a hug that spoke of lost time and newfound hope.

"This is Theo, my boyfriend," Ava said, stepping back just enough to pull Theo into the moment. "Theo, this is my brother Samuel."

Theo extended a hand toward Samuel, who took it in a firm grip. There was an immediate camaraderie in their handshake—a promise of friendship. Ava could see the beginnings of a bond that would only grow stronger with time.

They decided to celebrate Samuel's newfound freedom with the simple pleasures of life, and Molly's Diner was just the place for that. The diner was bustling with the lunch crowd, but they found a cozy booth, and Samuel ordered the biggest burger on the menu.

"This," Samuel declared after his first bite, his eyes almost comically wide, "is the best burger I've ever had. I missed this place so much. Prison food is nothing like Molly's food or what *Mamm* used to cook."

Samuel didn't want to talk about prison, so instead he asked Ava a string of questions, wanting to hear about her life. Between bites,

Theo and Ava shared stories of the house they'd refurbished, each anecdote a testament to their resolve and partnership.

She would wait to share her time in the city with him later on, when he was ready to hear about it. Right now, she wanted to keep the conversation positive. Who knew what he had gone through in prison?

***

After their meal, they drove to the Sullivan house.

"Wow, it looks great," Samuel observed, turning slowly in the kitchen. "This must have been a lot of work."

"The last tenants didn't take care of it, so Theo helped me fix it up, and Liz and Maria helped me clean. I couldn't have done it without them," Ava explained.

Theo smiled. "I enjoyed every minute."

"Have you...been downstairs?" Samuel asked. He paused, his hand hovering over the doorknob of the basement door.

"No. I haven't been down there since that day," she admitted, her voice carrying a tremor of resolve. "But we'll face it together."

Samuel nodded, bolstered by his sister's strength, and with a collective breath, they pushed the door open and made their way downstairs. Theo stayed a step behind, a silent guardian ready to offer support but respecting the moment.

The stairs creaked under their weight, the familiar sound now suddenly not so ominous sounding anymore. The shadows on the walls didn't seem so grim, and the basement didn't scare her like it used to at night when she was a young child. As the secret room came into view, Ava and Samuel moved closer, their shared history and unspoken emotions surrounding them like the musty air.

Together, they attacked the walls of the secret room with sledge hammers and a shared ferocity. As the walls came down, a tangible weight lifted from Ava's shoulders.

But then she noticed Samuel, silent sobs shaking his body. He sank to the floor.

She was by his side in an instant, her arms wrapping around him. "I forgave you, remember?" Ava whispered fiercely. "You were just a child, manipulated by our father. And when you did find out I was here, you were still afraid—I understand, Samuel. A few weeks couldn't undo his brainwashing, even if he was dead. You were still processing everything and the knowledge I was alive still had you in shock and some denial."

Samuel could only nod as he held back tears. On the cold concrete floor of the basement, the past seemed to claw its way toward them, eager to pounce.

"I can't imagine how hard it must have been on you," she said gently, her hand finding his arm. "You, Ian, and Jake... all of you being told by *Daed* that my death was your fault. It was so cruel of him to tell you that. You were just kids. No child should have to go through that."

Samuel's eyes were filled with pain and relief as he nodded again. "Yes," he said, his voice barely above a whisper, "it was...it's been a lot to carry."

In that moment, shared under the dim light of the basement, the air seemed to thicken with the weight of a past that they were ready to shed, together.

Samuel's voice was a hoarse whisper, "But after, when we knew you were alive...then that new guilt consumed me, Ava. We—*Mamm* and I—we kept you hidden. I've been drowning in it for years. My whole life I've lived with guilt. After being incarcerated, I have gotten a glimpse of what you must have experienced, but I know what you went through was worse, and for longer, and you were just a little girl. I am so sorry."

Ava pulled back, her hands on his shoulders, her gaze steely with determination. "Then let it go, Samuel. Smash it like the walls of this room. I'm ready to let it go. Don't you want to?"

Theo stood nearby, offering silent support while giving them space.

Fueled by Ava's words, they turned back to the secret room. With each swing of the tools, they obliterated the remnants of their haunted past, liberating themselves from its ghostly grip.

It was a seemingly insignificant, yet profoundly symbolic act—reclaiming the space that had represented some of their darkest days, transforming it with their very presence into nothing more than an empty basement.

With every shattered plank and broken board, Samuel and Ava felt lighter, freer—a new beginning etched into the very foundation of the home.

With the last nail hammered and the final coat of paint dried, Theo, Samuel and Ava stood in the kitchen of the renovated house, ready to hand over the fruit of their labor to Jacob and Sarah, the young Amish couple who had decided to make it their home, completely unaware of the trauma that had taken place within its walls.

Ava knew that finally, new, happy memories would replace her old ones with this new family.

In the kitchen, Ava extended the key to them with a bittersweet smile. "I hope this house brings you a lifetime of happiness," she said with heartfelt sincerity.

"Thank you so much," Jacob said. "We appreciate all the work you put into renovating it."

After a pause, Ava's gaze drifted towards the basement door. "Do you mind if I just...go down there again for one minute?" she asked, her voice steady but with a hint of underlying emotion.

"It's no problem. Take your time," Jacob replied warmly. "We are going to start unpacking the kitchen." Sarah was already opening a box on the table.

Ava opened the basement door and stood at the top of the steps, staring down into the dim basement like a child afraid of a monster lurking in the shadows.

"Do you want me to go with you?" Theo asked with a gentle hand on Ava's arm.

"No, I'll be right back. Thanks," she said.

Ava approached the top step, her hands gently brushing against the wall as she descended, each step deliberate and laden with memories. She reached the bottom, her eyes slowly scanning the now open space. With Theo and Samuel's help, they had demolished the secret room and the basement had been transformed, stripped of its dark history. Now, it looked like any other basement. No one would be able to tell what happened down here by looking at it.

"You have no hold over me anymore. I'm not afraid," Ava whispered into the stillness. With a resolute nod to herself, she turned her back on the basement that had once held her captive and ascended the stairs, each step lighter than the last, leaving the shadows of the past behind her.

***

About one year later, the picturesque farm field near the Amish community was transformed into a magical scene. Rows of white chairs were arranged neatly, facing a simple wooden arch adorned with flowers and greenery. Soft music played in the background, setting a serene and romantic ambiance.

Ava stood at the edge of the field, her heart fluttering with excitement and joy. She wore a stunning white gown, its delicate lace and flowing fabric catching the gentle breeze. Her bridesmaids—Liz, Maria, Natalie, and Freya—all looked radiant. Natalie and Freya wore matching soft pastel dresses, holding bouquets of wildflowers, while Liz and Maria wore their traditional Amish dresses.

Theo stood patiently near the pastor, looking dashing in his suit. His groomsmen—his father Mark, Adam, Detective Barrett, and his co-worker Detective Baker—stood by his side, all sharing in the joy of this special day.

The local pastor, a kind and gentle man, waited beneath the arch where the ceremony would take place. As the music swelled, Ava took a deep breath, linking her arms with Diana and Samuel. Diana was out of prison early on parole, and Ava was so grateful she and Samuel were both here for her special day. Together, they started down the aisle, each step bringing her closer to the love of her life.

As she walked toward Theo, Ava glanced around at first, taking in the faces of her friends and family, all gathered to celebrate this union—both Amish and *Englishers* alike. They were all here for her and Theo, united by their love. Then she locked eyes with her soul mate and didn't take her eyes off him.

Theo's eyes lit up as he saw Ava approaching, a smile spreading across his face that mirrored the love and happiness that filled her heart. Tears streamed down his face, which caused Ava to also shed tears of joy. As she reached the front, Diana and Samuel gave her hands a gentle squeeze and embraced her before stepping back, leaving Ava to stand before Theo.

The pastor began the simple yet beautiful ceremony, his words filled with warmth and sincerity. "We are gathered here today to join Ava and Theo in holy matrimony, a bond that is not to be entered into lightly but with love, commitment, and a promise to cherish each other always."

As the pastor spoke, the sun cast a golden glow over the field, and the soft breeze carried the scent of wildflowers through the air.

When it was time for their vows, Theo took Ava's hands, his voice steady and filled with emotion. "Ava, from the moment I met you, I knew you were special. Your strength, your kindness, and your unwavering spirit have taught me what it means to truly love someone. I vow to stand by your side, through every high and low, to support you, to protect you, to cherish you, and to love you for all my days."

Tears welled up in Ava's eyes as she took a deep breath and began her vows. "Theo, you have been my rock, my protector, and my soulmate. You've shown me that love can heal, that it can bring light to the darkest places. I vow to honor you, to support you, and to love you with all my heart, for as long as we both shall live."

The pastor smiled warmly as he pronounced them husband and wife. "By the power vested in me, I now pronounce you husband and wife. Theo, you may kiss your bride."

Theo leaned in, and as their lips met, the audience erupted into joyous applause. The world seemed to stand still for a moment, and she knew she would never forget this moment for the rest of her life.

Hand in hand, Theo and Ava walked back down the aisle, their hearts full and their future bright.

***

The bright lights of the studio shined down on Ava as she sat on the plush couch, facing the famous actress and TV host, Penelope Sterling. The audience buzzed with anticipation, excited to hear from the woman whose story had touched the heart of the nation. Penelope turned to the camera with a radiant smile.

"Tonight, we have a very special guest," Penelope began, her voice filled with genuine warmth. "She won America's heart as the Amish girl rescued from a basement after over a decade of captivity. Now, she's an accomplished, well-known author. Please welcome Ava Sullivan!"

The audience erupted into applause as Ava smiled, nodding appreciatively. Penelope turned to Ava, her expression kind and inviting.

"Ava, thank you so much for coming," Penelope said.

"Thank you for having me," Ava replied, her voice steady but filled with emotion.

Penelope continued, "You've had quite a journey. You started your author career by posting inspirational videos online about your life story, and your account became extremely popular over the course of a year. Can you tell us more about that?"

Ava nodded, "Writing is a very competitive industry, so it's very difficult to get an agent. I pitched to agents for two years straight and couldn't get anyone to represent me, even though I had been on national TV after I was rescued from the basement. I knew I needed to make myself stand out as a writer, so I started posting daily videos online about my life story—about growing up Amish, being locked up in the basement, and what happened to me in the city. I just didn't realize how much hope my message would give people. People relate to my struggles, and I get messages from people saying how my videos give them hope. I gained a large following quickly, so

I started querying agents again, and that's how I signed on with the wonderful agent I have now."

Penelope leaned in, her curiosity piqued. "Tell us about your debut book—your memoir, *Captive to Courageous*. What is it about?"

Ava took a deep breath, her eyes meeting the audience's. "My memoir is about my life in captivity—both in the basement and then how I was lured into prostitution and controlled by criminals. I went from one type of imprisonment to another. I faced tremendous hardships, but I wanted to share how I overcame them and rebuilt my life. It's a story of survival, resilience, and ultimately, hope."

Penelope's eyes glistened with empathy. "How do you want this book to impact people?"

"I want to spread awareness that many people in prostitution are forced into it," Ava said earnestly. "And I want to give hope to anyone in any situation. If you're struggling, you're not alone, and there is a way out. There is always hope. That's why I opened my shelter for women and their children. If any woman needs help, please, come to the shelter in Augusta, Maine." She provided the hotline phone number, keeping the location confidential for the residents' safety.

"I think it's wonderful that you are giving back."

"I feel called to help women who are in similar situations I was in. We teach women how to support themselves so they are not lured back into prostitution or go back to their abusive partners, which is often the case. Women should feel like they have choices and not feel trapped. I teach writing, and I have volunteers who teach budgeting, sewing, photography, cleaning, cooking, and more. My husband and his family help, and my friends also help. We are a community."

"That's incredible. Well, I want to help, so I will be offering a donation to the shelter, and I also invite all of you to donate," Penelope said to the audience. "You can donate by texting the number on your screen."

"Wow, thank you so much," Ava said, her eyes filled with tears. "I used the advance from my book to open the shelter, but there are so many expenses every month to keep running at maximum capacity. I appreciate your generosity."

"We are happy to help." Penelope leaned forward. "Now that your first book has been such a success, I imagine you will be writing more. What do you plan on writing in the future?"

Ava smiled, a glimmer of excitement in her eyes. "I've always wanted to write a fantasy novel. I worked on one for a few years but felt stuck. Then I realized I needed to write my own story first. Revisiting the darkest parts of my past was extremely difficult, but by writing it all down, it helped me heal. I want to give hope to others through different kinds of stories, but yes, I know now that it is time to finish my fantasy novel and hopefully publish that one next."

Penelope nodded, her admiration clear. "You're an inspiration, Ava. Thank you for sharing your story and for the incredible work you're doing to help others."

The audience erupted into applause, and Ava felt a profound sense of fulfillment. She had started this journey seeking to heal herself, but in the process, she had become a beacon of hope for others. As the interview wrapped up, she looked out into the audience and smiled, knowing she was right where she was meant to be, ready to continue making a difference—one page at a time.

***

Ava stood in the bustling kitchen of the women's shelter, the aroma of roasted chicken, vegetables, and freshly baked bread mingling warmly in the air. The sounds of laughter and chatter filled the spacious dining hall just beyond the kitchen, where eager faces awaited their evening meal. Many of the residents who wanted to improve their culinary skills helped cook the meals.

Next to her, Theo was diligently serving portions of food onto plates, his eyes twinkling with quiet satisfaction.

Thanks to the TV host's large donation to the shelter and the thousands of dollars from the audience and viewers at home, they had been able to move the shelter to a larger location down the street so they could house more women and their children.

"Here you go," Theo said, handing plates to one of the women and her toddler, his smile genuine and kind. Ava felt a swell of pride and love for him, grateful to have him as her partner, both as her husband and as her working partner here at the shelter.

In the corner of the dining hall, Carol, Theo's mother, sat with a group of volunteers, their hands busy with knitting needles and colorful yarn. A growing pile of hats and mittens lay at their feet, destined to warm the shelter's residents through the cold months ahead. Carol's gentle encouragement and infectious enthusiasm had inspired many to join her knitting circle, creating not just garments but also a sense of community. Carol also taught the women quilting and sewing.

Nearby, Mark, Theo's father, was teaching a group how to make wooden birdhouses. He also taught other woodworking projects.

Natalie was working alongside Diana and Samuel. They were sorting through a generous heap of donations—clothing, toys, pantry staples, toiletries, and other essential items dropped off by kind-hearted people from the town.

Ava paused in her work, a moment of reflection washing over her. She was exhausted, her muscles aching from the day's labor, yet she felt an overwhelming sense of fulfillment. This was the kind of tiredness that spoke of a day well spent, of lives touched and changed. Her dreams of running a shelter were now a reality, and she wasn't alone in this journey. Her husband, her new family, and a community that cared stood by her side.

As the last plate of food was served, Theo turned to Ava, wiping his hands on a towel. "Ready to join everyone for a moment?" he asked, his eyes reflecting the same contentment she felt.

Ava nodded, her heart swelling with gratitude. "Yes, let's take a break."

They walked out into the dining hall together, moving among the people they had come to know and care for. Sinking into a chair beside Theo, Ava glanced around the room, taking in the laughter and sense of belonging. It was in these moments, surrounded by love and purpose, that she knew with certainty she was right where she was meant to be.

An unfamiliar young woman was ushered through the door by her live-in manager. The woman stood hesitantly near the entrance, dressed in fishnet tights, high heels, a short skirt, and dark makeup. Her skittish, nervous demeanor struck a chord deep within Ava—it was like looking into a mirror of her own past, back when she was trapped in New York City, a victim of exploitation.

Ava felt a pang of empathy. She approached the young woman with a warm and gentle smile.

"Hi, I'm Ava," she introduced herself softly, making sure her tone was reassuring. "What's your name?"

"I'm Angel," the young woman said out of habit. "Actually, my real name is Elizabeth."

"Angel?" Ava choked out. "I'm sorry. It's just...that was the name my pimp gave me." Her eyes suddenly filled with tears. She longed to pull the young woman into her arms, but she knew that might not be what Elizabeth would want right now.

Ava saw herself in the young woman's eyes. Not so long ago, Ava was Angel.

"Elizabeth, you are safe here. We will take care of you, and we can get you help and protection," Ava managed to tell her. She held out her hand.

Elizabeth hesitated for a moment, her eyes darting around the room before they locked onto Ava's. She shook Ava's hand. Seeing the sincere kindness and understanding in Ava's eyes seemed to break through her defenses. She nodded, allowing Ava to guide her to a seat at one of the long tables.

"Let's get you something to eat," Ava said gently, handing her a plate of warm food. "You're among friends here."

As the young woman began to eat, her guarded posture slowly started to relax. Ava found a moment to herself, closing her eyes briefly in silent prayer.

"Dear God," she whispered in her heart, "thank You for bringing me out of that place of darkness and into this new life. Please use me to help others as You have helped me. Grant me the strength and wisdom to make a difference."

She opened her eyes to see the young woman looking back at her with a tentative smile. Ava smiled back, her heart swelling with gratitude. This was exactly why she had fought so hard to create the shelter—a safe haven for those who, like her, had been through the storm and survived.

Taking a seat beside the young woman, Ava began to talk to her about her options and about the shelter, letting her know that help was available when she was ready. They spoke quietly, their conversation a small refuge in the sea of activity around them.

Watching as the young woman began to eat more steadily, Ava felt tears of gratitude fill her eyes. This was where she belonged—using her experiences and newfound strength to guide others out of their suffering.

Today, it was one young woman. Tomorrow, it might be another. And with God's help, she would be there for each and every one of them.

Epilogue

Four years later...

The warm aroma of a Thanksgiving feast wafted through the air as Ava and Theo's home buzzed with laughter and the scamper of little feet. Their two young sons, Ezra and Joshua, chased each other between rooms, squealing with the sheer delight of play. Because they would be working at the shelter on Thanksgiving Day, they were celebrating a few days early.

Diana, her somber past a now distant memory, lived in the apartment attached to the main house that they had built for her, appreciative of her new chance at life. Diana and Samuel chose to remain Amish while Theo and Ava were *Englishers* who lived a simple life within the Amish community, just like some of their neighbors who lived there but were not Amish.

Ava laughed as Diana pretended to be "Mama Bear," chasing her grandsons down the hall as she used to do when Ava was a child. The children shrieked and squealed with laughter.

Samuel and his own family walked through the door, joining the celebration with his wife, Nancy, and their son and daughter, Matthew and Iris, who instantly joined in the bear game with their cousins and grandmother.

When the children were worn out from the bear game, Mark and Carol, Theo's parents, sat cross-legged on the floor with the children, laughing as they carefully placed wooden blocks, building towers destined to be knocked over by the toddlers. Nearby, Natalie and her new husband, Brandon, shared in the game, each block a testament to the familial bonds that had only grown stronger with time.

Ava finished cooking the Thanksgiving feast with Diana, and she stood side by side with her mother at the stove—something she had missed out on during years that the basement prison had stolen from her. Now, she was able to make up for lost time. Diana showed her how to make some of her favorite dishes for this elaborate feast over the past several months and weeks, and Ava was growing more confident in expanding her cooking skills every day, thanks to the countless happy hours she now was able to spend with her mother in the kitchen and cooking with her friends.

Amid this symphony of familial harmony, Ava gazed at her family. The happiness that punctuated every corner brought tears to her eyes. Theo, ever in tune with Ava's emotions, drew near and wrapped an arm around her, leading her a few steps into the hallway.

"Is something wrong?" he asked. "You're crying."

"No, everything is perfect. After so many hard years, I never imagined my life could be this full of joy, this wonderful. I'm so thankful to God," whispered Ava, her voice awash with gratitude.

"Me too," Theo replied, his eyes alight with the same thankfulness. "The Lord has truly blessed us."

Ava's hand drifted down to her belly, a tender smile spreading across her face. "There's one more blessing," she said, her gaze lifting to meet Theo's. "We're going to have another baby."

Overwhelmed with joy, Theo swept Ava into his arms and twirled her around, laughter bubbling from them both.

"Put me down! Be careful!" she exclaimed amidst her giggles.

With feet back on the ground, Theo beamed and said, "Let's go share the good news with everyone."

They moved into the living room, where the family gathered in a circle of love, ready to receive their joyous announcement.

GET 4 OF ASHLEY EMMA'S AMISH EBOOKS FOR FREE

www.AshleyEmmaAuthor.com

All of Ashley Emma's Books on Amazon

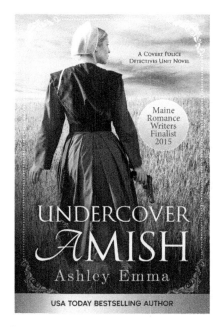

(This series can be read out of order or as standalone novels.)

Detective Olivia Mast would rather run through gunfire than return to her former Amish community in Unity, Maine, where she killed her abusive husband in self-defense.

Olivia covertly investigates a murder there while protecting the man she dated as a teen: Isaac Troyer, a potential target.

When Olivia tells Isaac she is a detective, will he be willing to break Amish rules to help her arrest the killer?

Undercover Amish was a finalist in Maine Romance Writers Strut Your Stuff Competition 2015 where it received 26 out of 27 points and has 455+ Amazon reviews!

Buy here: https://www.amazon.com/Ashley-Emma/e/B00IYTZTQE/

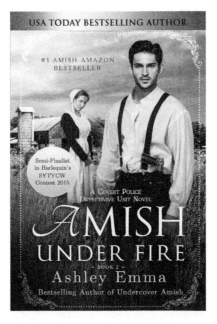

After Maria Mast's abusive ex-boyfriend is arrested for being involved in sex trafficking and modern-day slavery, she thinks that she and her son Carter can safely return to her Amish community.

But the danger has only just begun.

Someone begins stalking her, and they want blood and revenge.

Agent Derek Turner of Covert Police Detectives Unit is assigned as her bodyguard and goes with her to her Amish community in Unity, Maine.

Maria's secretive eyes, painful past, and cautious demeanor intrigue him.

As the human trafficking ring begins to target the Amish community, Derek wonders if the distraction of her will cost him his career...and Maria's life.

Buy on Amazon: https://www.amazon.com/Ashley-Emma/e/B00IYTZTQE/

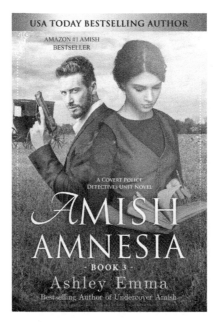

When Officer Jefferson Martin witnesses a young woman being hit by a car near his campsite, all thoughts of vacation vanish as the car speeds off.

When the malnourished, battered woman wakes up, she can't remember anything before the accident. They don't know her name, so they call her Jane.

When someone breaks into her hospital room and tries to kill her before getting away, Jefferson volunteers to protect Jane around the clock. He takes her back to their Kennebunkport beach house along with his upbeat sister Estella and his friend who served with him overseas in the Marine Corps, Ben Banks.

At first, Jane's stalker leaves strange notes, but then his attacks become bolder and more dangerous.

Buy on Amazon: https://www.amazon.com/Ashley-Emma/e/B00IYTZTQE/

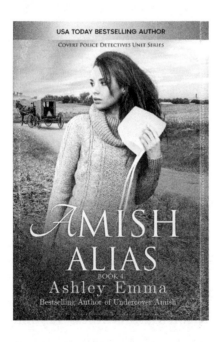

Threatened. Orphaned. On the run.

With no one else to turn to, these two terrified sisters can only hope their Amish aunt will take them in. But the quaint Amish community of Unity, Maine, is not as safe as it seems.

After Charlotte Cooper's parents die and her abusive ex-fiancé threatens her, the only way to protect her younger sister Zoe is by faking their deaths and leaving town.

The sisters' only hope of a safe haven lies with their estranged Amish aunt in Unity, Maine, where their mother grew up before she left the Amish.

Elijah Hochstettler, the family's handsome farmhand, grows closer to Charlotte as she digs up dark family secrets that her mother kept from her.

Buy on Amazon here: https://www.amazon.com/Ashley-Emma/e/B00IYTZTQE/

When nurse Anna Hershberger finds a man with a bullet wound who begs her to help him without taking him to the hospital, she has a choice to make.

Going against his wishes, she takes him to the hospital to help him after he passes out. She thinks she made the right decision...until an assassin storms in with a gun. Anna has no choice but to go on the run with her patient.

This handsome stranger, who says his name is Connor, insists that they can't contact the police for help because there are moles leaking information. His mission is to shut down a local sex trafficking ring targeting Anna's former Amish community in Unity, Maine, and he needs her help most of all.

Since Anna was kidnapped by sex traffickers in her Amish community, she would love nothing more than to get justice and help put the criminals behind bars.

But can she trust Connor to not get her killed? And is he really who he says he is?

Buy on Amazon: https://www.amazon.com/Ashley-Emma/e/B00IYTZTQE/

Ever wondered what it would be like to live in an Amish community? Now you can find out in this true story with photos.

Buy on Amazon: https://www.amazon.com/Ashley-Emma/e/B00IYTZTQE/

An heiress on the run.

A heartbroken Amish man, sleep-walking through life.

Can true love's kiss break the spell?

After his wife dies and he returns to his Amish community, Dominic feels numb and frozen, like he's under a spell.

When he rescues a woman from a car wreck in a snowstorm, he brings her home to his mother and six younger siblings. They care for her while she sleeps for several days, and when she wakes up in a panic, she pretends to have amnesia.

But waking up is only the beginning of Snow's story.

Buy on Amazon: https://www.amazon.com/Ashley-Emma/e/B00IYTZTQE/

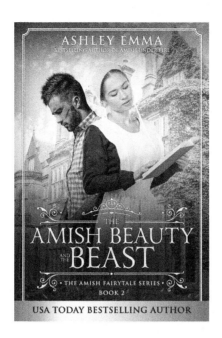

She's an Amish beauty with a love of reading, hiding a painful secret. He's a reclusive, scarred military hero who won't let anyone in. Can true love really be enough?

On her way home from the bookstore, Belle's buggy crashes in front of the old mansion that everyone else avoids, of all places.

What she finds inside the mansion is not a monster, but a man. Scarred both physiologically and physically by the horrors of military combat, Cole's burned and disfigured face tells the story of all he lost to the war in a devastating explosion.

He's been hiding from the world ever since.

After Cole ends up hiring her as his housekeeper and caretaker for his firecracker of a grandmother, Belle can't help her curiosity as she wonders what exactly Cole does in his office all day.

Why is Cole's office so off-limits to Belle? What is he hiding in there?

https://www.amazon.com/Ashley-Emma/e/B00IYTZTQE/

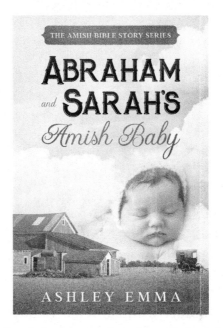

Abraham and Sarah know in their hearts that they are meant to have children, but what if they are wrong? And if they are meant to have children, how will God make it possible?

Just when all seems lost, God once again answers their prayers in a miraculous and unexpected way that begins a new chapter in their lives.

In this emotional family saga, experience hope and inspiration through this beloved Bible story retold.

https://www.amazon.com/Abraham-Sarahs-Amish-Baby-family-ebook/dp/B09DWCBD7M

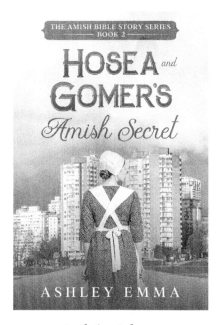

Gomer is not your typical Amish woman.
On the outside, Gomer seems like a lovely, sweet, young Amish woman, but she's hiding a scandalous secret.
Gomer was created to sing. Most of all, she loves to sing on stage for the audience--she loves the applause, the lights, and the performance--**but her Amish community forbids it.**

How can Hosea find his wife, bring her home, and piece their family back together again when it seems impossible?

https://www.amazon.com/Hosea-Gomers-Amish-Secret-family-ebook/dp/B09GQVCBM9

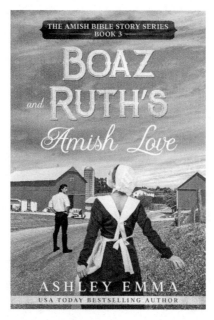

When Ruth's husband Mahlon dies one morning on his way out the door, she thinks she will never find love again--but little does she know that God has a miraculous plan for her future.

In Unity, Ruth catches the eye of successful farmer Boaz Petersheim. He's drawn to her not only because of her beauty, but because of her loyalty and devotion to her mother-in-law, **Naomi.** When Ruth asks for a job harvesting wheat in his fields, he immediately hires her because he can see how much she wants to take care of her mother-in-law, even though she is the only female worker among his male employees. □

When rumors sweep through the community after a near-death experience, who will Boaz believe?

https://www.amazon.com/gp/product/B09M7XV76C

OTHER BOOKS BY ASHLEY EMMA (EBOOKS)

Looking for something new to read? Check out my other books!
www.AshleyEmmaAuthor.com
GET 4 OF ASHLEY EMMA'S AMISH EBOOKS FOR FREE

More books by Ashley Emma available exclusively on Amazon in ebook and paperback

UNDERCOVER AMISH

(This series can be read out of order or as standalone novels.)

Detective Olivia Mast would rather run through gunfire than return to her former Amish community in Unity, Maine, where she killed her abusive husband in self-defense.

Olivia covertly investigates a murder there while protecting the man she dated as a teen: Isaac Troyer, a potential target.

When Olivia tells Isaac she is a detective, will he be willing to break Amish rules to help her arrest the killer?

Undercover Amish was a finalist in Maine Romance Writers Strut Your Stuff Competition 2015 where it received 26 out of 27 points and has 455+ Amazon reviews!

Buy here: https://www.amazon.com/Undercover-Amish-Covert-◻Police-◻Detectives-ebook/dp/B01L6JE49G

https://ashleyemmaamishbooks.myshopify.com/

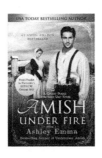

AMISH UNDER FIRE

After Maria Mast's abusive ex-boyfriend is arrested for being involved in sex trafficking and modern-day slavery, she thinks that she and her son Carter can safely return to her Amish community.

But the danger has only just begun.

Someone begins stalking her, and they want blood and revenge.

Agent Derek Turner of Covert Police Detectives Unit is assigned as her bodyguard and goes with her to her Amish community in Unity, Maine.

Maria's secretive eyes, painful past, and cautious demeanor intrigue him.

As the human trafficking ring begins to target the Amish community, Derek wonders if the distraction of her will cost him his career...and Maria's life.

https://ashleyemmaamishbooks.myshopify.com/

Buy on Amazon: http://a.co/fT6D7sM

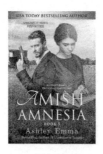

AMISH AMNESIA

When Officer Jefferson Martin witnesses a young woman being hit by a car near his campsite, all thoughts of vacation vanish as the car speeds off.

When the malnourished, battered woman wakes up, she can't remember anything before the accident. They don't know her name, so they call her Jane.

When someone breaks into her hospital room and tries to kill her before getting away, Jefferson volunteers to protect Jane around the clock. He takes her back to their Kennebunkport beach house along with his upbeat sister Estella and his friend who served with him overseas in the Marine Corps, Ben Banks.

At first, Jane's stalker leaves strange notes, but then his attacks become bolder and more dangerous.

https://ashleyemmaamishbooks.myshopify.com/

Buy on Amazon: https://www.amazon.com/gp/product/B07SDSFV3J

AMISH ALIAS

Threatened. Orphaned. On the run.

With no one else to turn to, these two terrified sisters can only hope their Amish aunt will take them in. But the quaint Amish community of Unity, Maine, is not as safe as it seems.

After Charlotte Cooper's parents die and her abusive ex-fiancé threatens her, the only way to protect her younger sister Zoe is by faking their deaths and leaving town.

The sisters' only hope of a safe haven lies with their estranged Amish aunt in Unity, Maine, where their mother grew up before she left the Amish.

Elijah Hochstettler, the family's handsome farmhand, grows closer to Charlotte as she digs up dark family secrets that her mother kept from her.

https://ashleyemmaamishbooks.myshopify.com/

Buy on Amazon here: https://www.amazon.com/Amish-Alias-Romantic-Suspense-Detectives/dp/1734610808

AMISH ASSASIN

When nurse Anna Hershberger finds a man with a bullet wound who begs her to help him without taking him to the hospital, she has a choice to make.

Going against his wishes, she takes him to the hospital to help him after he passes out. She thinks she made the right decision...until an assassin storms in with a gun. Anna has no choice but to go on the run with her patient.

This handsome stranger, who says his name is Connor, insists that they can't contact the police for help because there are moles leaking information. His mission is to shut down a local sex trafficking ring targeting Anna's former Amish community in Unity, Maine, and he needs her help most of all.

Since Anna was kidnapped by sex traffickers in her Amish community, she would love nothing more than to get justice and help put the criminals behind bars.

But can she trust Connor to not get her killed? And is he really who he says he is?

https://ashleyemmaamishbooks.myshopify.com/

Buy on Amazon: https://www.amazon.com/gp/product/B084R9V4CN

AMISH FOR A WEEK
Ever wondered what it would be like to live in an Amish community? Now you can find out in this true story with photos.
https://ashleyemmaamishbooks.myshopify.com/
Buy on Amazon: https://www.amazon.com/Ashleys-Amish-Adventures-Outsider-community-ebook/dp/B01N5714WE

AMISH SNOW WHITE
An heiress on the run.
A heartbroken Amish man, sleep-walking through life.
Can true love's kiss break the spell?
After his wife dies and he returns to his Amish community, Dominic feels numb and frozen, like he's under a spell.

When he rescues a woman from a car wreck in a snowstorm, he brings her home to his mother and six younger siblings. They care for her while she sleeps for several days, and when she wakes up in a panic, she pretends to have amnesia.
But waking up is only the beginning of Snow's story.
https://ashleyemmaamishbooks.myshopify.com/
Buy on Amazon: https://www.amazon.com/Amish-Snow-White-Standalone-Fairytale-ebook/dp/B089NHH7D4

AMISH BEAUTY AND THE BEAST

She's an Amish beauty with a love of reading, hiding a painful secret. He's a reclusive, scarred military hero who won't let anyone in. Can true love really be enough?

On her way home from the bookstore, Belle's buggy crashes in front of the old mansion that everyone else avoids, of all places.

What she finds inside the mansion is not a monster, but a man. Scarred both physiologically and physically by the horrors of military combat, Cole's burned and disfigured face tells the story of all he lost to the war in a devastating explosion.

He's been hiding from the world ever since.

After Cole ends up hiring her as his housekeeper and caretaker for his firecracker of a grandmother, Belle can't help her curiosity as she wonders what exactly Cole does in his office all day.
Why is Cole's office so off-limits to Belle? What is he hiding in there?
https://ashleyemmaamishbooks.myshopify.com/
https://www.amazon.com/gp/product/B089PR9ML

HOSEA AND GOMER'S AMISH SECRET

Gomer is not your typical Amish woman.
On the outside, Gomer seems like a lovely, sweet, young Amish woman, but she's hiding a scandalous secret. She sneaks out at night to sing in downtown bars, lying to her entire community while leading a double life.
Hosea hears from God in a dream, telling him to marry Gomer. Should he follow his heart and risk getting it broken?
https://ashleyemmaamishbooks.myshopify.com/
https://www.amazon.com/Hosea-Gomers-Amish-Secret-family-ebook/dp/B09GQVCBM9

EXCERPT OF UNDERCOVER AMISH

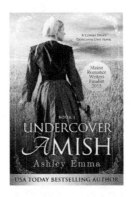

Chapter One

"Did you find everything you were looking for?" Jake asked.

Olivia Sullivan looked up to see her husband staring at her with furrowed brows and narrowed eyes. The anger flickering in them would soon grow into a hungry flame. He wouldn't yell at her here in the grocery store, but she should hurry to avoid a lecture later at home.

For a moment, she pondered his question. Had she found everything she was looking for?

No.

This was not the life she had signed up for when she had made her vows to Jake Sullivan.

"Olivia? Did you hear me?" His voice, low and menacing, came through clenched teeth.

"Sorry. I just need to find some toothpaste. I'll be right back."

"Hurry up. I'm hungry and want to go home."

Liv scurried with her basket toward the other end of the store, her long purple dress flapping on her legs. She tugged on the thin ribbons of her white prayer kapp to make sure it wasn't crooked and almost ran into her neighbor, Isaac Troyer.

She halted so fast, her basket tipped and her groceries clattered to the floor. "Hi, Isaac. I'm so sorry! I almost ran you over."

"It's all right, Liv. Don't worry about it!" He grinned, green eyes sparkling reassuringly. Then the smile slid from his face and concern shadowed his expression.

Fear swelled within her. Did he know?

She squirmed and avoided his gaze. "I'm so clumsy. I really should watch where I'm going." She shook her head, clearing her thoughts as she dropped to the floor to pick up her groceries. Isaac hurried to help her.

"Really, everyone does these things. So how are you, Liv?" he asked in all seriousness, using the nickname he used to call her when they had dated as teens. They had been so in love back then—until Jake came along and stole her heart with his cheap lies. Isaac was an old friend now and nothing more. The piece of her she had given to him when they had dated died the day she married Jake.

She told herself to act normal, even if he did suspect something. "I'm well. How are you?" She reached for a fallen box of cereal. Her purple sleeve rode up her arm, revealing a dark bruise. She took in a quick, sharp breath and yanked her sleeve down, turning away in shame.

Had he seen it?

Isaac rested his fingers on her arm. "Liv, be honest. Is Jake hurting you? Or did you 'walk into a door' again? You know I don't believe that nonsense. I've known Jake since we were children, and I know how angry he can get. And I know you might be silly sometimes, but you aren't that clumsy."

She sure wasn't silly anymore. Her silliness had also died the day she married Jake.

Olivia stared at Isaac wide-eyed, unable to breathe. He did know the truth about Jake. Her pulse quickened as the grocery store seemed to shrink around her, closing her in. Who else knew?

"You don't deserve this, Liv."

What would Jake do to her if he found out Isaac knew?

"Isaac... Promise me you won't say anything. If you do, he will hurt me terribly. Maybe even—"

"Olivia! Are you okay?" Jake strode over to them. He helped her up in what seemed like a loving way, and no one else noticed his clenching grip on her arm.

Except Isaac. His eyes grew cold as his jaw tightened.

He knew.

Oh, God, please don't let him say anything.

No one would believe him, even if he did. Jake was known for being a polite, helpful person. He was the kind of man who would help anyone at any time, even in the middle of the night or in a storm. No one would ever suspect him of hitting his wife.

He hid that side of himself skillfully, with his mask of deceptive charm that had made her fall in love with him so quickly.

Jake finished piling the groceries into the basket as Isaac stood.

"Good to see you, Isaac." Jake nodded to his former childhood friend.

"Likewise. Take care." Isaac offered a big smile as though nothing had happened.

When Liv glanced over her shoulder at him as she and Jake walked away, Isaac stared back at her, concern lining every feature of his face.

Most of the buggy ride home was nerve-wracking silence. They passed the green fields of summer in Unity, Maine. Horses and cows grazed in the sunlight, and Amish children played in the front yards. Normally she would have enjoyed watching them, but Olivia squeezed her eyes shut. She mentally braced herself for whatever storm raged in Jake's mind that he would soon unleash onto her.

"Want to tell me what happened back there?"

Jake's voice was not loud, but she could tell by his tone that he was infuriated. Who knew what awaited her at home?

"I bumped into Isaac and spilled my groceries. He was just helping me pick them up," she answered in a cool, calm voice. She clasped her hands together in her lap to stop them from shaking, acting as though everything was fine. Their buggy jostled along the side of the road as cars passed.

Did he know what had really happened?

"I was watching from a distance. I saw him touch your arm. I saw the way he smiled at you. And I saw the way you stared at him. You never look at me like that."

Here we go. She sucked in a deep breath, preparing for battle. At least he hadn't heard what Isaac had asked her. Jake was always accusing her of being interested in other men, but it was never true. He was paranoid and insecure.

"You know I love you, Jake."

"I know. But did you ever truly let go of Isaac before you married me? Does part of you still miss him?"

"No, of course not! You have all my love."

"Then why don't you act like it?" His knuckles turned white as he clenched his fists tighter around the reins. "Why don't you ever look at me like that?"

How could he expect her to shower him with love? She tried, but it was so hard to endure his rampages and live up to his impossible standards. Yes, she had married him and would stay true to her vows. She would remain by his side as his wife until death.

However soon that may be. Every time he had one of his rampages, she feared for her life more and more.

She had given up on romance a long time ago. Now she just tried to survive.

If only her parents were still alive... but they had been killed along with the rest of her family in a fire when she had been a teenager. How many times had Liv wished that she could confide in her mother about Jake? She would have known what to do.

"I'm sorry, Jake. I'll try to do better." She told him what he wanted to hear.

"Good." Smugness covered his face as he glanced at her and sat up a bit taller.

When they arrived home, he helped her unload the groceries without saying a word. She knew what was coming. He internalized all his anger, and one small thing would send him over the edge once they were behind closed doors.

When everything was put away, he stalked off to the living room to wait as she prepared dinner. She began chopping vegetables, and not even ten minutes had passed when he stomped into the kitchen. As he startled her, the knife fell on the counter top.

Jake snarled through clenched teeth, crossing the room in three long strides. "You love him, don't you?"

"No, Jake! I told you I don't love him. I love you." She struggled to keep her voice steady. They had had this fight more than once.

"Are you secretly seeing each other?"

She spun around to face him. "No! I would never do that." She might wonder sometimes what her life would have been like if she had married Isaac, but that didn't mean she loved him or had feelings for him, and it certainly didn't mean she would have an affair with him. Happy or not, she was a married Amish woman and would never be unfaithful to her husband.

"I can see it all over your face. It's true. You are seeing him." He lunged toward her, pinning her against the counter top.

She tried to shield her face with her hands. The familiar feeling of overwhelming panic filled her. Her heart pounded as she anticipated what was coming. "No, that's not true!"

"After everything I've given you!" His eyes burned with an angry fire stronger than she had ever seen before. He raised his clenched fist and swung.

Pain exploded in her skull. Her head snapped back from the impact. Before she could recover, he wrapped his hands around her neck, squeezing harder and harder until her feet lifted off the floor.

She clawed at his hands, but he only clenched tighter. Her lungs and throat burned; her body screamed for oxygen.

This was it. She was going to die. She was sure of it.

A strange calm settled over her, and her eyes fluttered shut. It was better this way.

Her eyes snapped open.

No. Not today. For the first time in her life, she had to fight back.

She tried to punch him, but it was as if he didn't feel a thing. She tried to scream for help, but her vocal chords were being crushed. She reached behind her for anything to use to hit him in the head. Her fingers fumbled with something sharp, and it cut her hand. But she ignored the pain.

The knife.

She gripped the handle. Before she could reconsider, she thrust the knife as hard as she could into the side of his neck.

Blood spurted from the wound as his grip loosened. His eyes widened in shock, and his knees gave out as he crumpled to the floor.

"What have I done?" She inhaled shaky breaths, struggling to get air back into her lungs. Tears stung her eyes. Bile crept up her throat, and she clamped a hand over her mouth. Panic and fear washed over her and settled in her gut.

She had stabbed her own husband.

A sob shook her chest. "Oh, dear Lord! Please be with me."

There was so much blood. Her stomach churned, and her ears rang. Her head was weightless, and her vision tunneled into blackness. She slid against the handmade wooden cabinets to sit on the floor.

She should run to the phone shanty and call an ambulance, but she couldn't move. There was no way she could run or even walk all the way to the shanty without passing out. She would have gone next door to her uncle's house, but her relatives were out of town.

As her vision tunneled, she wasn't sure if she was possibly losing consciousness or dying from being choked.

Either way, she was free.

Buy Undercover Amish here: https://www.amazon.com/Undercover-Amish-Covert-Police-Detectives/dp/1732987912

About the Author (Ashley Emma)

Visit www.AshleyEmmaAuthor.com to download free eBooks by Ashley Emma!

Ashley Emma wrote her first novel at age 12 and published it at

16. She was home schooled and knew since she was a child that she wanted to be a novelist. She's written over 20 books and is now an award-winning USA Today bestselling author of over 15 books, mostly Amish fiction. (Many more titles coming soon!)

Ashley has a deep respect and love for the Amish and wanted to make sure her Amish books were genuine. When she was 20, she stayed with three Amish families in a community in Maine where she made many friends and did her research for her Amish books. To read about what it was like to live among the Amish, check out her book Amish for a Week (a true story).

Ashley's novel Amish Alias was a Gold Medal Winner in the NYC Book Awards 2021. Her bestselling book Undercover Amish received 26 out of 27 points as a finalist in the Maine Romance Writers Strut Your Stuff novel writing competition in 2015. Its sequel Amish Under Fire was a semi-finalist in Harlequin's So You Think You Can Write novel writing competition also in 2015. Two of her short stories have been published online in writing contests and she co-wrote an article for ProofreadAnywhere.com in 2016. She judged the Fifth Anniversary Writing Contest for Becoming Writer in the summer of 2016.

Ashley owns Fearless Publishing House in Maine where she lives with her husband and four children. She is passionate about helping her clients self-publish their own books so they can build their businesses or achieve their dream of becoming an author.

Download some of Ashley's free Amish books at www.AshleyEmmaAuthor.com.

ashley@ashleyemmaauthor.com

>>>>Check out Ashley's TV interview with News Center 6 Maine!

https://www.newscentermaine.com/article/news/local/207/207-in

terview/what-led-a-writer-to-the-amish/97-5d22729f-9cd0-4358-8
09d-305e7324f8f1

Printed in Great Britain
by Amazon